I *believe in the Church of Baseball.*

I've tried all the major religions and most of the minor ones—I've worshipped Buddha, Allah, Brahma, Vishnu, Siva, trees, mushrooms, and Isadora Duncan . . .

I know things. For instance—

There are 108 beads in a Catholic rosary. And—there are 108 stitches in a baseball.

When I learned that, I gave Jesus a chance.

But it just didn't work out between us . . .
The Lord laid too much guilt on me. I prefer metaphysics to theology.

You see, there's no guilt in baseball . . . and it's never boring.

Which makes it like sex.

There's never been a ballplayer slept with me who didn't have the best year of his career.

Making love is like hitting a baseball—you just got to relax and concentrate.

Besides, I'd never sleep with a player hitting under .250 unless he had a lot of RBI's or was a great glove man up the middle.

A woman's got to have standards.

The young players start off full of enthusiasm and energy but they don't realize that come July and August when the weather is hot it's hard to perform at your peak level.

The veterans pace themselves better. They finish stronger. They're great in September.

While I don't believe a woman needs a man to be fulfilled, I do confess an interest in finding the ultimate guy— he'd have that youthful exuberance but the veteran's sense of timing. . . .

Y'see there's a certain amount of "life-wisdom" I give these boys.

I can expand their minds. Sometimes when I've got a ballplayer alone I'll just read Emily Dickinson or Walt Whitman to him. The guys are so sweet—they always stay and listen.

Of course a guy will listen to anything if he thinks it's foreplay.

I make them feel confident. They make me feel safe. And pretty.

'Course what I give them lasts a lifetime. What they give me lasts 142 games. Sometimes it seems like a bad trade—but bad trades are part of baseball— who can forget Frank Robinson for Milt Pappas, for Godsakes!

It's a long season and you got to trust it.

I've tried 'em all . . . I really have . . .

. . . and the only church that truly feeds the soul—day in, day out—is the Church of Baseball.

ANNIE SAVOY'S SOLILOQUY
(from Bull Durham)
Ron Shelton

INTO

the Temple of

BASEBALL

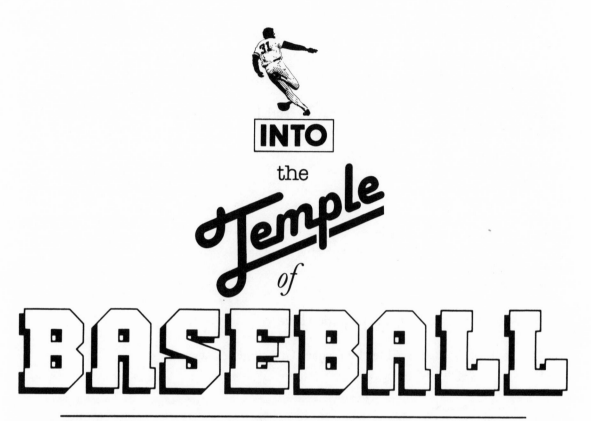

INTO

the

Temple

of

BASEBALL

EDITED by RICHARD GROSSINGER & KEVIN KERRANE

CELESTIALARTS

Berkeley, California

Celestial Arts
P.O. Box 7327
Berkeley, California 94707

Cover and text design by Ken Scott
Cover painting of Roberto Clemente © 1985 by Tom Clark
Composition by Wilsted & Taylor
Set in Aldus

Library of Congress Cataloging in Publication Data

Into the temple of baseball / edited by Richard Grossinger & Kevin
    Kerrane.—1st paperback ed.
        p.   cm.
     ISBN 0-89087-598-7 :
     1. Baseball—Literary collections.   2. American literature.
   I. Grossinger, Richard, 1944–   .   II. Kerrane, Kevin.
   PS509.B3715   1990
   810.8′0355—dc20

First paperback edition, 1990
1   2   3   4   5   -   94   93   92   91   90

Manufactured in the United States of America

CREDITS

ON THE BALL, from *Five Seasons* © 1972, 1973, 1974, 1975, 1976, 1977 by Roger Angell. Reprinted with permission of Simon & Schuster, Inc.

BUYING A BASEBALL © 1990 by Jonathan Holden. Reprinted with permission of *Minnesota Review.*

THE GREEN FIELDS OF THE MIND, from *Yale Alumni Magazine* (November 1977) by A. Bartlett Giamatti. Reprinted with permission of Toni S. Giamatti, executrix of the estate of A. Bartlett Giamatti.

EXCERPT from *The Carmen Miranda Memorial Flagpole* © 1978 by Gerald Rosen. Reprinted with permission of the author.

LEO 1675, from *Penny Lane, A Novel* (Black Sparrow Press, 1977) © 1977 by Fielding Dawson. Reprinted with permission of the author.

RIVERFRONT © 1978 by Sandra Soto Hatfield. Originally published in *Baseball I Gave You All the Best Years of My Life.*

EXCERPT from *Desolation Angels* © 1964 by Jack Kerouac. Reprinted with permission of Sterling Lord Literistic, Inc.

THE MYSTICAL INDIAN PENNANT VISION © 1989 by Dennis J. Kucinich. Reprinted with permission of the author.

BROOKLYN AUGUST © 1977 Stephen King. Originally published in *Baseball I Gave You All the Best Years of My Life.*

THE MINDS REEL IN DREAM AT-BAT © 1989 by Peter Richmond. Reprinted with permission of *The Miami Herald.*

REDS, YANKS AND O'S, from *Wigwag* (October 1989) © 1989 by Dwight Allen. Reprinted with permission of the author.

FROM FATHER, WITH LOVE © 1987 by Doris Kearns Goodwin. Originally published in *Diamonds Are Forever* (Chronicle Books, 1987).

"IT'S DONE"—WILL CLARK © 1989 by Thom Ross. Reprinted with permission of the author.

NOTES ON THE 1986 PLAYOFFS AND WORLD SERIES © 1986, 1990 by Richard Grossinger. Reprinted with permission of the author.

O FOR A MUSE OF FIRE! © 1969 by Jonathan Williams. Reprinted with permission of the author.

EXCERPT from *Growing Up Bronx* (North Atlantic Books, 1984) © 1984 by Gerald Rosen. Reprinted with permission of the author.

BLUES FOR A LOST OCTOBER from *The East Bay Express* (November 1989) © 1989, 1990 by John Krich. Reprinted with permission of the author.

THE LANGUAGE OF SCOUTING from *The Dollar Sign on the Muscle* © 1984 by Kevin Kerrane. Reprinted with permission of Simon & Schuster, Inc.

JAPANESE HOME RUN KING © 1984 by Jim Cohn. Originally published in *The Temple of Baseball.*

EXCERPT from *Sadaharu Oh: A Zen Way of Baseball* (Times Books, 1984) © 1984 by Sadaharu Oh and David Falkner. Reprinted with permission of Times Books.

EXCERPT from *The Wrong Stuff* (Viking Penguin, 1984) © 1984 William Francis Lee and Richard Lally. Reprinted with permission of Penguin USA Inc.

UNDERSTANDING ALVARADO from *The Oranging of America* (Viking Press, 1976) © 1976 by Max Apple. Reprinted with permission of Penguin USA Inc.

BACKYARD © 1987 by Rochelle Nameroff. Reprinted with permission of the author.

TIME LOVES A HAIRCUT from *Harper's* (April 1987) © 1987, 1990 by Bill Cardoso. Reprinted with permission of the publisher.

HOWL FOR CASEY © 1978, 1980 by Mikhail Horowitz. Reprinted with permission of the author.

STAN'S RING from *Take One As Needed* (Ten Speed Press, 1989) © 1989 by Oscar London. Reprinted with permission from the publisher.

FIDEL'S LAST PITCH from *A Totally Free Man: An Unauthorized Autobiography of Fidel Castro* (Creative Arts, 1981) © 1981 by John Krich. Reprinted with permission of the author.

DOCTOR K © 1984 by Jim Hydock. Reprinted with permission of the author.

BABE & LOU © 1977 by Franz Douskey. Originally published in *Baseball I Gave You All the Best Years of My Life.*

THREE NEW TWINS JOIN CLUB IN SPRING from *The New Yorker* (February 1988) © 1988 by Garrison Keillor. Reprinted with permission of the author.

WHITE LIKE ME from *Pete Rose Agonistes* © 1987 by Mike Shannon. Reprinted with permission of the author.

HOW I GOT MY NICKNAME from *The Thrill of the Grass* (Viking Penguin, 1984) © 1984 by W. P. Kinsella. Reprinted with permission of Penguin USA Inc.

UNTITLED (poem) © 1987 by Tom Clark. Reprinted with permission of the author.

TO BILL LEE © 1977 by Tom Clark. Reprinted with permission of the author.

VAN LINGLE MUNGO by Dave Frishberg © 1969, 1985 Kohaw Music Inc. All Rights Reserved. Used by permission.

THE GREAT DYNASTIES OF THE WORLD © 1990 by Thom Ross. Reprinted with permission of the author.

CREDITS

CONTENTS

SECOND BASE:
THE PLAYERS

THIRD BASE:
THE MYTH

HOME PLATE

INTRODUCTION

Richard Grossinger

Into the Temple of Baseball is the realization of almost twenty years of "baseball literature" anthologizing by Kevin Kerrane and me. We began independently in the late 1960s, Kevin with a course in Baseball Literature at the University of Delaware and me with the "Baseball Issue" of *Io*, a countercultural journal Lindy Hough and I had launched in 1964. *Io* #10, on baseball, appeared in 1971 in Cape Elizabeth, Maine, as a loose compilation of baseball poems and essays, original documents on the game (and its forerunners in both European and American Indian games), excerpts on history of baseball, and assorted similar material on other "games," ranging from football and volleyball to bowling and sledding. Kevin Kerrane adopted this collection for his course soon after it appeared, and in 1975 he invited me to speak to his class. Afterwards, in his office, he showed me his voluminous files of baseball literature. In scope, variety, and quality, these far overshadowed the "Baseball Issue"; they were the basic corpus of fine writing on baseball to that point. On the other hand, I had a few odd things he had missed (or that were unpublished) and, in general, had enacted a more radical mythologization of baseball into art form and metaphor. We left his office with the goal of putting together the monster baseball literary anthology of all time.

For the next year Kevin and I sent out query letters throughout the country and were flooded with thousands of pages of submissions (in addition to what Kevin had already found and what he and I both came up with from novels, poetry collections, newspapers, magazines, etc., and the work in *Io* #10). In the fall of 1977, our version of the best 400 pages of this material appeared under the title *Baseball I Gave You All the Best Years of My Life*, published by North Atlantic Books (an outgrowth of *Io*) from Oakland, California, where I had moved. During the next two years it was followed by two more editions under the same title, each reedited and enlarged, and then, in 1980, by a Doubleday Anchor abridged version of the material under the title *Baseball Diamonds: Tales, Traces, Visions, and Voodoo from a Native American Rite*.

Arguably, these four editions of the same collection gave birth to the "Baseball Literature" movement of the 1980s. Of course, there was no one progenitor (there rarely is in cultural innovations), but, for instance, *Baseball I Gave You . . .* was later credited by Mike Shannon, founder and editor of *Spitball* (the first national baseball literary magazine, out of Cincinnati) as having been his inspiration, and the anthology was also used as the basis for a dozen or so other anthologies and magazines, many of which reanthologized large portions of its work. Peter H. Gordon, curator of the travelling exhibition *Diamonds Are Forever: Artists and Writers on Baseball* (which has appeared in museums throughout the country in association with the Smithsonian), has cited *Baseball I Gave You . . .* as a primary reference (and told me last year in Oakland that our book gave him the formative idea). I have also heard, indirectly, that the Tibetan tangka paintings of the later North Atlantic anthology *The Temple of Baseball* inspired Susan Sarandon's shrine in the movie *Bull Durham*. In the June 1989 issue of *Small Press*, Doctor Baseball Peter C. Bjarkman, historian of the baseball literary movement, writes: "Grossinger [and Kerrane] stand at the fulcrum of the baseball-book renaissance . . . launching the current boom of interest in baseball as a literary art form. . . . [Their] earliest anthologies were the original sourcebooks for the baseball literature and history courses that began as part of the popular-culture movements in the early 1980s . . . huge volumes of expertly selected baseball poems, essays, fiction, philosophical treatises, photography, and multimedia new-age artwork that are still unsurpassed as the consummate classroom baseball anthologies."

In truth, though *Baseball I Gave You . . .* was a success for the independent publishing world of its era (going through three editions and 6000 copies of an expensive oversize paperback), Doubleday's subsequent watered-down *Baseball Diamonds* was a failure (and a mistaken ambition on our part). It went out of print within a year. For a variety of reasons, Kevin chose not to continue the project at that point, but I used continued submissions of new writing to publish two subsequent anthologies—*The Temple of Baseball* in 1985 and *The Dreamlife of Johnny Baseball* in 1987, and these were popular enough to justify continued anthologizing of ongoing work. However, Celestial Arts stepped into the picture in 1989, and the enthusiastic and expert editing and design work of Sal Glynn, David Hinds, and Ken Scott has enabled the entire series to be reborn under Kevin's and my co-editorship.

Into the Temple of Baseball selects from all editions of the three past anthologies and also uses a considerable amount of new work, right through the 1989 World Series. It replaces the generally unavailable *Baseball I Gave You . . .* as the primer of baseball literature, while updating it. It also may launch a new series of baseball literary anthologizing under the Celestial Arts imprint.

Berkeley, 1990

"...the greatest skill learned by the fanatic is
an ability to rationalize anything—even optioning out your own mother to the minor leagues.
It isn't a skill that stands you in good stead when it comes to real life."

FIRST BASE:

THE
GAME

ON THE BALL

Roger Angell

It weighs just over five ounces and measures between 2.86 and 2.94 inches in diameter. It is made of a composition-cork nucleus encased in two thin layers of rubber, one black and one red, surrounded by 121 yards of tightly wrapped blue-gray wool yarn, 45 yards of white wool yarn, 53 more yards of blue-gray wool yarn, 150 yards of fine cotton yarn, a coat of rubber cement, and a cowhide (formerly horsehide) exterior, which is held together with 216 slightly raised red cotton stitches. Printed certifications, endorsements, and outdoor advertising spherically attest to its authenticity. Like most institutions, it is considered inferior in its present form to its ancient archetypes, and in this case the complaint is probably justified; on occasion in recent years it has actually been known to come apart under the demands of its brief but rigorous active career. Baseballs are assembled and handstitched in Taiwan (before this year the work was done in Haiti, and before 1973 in Chicopee, Massachusetts), and contemporary pitchers claim that there is a tangible variation in the size and feel of the balls that now come into play in a single game; a true peewee is treasured by hurlers, and its departure from the premises, by fair means or foul, is secretly mourned. But never mind: any baseball is beautiful. No other small package comes as close to the ideal in design and utility. It is a perfect object for a man's hand. Pick it up and it instantly suggests its purpose; it is meant to be thrown a considerable distance—thrown hard and with precision. Its feel and heft are the beginning of the sport's critical dimensions; if it were a fraction of an inch larger or smaller, a few centigrams heavier or lighter, the game of baseball would be utterly different. Hold a baseball in your hand. As it happens, this one is not brand-new. Here, just to one side of the curved surgical welt of stitches, there is a pale-green grass smudge, darkening on one edge almost to black—the mark of an old infield play, a tough grounder now lost in memory. Feel the ball, turn it over in your hand; hold it across the seam or the other way, with the seam just to the side of your middle finger. Speculation stirs. You want to go outdoors and throw this spare and sensual object to somebody or, at the very least, watch somebody else throw it. The game has begun.

BUYING A BASEBALL

Jonathan Holden

As I turned over in my palm
that glossy little planet
I was going to hand my son
I was wondering how
it could still cost the same
as when I was his age.
Around came the brand:
Rawlings. Made in Haiti.
Like those poor city kids
I'd heard have no idea
that milk came from a cow,
I'd never known before
where baseballs come from.
They were always there
in the stores in bins, stitched
tight as uncracked books,
each with its tiny trademark,
Made in Hell.
We'd test the tough seams
along both fingers' links
to get a thrill of power
remembering how to fake
a staggering grounder out
so it would leap to the mitt
at our convenience,
how that black magic squeezed
in the core would make it
spark off the bat
with a high, nasty *crack*
you could mistake for no
other sound in the world.

THE GREEN FIELDS OF THE MIND

A. Bartlett Giamatti

I t breaks your heart. It is designed to break your heart. The game begins in the spring, when everything else begins again, and it blossoms in the summer, filling the afternoons and evenings, and then as soon as the chill rains come, it stops and leaves you to face the fall alone. You count on it, rely on it to buffer the passage of time, to keep the memory of sunshine and high skies alive, and then just when the days are all twilight, when you need it most, it stops. Today, October 2, a Sunday of rain and broken branches and leaf-clogged drains and slick streets, it stopped, and summer was gone.

Somehow, the summer seemed to slip by faster this time. Maybe it wasn't this summer, but all the summers that, in this my fortieth summer, slipped by so fast. There comes a time when every summer will have something of autumn about it. Whatever the reason, it seemed to me that I was investing more and more in baseball, making the game do more of the work that keeps time fat and slow and lazy. I was counting on the game's deep patterns, three strikes, three outs, three times three innings, and its deepest impulse, to go out and back, to leave and to return home, to set the order of the day and to organize the daylight. I wrote a few things this last summer, this summer that did not last, nothing grand but some things, and yet that work was just camouflage. The real activity was done with the radio—not the all-seeing, all-falsifying television—and was the playing of the game in the only place it will last, the enclosed green field of the mind. There, in that warm, bright place, what the old poet called Mutability does not so quickly come.

But out here on Sunday, October 2, where it rains all day, Dame Mutability never loses. She was in the crowd at Fenway yesterday, a gray day full of bluster and contradiction, when the Red Sox came up in the last of the ninth trailing Baltimore 8-5, while the Yankees, rain-delayed against Detroit, only needing to win one or have Boston lose one to win it all, sat in New York washing down cold cuts with beer and watching the Boston game. Boston had won two, the Yankees had lost two, and suddenly it seemed as if the whole season might go to the last day, or beyond, except here was Boston losing 8-5, while New York sat in its family room and puts its feet up. Lynn, both ankles hurting now as they had in July, hits a single down the right-field line. The crowd stirs. It is on its feet. Hobson, third baseman, former Bear Bryant quarterback, strong, quiet, over 100 RBIs, goes for three breaking balls and is out. The goddess smiles and encourages her agent, a canny journeyman named Nelson Briles.

Now comes a pinch hitter, Bernie Carbo, one-time Rookie of the Year, erratic, quick, a shade too handsome, so laid back he is always, in his soul, stretched out in the tall grass, one arm under his head, watching the clouds and laughing; now he looks over some low stuff unworthy of him and then, uncoiling, sends one out, straight on a rising line, over the center-field wall, no cheap Fenway shot, but all of it, the physics as elegant as the arc the ball describes.

New England is on its feet, roaring. The summer will not pass. Roaring, they recall the evening, late and cold, in 1975, the sixth game of the World Series, perhaps the greatest baseball game played in the last fifty years, when Carbo, loose and easy, had uncoiled to tie the game that Fisk would win. It is 8-7, one out, and school will never start, rain will never come, sun will warm the back of your neck forever. Now Bailey, picked up from the National League recently, big arms, heavy gut, experienced, new to the league and the club; he fouls off two and then, checking, tentative, a big man off balance, he pops a soft liner to the first baseman. It is suddenly darker and later, and the announcer doing the game coast to coast, a New Yorker who works for a New York television station, sounds relieved. His little world, well-lit, hot-combed, split-second-timed, had no capacity to absorb this much gritty, grainy, contrary reality.

Cox swings a bat, stretches his long arms, bends his back, the rookie from Pawtucket, who broke in two weeks earlier with a record six straight hits, the kid drafted ahead of Fred Lynn, rangy, smooth, cool. The count runs two and two, Briles is cagey, nothing too good, and Cox swings, the ball beginning toward the mound and then, in a jaunty, wayward dance, skipping past Briles, feinting to the right, skimming the last of the grass, finding the dirt, moving now like some small, purposeful marine creature negotiating the green deep, easily avoiding the jagged rock of second base, traveling steady and straight now out into the dark, silent recesses of center field.

The aisles are jammed, the place is on its feet, the wrappers, the programs, the Coke cups and peanut shells, the detritus of an afternoon; the anxieties, the things that have to be done tomorrow, the regrets about yesterday, the accumulation of a summer: all forgotten, while hope, the anchor, bites and takes hold where a moment before it seemed we would be swept out with the tide. Rice is up, Rice whom Aaron had said was the only one he'd seen with the ability to break his records, Rice the best clutch hitter on the club, with the best slugging percentage in the league, Rice, so quick and strong he once checked his swing halfway through and snapped the bat in two, Rice the Hammer of God sent to scourge the Yankees, the sound was overwhelming, fathers pounded their sons on the back, cars pulled off the road, households froze, New England exulted in its blessedness, and roared its thanks for all good things, for Rice and for a summer stretching halfway through October. Briles threw, Rice swung, and it was over. One pitch, a fly to center, and it stopped. Summer died in New England, and like rain sliding off a roof, the crowd slipped out of Fenway, quickly, with only a steady murmur of concern for the drive ahead remaining of the roar. Mutability had turned the seasons and translated hope to memory once again. And once again, she had used baseball, our best invention to stay change, to bring change on. That is why it breaks my heart, that game—not because in New York they could win because Boston lost; in that, there is a rough justice, and a reminder to the Yankees of how slight and fragile are the circumstances that exalt one group of human beings over another. It breaks my heart because it was meant to, because it was meant to foster in me again the illusion that there was something abiding, some pattern and some impulse that could come together to make a reality that would resist the corrosion; and because after it had fostered again that most hungered-for illusion, the game was meant to stop, and betray precisely what it promised.

Of course, there are those who learn after the first few times. They grow out of sports. And there are others who were born with the wisdom to know that nothing lasts. These are the truly tough among us, the ones who can live without illusion, or without even the hope of illusion. I am not that grown-up or up-to-date. I am a simpler creature, tied to more primitive patterns and cycles. I need to think something lasts forever, and it might as well be that state of being that is a game; it might as well be that, in a green field, in the sun.

From THE CARMEN MIRANDA MEMORIAL FLAGPOLE

Gerald Rosen

love stadiums. Especially old baseball parks. You see, my brother and I grew up near Yankee Stadium. We used to go there all the time. And to the Polo Grounds, too. We'd walk across the old walking bridge from the Bronx to Manhattan. The one with the two-car subway shuttle on it. They tore down the Polo Grounds to build a housing project. They even tore down the old walking bridge.

We loved to go out to the ballpark. We'd go early and pay our sixty cents and sit out in the sunshine in the bleachers and read Russian novels until the game started. I finished the last couple chapters of _The Brothers Karamazov_ at the Polo Grounds one day before a Giant-Dodger game. What a great day that was. First all those kids shouting, "Hooray for Karamazov!" to Alyosha, and then Carl Furillo throwing the ball at Leo Durocher after Sal the Barber Maglie gave him too close a shave at the plate.

Life was full then. At the ballpark. When I could forget about my "real" life. Outside.

Sometimes I would go by myself. You'd be surprised how alone you can feel, sitting in an old ballpark. Even with ten thousand people around. If you didn't grow up in the country with trees and all, it's the only place you could go to think about things.

"Root, root for old Notre Dame," Jack is singing as he pulls out to pass a big Safeway truck, "You take the Notre and I'll take the Dame."

We smile together. Another Junior High School 82 Special.

"Jack, you remember that time we went to Griffith Stadium in Washington?"

"Sure do. Four hundred six feet down the left-field line. It took a Paul Bunyan to hit one out of there . . . You think it's still there?"

"Nah . . . I imagine they tore it down when they built that new RFK Stadium."

"I don't like these new suburban stadiums."

"Me neither," I said.

"They all look alike."

"Anyone can build a big bowl in the middle of a field."

"Yeah, but you give a guy a little odd-shaped lot in the center of a city and you tell him to build a ballpark on it . . . man, that's *architecture!*"

Hark reached his head over the seat and nuzzled my ear with his wet nose. I patted him on his head. Jack said, "You know what I would've liked to have done? Taken a trip across country going from ballpark to ballpark. Then we could've *seen* the places we used to hear about on the radio when the teams were on the road."

"We could've taken a quick trip to Boston to look at the short left-field wall in Fenway Park."

"No, I mean all of them, Jerr. Shibe Park in Philly, and Forbes Field in Pittsburgh, and Crosley Field in Cincinnati . . ."

"They're all gone now."

"I know . . . Damn it, any other country would've preserved them. It isn't right. They were our Gothic cathedrals."

LEO 1675
From PENNY LANE, A NOVEL
Fielding Dawson

Von Joshua led off for the Giants, hitting .326 on a cool cloudy Saturday afternoon out at Shea.

Asa and I were sitting in the third deck along with a whole slew of kids and a good sprinkling of cigar-smoking beer-drinking World War One & Two vets and other assorted pensioners and creature people applauding as Joshua flied out to Unser.

After the catch he threw it in to Phillips at short and after the ball was tossed around, then it went back to Seaver as Derrel Thomas stepped in, bounced a hard shot to Phillips who went to

Torre at first (6-3), and after they again threw the ball around it went to Seaver as Willie Montanez dug in hitting .295. The first pitch was a ball, the second a strike, the third a strike and so was the fourth, and me and Asa and the fans cheered as the Mets ran in.

They're lovely, Asa smiled. In their sparkling white uniforms.

I nodded, marking down the totals on my scorecard. K for Montanez, as I said: white at home, gray on the road. An American Airlines jet made an arc not all that high over left field, like a lazy mechanical fly, and headed east to—Suez, its roaring breezy racket trailing after. Del Unser got the bat he wanted and walked out to the plate. Dave Rader threw the last of Montefusco's warm-up pitches to second base and the Giant infield peppered it around, tossed it to their pitcher, and the bottom of the first inning began as Unser, hitting .288, hit a drive toward the left field corner.

Which I thought had Gary Matthews in a flicker the way he leaned forward, and then saw it, made a little misjudge, but then he began to run back as Unser was around first and digging hard to second, Matthews, with his back to the infield yet watching the ball over his shoulder and his left (glove) hand outstretched, in two deerlike leaps, and in the middle of the last leap, glove extended, his right arm outstretched laterally but on a downward angle and his whole body diving up and out to the extreme of its reach as he snagged it, round, small, white, against the sienna and black of his glove as his body came down hard in a forward pitch, lunging forward, right hand out to cushion the impact when he slammed against the wall as Unser rounded second and slowed while Matthews managed to brake without hitting the wall and Unser jogged across the infield into the dugout. Matthews threw the ball in to Chris Speier, say it like spire, who even without throwing pebbles still reminds me of Marty Marion, more than anyone, in fact, and I made the mark on my scorecard (7), and there was one out. The Met fans showed their curious courtesy—it was the first inning—and cheered the catch, as Millan, say it me-yahn, with his respectable .294 second baseman's average, slashed a drive down the right-field line which Montanez intercepted with a fine backhanded catch, and in a little trot stepped on first. I marked down 3, there were two down, Millan ran back into the dugout and I thought that the first two hits had been pretty hard, but Kranepool came in to strike out and straighten out my thinking. The fans made unhappy noises because Kranepool is a favorite, as he should be. He's hit in the desperate clutches only the Mets create, those weird late-in-the-game trickster situations that call for the level force of Kranepool, and on the hit which extricates his team, the Met fans spin off into Met-ecstasy, and prove somebody's point whoever it is, for every warp there's a whap, and besides Kranepool is the only original Met left, what's that, Joel? Thirteen years?

I did the totals and Asa remarked it was looking more like rain than ever. I raised my eyes and saw that the sky was in too many different levels, and said no, it won't rain (it didn't), and she said how do you know and I said I used to play outfield I know what rainclouds look like.

But, she said, pushing a finger into my left shoulder: that was over twenty-five years ago! Don't bug me, I said.

Aw, she pouted, gee Lucky.

Some things you don't forget, I explained, and besides I did a lot of farm work, in my day. What a bore.

I don't talk much at ballgames, I said.

We should come more often, she said, and Gary Matthews stepped in. Seaver rubbed the ball around and looked at Matthews, and then, in about fourteen pitches struck out the side: Matthews .283, Speier .280, and Thomasson .219, as it might be remembered that the high batting averages of yesteryear that glamorized the game have vaporized in the modern baseball that's all pitching. On my scorecard, in the vertical column of the top half of the second inning it was all Ks and I wrote at the bottom, in the little box divided by a diagonal line, an ideogram not unlike the sign which stands for percent, as Asa yawned, lit a filter, scratched the back of my neck and slumped back in the seat humming he's a reeeeeel nowhere man and I laughed looking out over the field. No hits, no runs, and maybe Seaver's gotta no-hitter (wrong. Wuzza 5-hitter).

The big curly red-headed batter Montreal had loved stood outside the batter's box watching the Giant infield snap the ball around, and then he stepped in with, as is his style, his pants high on the leg and his hard plastic batter's cap clamped down over his curls with the bill so low he has to tip back his head to see, or at least it looks like that, and for some reason I think of Christopher Robin, and an old-fashioned biglittleboy image of a major leaguer like the tiger in the coloring book and the tiger in the zoo, on Leo 1675 when Rusty Staub stepped in. Very cool. Casual a man as you could see, except when he makes those running catches and doesn't dive for it like Mays and the others, but in the flash before he gets it, he sits down and with his feet out makes the catch in his lap while he slides along the grass as the kids go wild.

What's he like? Asa asked, I've heard of him.

While the fans cheered Staub leading off the Met second, I said, remembering the Pete Rose incident, that Staub was a fine ballplayer, and evidently responsible, and I yet see him out there in left with Berra, facing the furious crowd, making the gesture of no more throwing things at Rose. Pete Rose is as popular at Shea as Ted Williams was at Fenway in the Forties.

Staub is, I said, a bachelor, popular with the ladies, and a great cook. They called him *Le Grand Orange* in Montreal.

The delight of the fans, whose bounding hopper Speier turned into an easy out 6-3, as in telling Asa about him, Staub, I suddenly remembered a fifteen-year-old girl I once knew who would have called him cute: he the cleanup hitter, the cool red-headed Christopher Robin tiger, he whose first-definition German name means powder, dust as on the wings of butterflies, made the righthanded turn at first and loped back into the dugout as casual as if he was out in the hallway and went back to get the cigarettes he forgot.

Staub out, 6-3. Joe Torre walked, Garrett struck out and Jerry Grote slapped a liner to first which Montanez fielded (unassisted, 3), and the Mets were down 0/0 on my scoreboard as a big United jet glided across the first-base side of the sky and banked down over left out of sight.

I like the white little ball rolling around, Asa said as I was writing. Me too, I said. She slipped her arm through mine and we sat back close together looking out beyond the big black cliff of the scoreboard to the parking lot and Queens County beyond, in soft Saturday smog, in New York. Staub means a lot of things.

I smiled to myself all this fuss over that little white ball: *must* be psychic, I thought.

She nodded. Chasing the world, I thought. The Bird.

Yes, I continued to think. I thought eagerly. We looked at each other warmly as Seaver looked in to Grote for the sign. Rader was on first with a single which goes to show what love will do, you miss things, and then Steve Ontiveros (.272) walked, which put men on first and second with nobody down and Seaver's no-hitter gone. Montefusco, the Giants' pitcher (10-6

ERA 3.23), came to bat. Seaver struck him out. The leadoff hitter, Von Joshua again, who had flied out to Unser in the first, came up and hit a hard shot about two feet to the right of second base, and as the ball was clearly destined for the alley up right center, and Rader was on his way into and then around second, and Ontiveros was coming into second, Millan, in a headlong, but not utterly headlong, dive with his glove out blocked the ball, and in his forward momentum did a sort of three-quarter somersault in a cloud of dust scrabbling around to get it he got it and flipped over somehow so when the dust cleared and Ontiveros was almost to second, Millan lay on his back in the dirt about fifteen feet to the right of but behind the base with the ball in his hand and his head up, he had a calm and patient expression on his face as he watched Phillips, the Met shortstop, flash to second, and just before Phillips got there, Millan lobbed the ball to the bag. And the ball looped in no hurry as Phillips crossed the bag in a roar as Ontiveros was in the middle of his slide and the force out was made, there were two down and, most importantly, the run didn't score nor were the bases loaded, and as Millan got to his feet and dusted himself off the threat was no longer so great. Asa tapped me on the shoulder, her eyes wide and bright from the remarkable play, she pointed, and there was the beer vendor! So as Thomas stepped in I saw the union man at the keyboard of the linotype machine typing away what the sportswriter had written and the editor had polished up, tomorrow's subhead under the Met victory calling Millan's play the play of the game, which it was and which they printed, right there in tomorrow's paper, without the sound of the crowd, the cloud of dust, Millan's head-up calm and patient expression, and the sense of the sight of the touch in the vision surrounding that little white ball floating through the air to second base as Phillips snatched it and the force was made. No sense of the collective heightened empathetic impact—never. No sense of the beautiful girls who are at every game—no sense of Asa in her cutoffs, of her gorgeous legs, her sneakers without socks, and the brief crisp white tanktop, those spare garments over her long and elegant figure, tan from the beaches and the sun, no sense of her long glowing coal black hair, combed straight back from her forehead, so her whole face shone—no sense of any *body*, not even of those on the field, whose bodies are what the game consciously is intuitively, as I descended—carefully—the steps to the beer vendor and Derrel Thomas took a strike. I made the happy purchase and returned up to Asa, sat down beside her and as one of the World War One soldiers in the section to our right lit a cigar, watching me over the flame, he smiled, and as Asa took the beer she saw him and smiled and so did I she was so madly lovely. Strike one. We both sipped beer.

Jesus that's good, she said, and with Hey Lucky and a little nudge—how about some vodka!

Well, I am. Lucky scores again! reaching into my raincoat pocket and took out the small glass jar that had previously, once, contained herring in sour cream, but which this Saturday held (80 proof) vodka, and after I, after I myself sipped it was delicious as she sipped and Thomas smacked a grounder to Millan who flipped to Phillips for the force and the Mets were out of the inning. I marked down, at the bottom, 1/0, also marking in the H (hit) column at the far right, 1 (for Rader), he'd gotten the single, as Asa sipped again and swallowed and cried out as the old vet watched her, as he puffed on his cigar, the jealous old lech, and Asa said holy *shit*, It ain't beer, I said, and she handed the jar to me and I sipped and capped it, returned it to my raincoat pocket and sipping beer I watched the Giants toss the ball around in the pre–third inning warm-up.

I looked into the great space before me.

And as baseball is ninety-nine percent consciousness and concentration the one percent of sensation happens in a step by step process that to those who don't know happens all of a sudden, but to those who know, one thing creates the next thing, and in all that space where fractions count and something happens, guys who have played a lot of ball get to in a certain way know when something's gonna happen before it does, and in the bottom of the third as Phillips stepped in I had that old feeling again, and I smiled.

Phillips took a strike.

My vision crystallized, and on the next pitch my body felt like a tuning fork as Phillips swung and me and Asa rose to our feet as the ball flew on one great straight line over the second baseman's head up the right center alley, and Phillips raced in to first and around on his way to second as the two Giant outfielders Thomasson (right) and Joshua (center), converged to it in a roar and the glory of a cloud of dust Phillips slid hard into second with the throw too late and we had a man on second, nobody out, and Seaver who is a helluva hitting pitcher at bat and everybody from here to Rangoon knowing he was gonna bunt, which he did, and lemmie tell ya Ontiveros at third had to *hustle* on his throw to first to get Seaver, which he did, he got him on a perfect bunt, and there was one out, with.

Phillips was on third.

All the fans sat down, and got that hard-eyed look fans get when they *know* they're gonna get a run. Unser was up and the kids began to pipe.

The Mets are a trickster team and fans are tricksters too, and when Unser slammed the double into left center and Phillips scored it was a trickster hit in a refreshing new definition of the word team-ster—smacked with authority, and after Asa and I had finished clapping and cheering and had sat down again, we had a little more of that (Russian) water followed by a slug of beer as I made the appropriate signs on my scorecard and Felix Millan came to bat, and after a lull and a little hum, he sent a thunderbolt to Montanez at first who caught it and stepped on first for the out, and then Kranepool came up and much to the distress of the fans, flied out to center and Unser got stranded at second. But.

We'd had two hits and we gotta run! It was us ONE, them nix.

As the Giants came to bat.

Top of the fourth.

I looked at Asa who was looking at my scorecard and asking me what the numbers meant, and while I explained, I thought about her, objectively, as well as the other way.

She was lovely in a disturbing way. Her skin was rich, resilient, and tawny. She had long dark hair and very dark emotional eyes above a little button of a nose, round cheeks and her constant and helpless full-lipped pout, which with her lean and graceful figure, and style of (marching) walking (head high), generally sent guys on the streets into fits. She was nineteen.

She had, and it was true, a heart of gold. And following the metaphor in metals, she was as tough, or as defensively hard, as iron. The gold was given, but she had become iron the hard way, forged out of a miserable childhood in a rotten city across the gray river.

I had a sort of haggard look, gazing at her: call me Mary Shelley. Call me Dr. Frankenstein. Call me Lucky.

I'm hungry, she said.

So am I, I said, but the lines at the refreshment stand are each a mile long and in each line ten thousand kids drive countermen and women crazy because the kids forget.

You should write an essay, she interrupted.

Maybe I will, I said.

Maybe I mean it, she said.

Maybe I will, I repeated.

I bet you won't.

We'll see, I said, watching Seaver warming up.

She lay her head on my shoulder and slipped her arm through mine and yawned, saying she thought she was getting drunk. Then she took her arm away, raised her head, sat back, folded her hands in her lap and scowled. I watched her.

She looked at me and her eyebrows went into an upside down V as her eyes got imploring, and she said I really *am* hungry, Lucky, couldn't you get us a couple of hot dogs and some more beer?

Montanez stepped in and Seaver looked for the sign as I said oh well Goddamn and handed her the scorecard and pencil. Told her to write down what happened, and walked down the steps finishing my beer and watching Montanez's hit drift lazily over Phillips's head into left where Kranepool caught it as the crowd applauded and cheered. A big United jet glided up on a rising curve from left field, and headed east. I turned and flashed a seven sign up to Asa, saw her write it down, and continued on my way.

Down the walkway under the stands to the long lines at the refreshment stand. I tossed the plastic cup in a trashcan and took my place at the rear of what looked like the shortest line, and set myself to be patient. There were about sixteen kids, and in the line to my left I saw another adult, standing just ahead of me. He was wearing a porkpie hat and a plaid sportscoat. He was over forty, around five eight, plump and husky, and sweat ran down the side of his face. He sighed, and sensing me watching him he turned, and our eyes met. We smiled, and we each shook our head at being back in line again and the hopelessness of it all ho hum *fuck*. As a matter of fact he looked like a cop. White. Pockmarked in the hollows of his cheeks. White shirt open at the collar, and actually he looked—he looked like the Continental Op! Was this *The Shea Caper*? Maybe! as around us kids chirped, laughed, and cried out as they messed around clutching their Met pennants with their blue Met ballcaps askew, and like Rusty Staub, so low on their foreheads they had to raise their heads to see before them, which was kind of amusing, but not to the people behind the counter at the refreshment stand who served them, who were just about to explode from frustrating rituals that'd driven even Jesus to wits end.

Watcha want! barked the counterman.

Little voice, eyes wide, peering up: a hot dog.

The counterman took the dog off the rotating grid, put it in a bun and gave it to the boy who said Two.

The counterman took a deep breath. His eyes bugged out of his head, and his face got red as he prepared by rote the other hot dog thinking ahead—the kids were too small to reach up to the mustard and ketchup dispensers, so the counterman took a good grip on reality and went through his sequence which began with which did they want mustard or ketchup, thus oh gee whiz, gosh, golly, decisions, decisions, a grimy index finger between parted lips ummmm mustard mustard ketchup ketchup ketchup mustard with questions written in his eyes while the gang behind him carried on and the adults in the line ground their teeth and stared at the floor, remembering.

Ketchup! cried the boy.

The counterman, cursing architects that designed refreshment stand counters so high, slopped ketchup on the two hot dogs and handed them back to the boy, each dog in shallow paper containers with a napkin for each, and after the boy paid the counterman he, the counterman, with an incredible, yet sort of doomed expression, like a bee in a blizzard, and his face crisscrossed with broken capillaries, glanced at the next kid, who was in a batch—who was a batch—began to relate, while yet the first little boy looked up, and with the two hot dogs in his hand, he remembered Mommy had said ice cream.

I laughed, and saw the agency detective grinning.

The counterman turned the color of raspberry sherbert, leaned partly over the counter and asked what kind d'ya want, in a tone of Huckleberry Hound gone mad, and the boy bit his lip and looked up at that big face and didn't say anything as his little face under that big major-league Rusty Staub ballcap went pink and then red and then pale white as he gathered courage, and then, in an awfully small voice asked what kind did the counterman have?

Vanilla/chocolate vanilla/strawberry growled the counterman in an evil voice, and the boy lowered his head and sighed, looked at the hot dogs in his hands and thought, hard, in fact, the bill of his ballcap all but obscuring his face, and he thought and thought, and thought and thought and thought and then looked up to the counterman who was turning a darker color, heading toward plum, and the boy parted his lips, and with his eyes wide and honest injun, said, but almost in a whisper,

I don't know!

The counterman's face was heading toward a funny green and I thought he was going to flip, VANILLACHOKLIT cried the boy, which he got, along with a plastic spoon. The counterman took the boy's money, made change and gave it to the boy and the boy left and that's the way it went until it finally came my turn. I made my order which I quickly received, and as he rang up the sale I put mustard on the four hot dogs, and put them along with two cold beers in the box, and when the counterman gave me my change I took the singles and gave him the silver as a tip, for which he thanked me, and as our eyes met we both smiled.

You gotta be patient, I said.

It's a lousy job, he said, and I agreed. It was, as he sipped from a paper cup, something kin but amber to my little water in my herring & sour cream jar, tossing me a wink over the rim, and we grinned. I moved out of the shrill swirl of waiting kids, and headed toward the ramp and as I emerged into the vista of the stadium Staub stepped into the batter's box. I finally made my way up the steps to Asa, and as I sat down I saw the distant figure of the agency detective settle himself in his seat on the far end of the next section, and take a bite from his hot dog and a long pull of beer. He was alone.

"Hot dog!" Asa laughed. She took 'em and bit one hungrily, and chewed and drank beer thirstily. As she told me what had happened I made the marks on my scorecard.

Matthews had grounded out third to first, Garrett had made a fine play, Speier had walked and somehow, which neither of us could figure out, there had been two out when Thomasson flied out to left to end the inning. So the bottom of the fourth and the Mets were up. I ate a hot dog and drank beer. Asa put her arm around my neck, kissed my cheek, told me this was wonderful, more fun than she'd ever dreamed. She'd never been to a major-league game. I took her hand in mine and kissed her fingers, looked in her eyes and said a word or two. She agreed, and we breathed hot dogs, mustard, beer, vodka and cigarette tar on each other as we laughed, and Staub took a strike and, as is his habit, looked back to the umpire. Strike confirmed. Staub resumed his forward bending stance, bat straight up. Asa finished her second dog, sipped beer, sat back, lit up a cigarette and watched him with a neat little smile.

It was I guess because of the cool cloudiness that the big crowd stayed away, but I was glad because we could stretch our feet across the seats before us, as the two rows of seats were empty. Thought of Penny Lane. I hummed some. Staub hit a liner foul down the first-base line and one of the vets to our right yelled Hit one like that *fair*, and when, on the next pitch Staub hit down the *third*-base line foul, the vet yelled the same thing, and on the next pitch, which was a ball, which the red-headed power as on the wings of butterflies took, he, on the next pitch, fouled it onto the screen behind home and the old guy on our right shouted The other way! pointing to center field, and half out of his seat, cigar butt between fingers around a beer.

Staub hit the next pitch into center for a single.

I bet that vet felt like Babe Ruth.

Staub stood on first base casually taking off his batting glove like he was waiting for a streetcar in a small town in Ohio, and then took his lead. But Torre struck out. Garrett walked and Staub jogged down to second as Grote came up, dug in, and in an effort to hit into right field behind the runners, unusually good Met thinking, he sent a smart hopper to Thomas at second who tossed to Speier crossing second who on the pivot threw a straight line to Montanez at first for the double play and the Mets were down. One hit no runs, and I filled everything in on my scorecard. So far, going into the top of the fifth, Seaver had pitched a one-hit shutout, walking only one and striking out five.

I have a hunch this is going to be Seaver's all the way, I said to Asa, also thinking it might be his best year yet. She said she wished she knew more about it, although she admitted she had played softball and was, in fact, a good player, but still, she further admitted, she wished she had kept up with *base*ball and I said I wished I had too. A Pan Am 747 drifted over the ballpark, heading east to exotic places with a trailing rushing roaring wind behind, and Dave Rader, who had gotten the only hit off Seaver so far, came to bat as the Mets finished throwing the ball around. Garrett threw it to Seaver and Seaver rubbed it around and watched Rader dig in, and I think it was on a two and one count that Rader hit a hard grasscutter to Phillips who grabbed it, and in a motion like conductors make to the trumpets in the approach to the end of the fourth movement, Phillips laced it to first for the out. 6-3, one down and a ripple of applause swept over the crowd. The infield fired the ball around and again Garrett tossed it to Seaver who rubbed it hard and looked in to Grote for the sign, as Ontiveros, the Giant third baseman, waited for the pitch which he subsequently drilled into left for a single BUT then bingo suddenly another terrific play.

The Giant pitcher, Montefusco, hit a high hopper to the mound which Seaver went up for and got, turned and threw to Phillips as Phillips swept across second base and in a slashing motion threw to Millan at first for the double play bam, like that, except it had been slightly different, because Met second baseman Millan covered first because Met first baseman Torre had gone in toward home on the chance of a bunt, and it was really nifty to see 'em move so professionally and that Millan was so absolutely there for Phillips's throw. Millan made a gesture of excellence to Phillips who acknowledged it with a nod and they ran off the field together. I wondered if Millan was getting Phillips ready to take control of the infield, as Harrelson (out on injuries), seemed to have lost, and that cannot be.

One hit, no runs: 1/0. Seaver had again figured in the vital sense.

It was the bottom of the fifth, and, in the mystery of order, as in the secret surprise in the unfolding of normal expectations, suddenly, marvelously, Phillips was up.

You could almost see it—we all felt it. A certain restless happy apprehension, a certain sparkle, something almost invisible, but not quite, like a shimmer in the air, a subtle tingle in the sensibilities which felt great, and I leaned forward intently. Asa was absorbed in it too, and was reading my scorecard, murmuring to herself. I said,

How about a little water?

She laughed and nodded, eagerly, so we had a nip and a chaser of beer, good, I lit up a smoke and waited for what I was certain would happen, yet not knowing how it would, and I rubbed my hands. She made a merry little laugh as Phillips took a strike.

The clouds had seemed to lift a bit, and I was certain it wasn't going to rain. Another one of those in-between days. The crowd, not being able to stand the suspense, began to clap and a scattering of kids across the park began to chant Let's go Mets, in their piping voices, and Phillips took a ball, and in my own pleased apprehension I put my beer, scorecard, and pencil on the empty seat before me.

Why are you doing that? Asa asked.

Just in case, I grinned, and the fans clapped louder and in more volume as he took ball two, but it died down and the ballpark got quiet when he took a strike, and in the tingling and silent suspense in the crowd the place was so quiet you could hear a glove drop, but on the next pitch— on a two and two count—on what looked like an outside fastball Phillips met it perfectly: a fraction too late and right on the button sending a long *hard* hummer over the second baseman's head into and up the alley in right center and as he dug around first the ballpark was on its feet, me and Asa too, as Joshua and Thomasson converged on it, Joshua getting the jump, but the hand of Fate gave the Giants a raw deal, for as Joshua, the Giant center fielder, got there and was correctly prepared to hold Phillips to a long single, the ball hit a pebble in the grass, or a tiny ridge made from someone's spikes, and took a bad hop and went behind Joshua, and Phillips raced toward second. Thomasson overran the ball, and Joshua ran hard toward the wall, chasing the bounding ball, which he got as Phillips rounded second and went toward third with everything he had as Joshua made the long throw to second which Thomas took, pivoted, and threw a strike to Ontiveros at third *just about* when Phillips slid in—but not quite, because Phillips came in under the glove and before the tag and when Ontiveros made the tag the umpire, in the drama some of them love, quickly stooped and threw his arms out wide: hands down and Phillips was in safe with a triple—a buckeye triple, but still a triple—and the cheers and the applause rocked the stadium.

We had a guy on third. Nobody out.

Seaver came to bat and everybody remained standing standing as on the end of the diving board happily, while Seaver took a couple of pitches and we all gradually sat back down again, and on what looked like a low curve strike that hung a little on the outside corner Seaver swung down, and hit the ball hard, on the nose, sending it bouncing between first and second into right field for a single and Phillips scored and everybody in tumult, the ballpark on its feet again all of us crazy and hollering and all and me and Asa with our arms around each other, oh those sluggin' pitchers! the score was two to *nuthin'*! as the batboy ran out and Seaver put on the blue jacket, and stood on first base as people clapped and cheered and the batboy ran back into the dugout.

Seaver took a couple of steps off the bag as the Giant pitcher went into his motion, and Unser, at bat, waited.

But he flied to center. Joshua got it handsomely and threw it in to Speier. One down.

We were in our seats again and I said: Phillips has two hits, a double and a chancy triple, he's scored twice and both those runs are because of Seaver. Not bad!

She nodded, and I warmed at the sight of her profile, and her intense gaze on Millan as he crossed himself as he walked to the plate. Then he stepped in and took his stance. Choking the bat, like he does, way up, the Braves were fools to let him go, but they did and there he was, and he whacked a liner about two inches off the ground on the chalk line—all the way down into the right-field corner, and went into and tore around first, lost his cap, and then went into second at the last moment slowing for a stand-up double as the ballpark tilted in a solid cheer and Seaver ran and ran and ran and ran as we cheered and cheered and he slid safely into third—well WELL!

Thus Kranepool walked and Staub came up with the bases loaded. The kids were piping, shrilling, shouting and yelling and cheering and carrying on somethin' terrific. Staub took a couple & then—he hit the ball into left center, just a shade toward center, but in left field, and not very deep as Seaver tagged up and the tension was wonderful! The ball wasn't in any hurry, it hung around in the air, but after a while it dropped into Joshua's waiting glove and Seaver took off as fast as he could toward home, and as he came in positioning his body for the slide, Torre, the next batter, held his hands up like Hands Up! and Seaver stayed on his feet and crossed home plate on a run, the throw was cut off, there were two out and the runners held. Score, three zip.

Seaver ducked down into the dugout and his teammates surrounded him as Torre stepped in.

Oh, Asa said, Seaver's *beautiful*.

Want a beer? I asked, there's the beer man—

She shook her head and I walked down and got one, came back, sat down drinking, Torre took strike two, and as I marked everything down on my scorecard, he struck out, so at the bottom of the fifth it was total five hits and three runs for us and two hits and *nuthin'* for them.

Seaver lasted the sixth and the seventh and big jets flew east to Kipling-land, but in the top of the eighth after Rader flied out, Ontiveros walked, and Adams, pinch-hitting for Giant pitcher Montefusco, singled, McMillan came out and we saw Seaver nod, and as he walked off the field he got a standing ovation, as pitcher Jerry Koosman came in. Berra wouldna done that.

But it was a good move, as Seaver was exhausted. On one of the last pitches he threw, we saw him pushing, trying too hard—the hitting and all that running he'd done did it.

Asa laughed seeing that bizarre auto in the form of a baseball with a Mets cap on top putter in, Koosman got out, went to the mound and began his few warm-ups, and I wondered. I'd seen enough of Koosman to know how good he is, but—well, in the (this) clutch, I wasn't sure.

But he got 'em. On a force at second and a snappy 6-4-3 Phillips to Millan to Torre double play to end the inning. And after Speier pulled off a dazzling double play of his own, which wiped out the Mets in their eighth, the Giants came to bat in the top of the ninth. Montanez singled, Koosman took a hard *mean* grounder from Matthews, whirled, and because Phillips, on the right-handed hitter, was playing for the ball to come on that side, Millan covered second and was the pivot man for a terrific double play.

Two down, and all the crowd—everybody—kids, vets, vendors, cops, poets, and other types including me and Asa—watched Koosman strike out Speier to end the game, as in a universal cheer *hooray*.

We sat down, and leaned back, and then, as everybody rose and began to leave the ballpark, I notated the K, made the totals, lit up a smoke and then lit Asa's smoke, and we shared the last of the beer and watched the cops line up along the first- and third-base lines, as the field attendants rolled out the big tarp cylinder and began covering the infield, and, like memories of me, pieces of stray paper blew across the deserted outfield. Days gone by.

Then we stood up too, stretched, and walked down the steps to begin the long journey home. That long walk to the subway, and the long subway ride, the transfer, and then—at Grand Central we decided to take a cab, which we did, and Asa, who said she wanted to go home and clean up her place, it was a mess, she said, & we crossed the city. She got out on the corner of the street where she lived—not, however, before I'd gotten a warm hug and a kiss that is yet on my lips. Just as her words are still in my ear: *Thanks Lucky, it's been wonderful.*

I watched her elegant figure walk briskly away as the machine I was in moved off on a tangent, and so I went my way too, suddenly deciding right then and there that the next day's papers would, in their usual dry style, report the same dull shit about Seaver's beautiful 17th win. More news in the same old language written by the same old hack reporters who work for the same old editors who work under the fist of the same old publishers, so! as I had my scorecard, and all the people, the ballpark, and the whole feel of the whole game in my mind, why not write it the way it really *ought* to be written? Something I'd wanted to do anyway, just about all my life. I'd suffered that dull old daily baseball reportage frustration in daily newspapers since I was a boy, and even then, when I was fifteen & I'd gotten my first typewriter, a black Royal portable, secondhand, I'd wanted to write about DiMaggio, & Musial, & Mize, Jack Robinson and Ned Garver and Williams in *my* way—

Thus this story.

I didn't go to the ballgame with Asa. I went by myself. But that's what the reporters called reality, which I, being real, will know in another, different story which one day I'll write—but anyway I don't much bother with what they call real. Being forty-five years old, alone at a major-league ballgame with my memories. That's real, okay. But I do something else—I do what I do, and what I do is what I call my art, my mythology, my self.

And there, as Kipling wrote, in the last sentence of a story called *The Man Who Would Be King*, the matter rests.

RIVERFRONT

Sandra Soto Hatfield

Fine drops of rain
run down like young streams from
plastic summer parkas
down the arms of curved chairs
falling from the hair of
three men in row 38B
in row C
an elegant young face intense
carved mahogany, small rivulets
carelessly sliding from aquiline nose
upon a knee
make random patterns
merge with cement water then
continue through the human sea
past soggy red-hots Hudepohl and
staggering shells from peanuts delved
now forgotten in one
unanimous need for sun.

billows of tarp begin to wave
rolling tossing toward home plate
slowly moving to the low buzz-sung
stanza of hawkers, families, fans
a man wearing a blue hat
is on the mound
reds near the dug-out
swing various wooden bats
rhythmic oars skimming water from air
beating the haze clear
at last
high up near the flying flags
sings an accented bird-like voice
"vaya, Perez, vaya"
far below a small voice echoes
"let's go Bench"
sun drenches the stands.

From **DESOLATION ANGELS**

Jack Kerouac

To while away the time I play my solitaire card baseball game Lionel and I invented in 1942 when he visited Lowell and the pipes froze for Christmas—the game is between the Pittsburgh Plymouths (my oldest team, and now barely on top of the 2nd division) and the New York Chevvies rising from the cellar ignominiously since they were world champions last year. I shuffle my deck, write out the lineups, and lay out the teams—For hundreds of miles around, black night, the lamps of Desolation are lit, to a childish sport, but the Void is a child too—and here's how the game goes:—what happens:—how it's won, and by whom:—

The opposing pitchers are, for the Chevvies, Joe McCann, old vet of 20 years in my leagues since first at 13 age I'd belt iron rollerbearings with a nail in the appleblossoms of the Sarah backyard, Ah sad—Joe McCann, with a record of 1-2, (this is the 14th game of the season for both clubs), and an earned run average of 4.86, the Chevvies naturally heavily favored and especially as McCann is a star pitcher and Gavin a secondrater in my official effectiveness rulings—and the Chevvies are hot anyway, comin up, and took the opener of this series 11-5 . . .

The Chevvies jump right out ahead in their half of the first inning as Frank Kelly the manager belts a long single into center bringing home Stan Orsowski from second where he'd gone on a bingle and walk to Duffy—yag, yag, you can hear those Chevvies (in my mind) talking it up and whistling and clapping the game on—The poor greenclad Plymouths come on for their half of the opening inning, it's just like real life, real baseball, I cant tell the difference between this and that howling wind and hundreds of miles of Arctic Rock without—

But Tommy Turner with his great speed converts a triple into an inside-the-park homerun and anyway Sim Kelly has no arm out there and it's Tommy's sixth homerun, he is the "magnificent one" all right—and his 15th run batted in and he's only been playin six games because he was injured, a regular Mickey Mantle—

Followed immediately back to back by a line drive homerun over the rightfield fence from the black bat of old Pie Tibbs and the Plyms jump out ahead 2-1 . . . wow . . .

(the fans go wild in the mountain, I hear the rumble of celestial racing cars in the glacial crevasses)

—Then Lew Badgurst singles to right and Joe McCann is really getting belted (and him with his fancy earned run average) (pah, goes to show)—

In fact McCann is almost batted out of the box as he further gives up a walk to Tod Gavin but Ole Reliable Henry Pray ends up the inning grounding out to Frank Kelly at third—it will be a slugfest.

Then suddenly the two pitchers become locked in an unexpected brilliant pitching duel, racking up goose egg after goose egg, neither one of them giving up a hit except one single (Ned Gavin the pitcher got it) in the second inning, right on brilliantly up the uttermost eighth when Zagg Parker of the Chevs finally breaks the ice with a single to right which (he too for great super runner speed) unopposed stretches into a double (the throw is made but he makes it, sliding)— and a new tone comes in the game you'd think but no!—Ned Gavin makes Clyde Castleman fly out to center then calmly strikes out Stan the Man Orsowski and stalks off the mound chewing his tobacco unperturbed, the very void—Still, a 2-1 ballgame favor of his team—

McCann yields a single to big bad Lew Badgurst (with big arms southpawing that bat) in *his* half of the eighth, and there's a base stolen on him by pinch runner Allen Wayne, but no danger as he gets Tod Gavin on a grounder—

Going into the final inning, still the same score, the same situation.

All Ned Gavin has to do is hold the Chevvies for 3 long outs. The fans gulp and tense. He has to face Byrd Duffy (batting .346 up to the game), Frank Kelly, and pinch hitter Tex Davidson—

He hitches up his belt, sighs, and faces the chubby Duffy—and winds up—Low, one ball. Outside, ball two.

Long fly to center field but right in the hands of Tommy Turner.

Only two to go.

"Come on Neddy!" yells manager Cy Locke from the 3rd base box, Cy Locke who was the greatest shortstop of all time in his time in my appleblossom time when Pa was young and laughed in the summernight kitchen with beer and Shammy and pinochle—

Frank Kelly up, dangerous, menacing, the manager, hungry for money and pennants, a whiplash, a firebrand—

Neddy winds up: delivers: inside.

Ball one.

Delivers.

Kelly belts it to right, off the flagpole, Tod Gavin chases, it's a standup double, the tying run is on second, the crowd is wild. Whistles, whistles, whistles—

Speedboy Selman Piva is sent out to run for Kelly.

Tex Davidson is a big veteran chaw-chawin old outfielder of the old wars, he drinks at night, he doesnt care—He strikes out with a big wheeling whackaround of the empty bat.

Ned Gavin has thrun him 3 curves. Frank Kelly curses in the dugout, Piva, the tying run, is still on second. *One more to go!*

The batter: Sam Dane, Chevvy catcher, old veteran chawidrinkbuddy in fact of Tex David-son's, only difference is Sam bats lefty—same height, lean, old, dont care—

Ned pitches a call strike across the letters—

And there it comes:—a booming homerun over the centerfield barrier, Piva comes home, Sam comes loping around chewing his tobacco, still doesnt care, at the plate he is mobbed by the Kellies and the crazies—

Bottom of the 9th, all Joe McCann has to do is hold the Plymouth—Pray gets on an error, Gucwa singles, they hold at second and first, and up steps little Neddy Gavin and doubles home the tying run and sends the winning run to third, pitcher eat pitcher—Leo Sawyer pops up, it looks like McCann'll hold out, but Tommy Turner simply slaps a sacrifice grounder and in comes the winning run, Jack Gucwa who'd singled so unobtrusively, and the Plymouths rush out and carry Ned Gavin to the showers atop their shoulders.

Tell me Lionel and I didnt invent a good game!

THE MYSTICAL INDIAN PENNANT VISION

Dennis J. Kucinich

Two Sioux did a pas de deux as Leonard Crow Dog, M.M., blew sacred smoke at the Great Spirit to break the drought which had been microwaving the soybeans on a hard brown dish once called a farm in Clyde, Ohio.

One hundred miles east, eight Cleveland Indians invoked the One Great Scorer. They took their ritualistic positions around a green diamond while a sphere of white smoke floated from the right hand of a mound builder named Chief Candy Man, past the transfixed eyes of the Men in the pinstriped White Coats, while fifty thousand brave fans inhaled deeply and saw championship visions.

Cleveland, eleven runs, ten hits, no errors. New York, three runs, six hits, no errors. Cleveland two games to one in a home weekend series with the Yankees. Cleveland, two games out of first place, locked into a three-way race with the Yankees and the Tigers.

We believe. We believe.

That crafty journeyman from Ixtlan, Carlos Castaneda, once said if you take your attention away from the world for one moment the world collapses, so you can imagine what looking at Tom Candiotti's knuckleball most of the day would do to the cash-register brains of the Martinets from Manhattan. Was it just Candiotti's paper-rags routine he learned last year from that old junkman Phil Niekro that started the Yankees' fall from first place? Or was it Joe Montana's crimson and gold Forty-Niner's jersey Candiotti wore underneath his Indian slicks, like some Bay Area version of Superman? Did Leonard Crow Dog, M.M., and his feathered friends fan the holy smokes all the way to Cleveland? Is Cleveland about to break a thirty-four-year pennant drought?

Where's that *Sports Illustrated* cover from the Opener in 1987? You know, where the Indians were predicted to win The Big One. They finished in the basement, instead. So the Baseball Scribes United Against White Space augured a year early. It's like baseball and the Bible, the first shall be last and the last shall be first: In the BigInning, Genesis 1.

My God, I haven't been this excited about Cleveland baseball since I tossed the first pitch at the home opener in 1978 while wearing a bulletproof vest as thirty sharpshooters watched nervously from the roof of the packed Municipal Stadium. People were yelling "Throw the bum out," yet no umpire had taken the field, only me walking toward the mound to claim my ceremonial propers. Strange. As I recall, all I did was to fire Dick Hongisto as manager of the police athletic league or something. I got a standing boo. Me, duh Mayuh. But I couldn't be distracted by the pressure. I had a job to do. I visualized a strike, saw the ball rocket from my arm straight and true to the Indians' catcher waiting at the plate to get this mess over with. I shook off some totally inappropriate signals from the catcher. I threw a strike. The boos turned to cheers. Baseball is a lot like politics.

If Dick could have played Billy Martin to my Steinbrenner, there is no telling how far we could have taken that act.

Cleveland is great sports town. Show me one other city whose population keeps dropping as its home attendance is soaring, from 562,117 in the first thirty-five games in 1987 to 746,307 for thirty-five games in 1988.

Last year at this time, the Indians were sixteen games back, praying for rain-outs, making repeated attempts to kill themselves, but you can't commit suicide jumping out of a basement window. This year they continue to have a respectable offensive punch led by MVP contender Joe Carter, with strong assists by Julio Franco, Mel Hall, Cory Snyder, and streak hitter Ron Kittle.

But if Connie Mack was right, about pitching being 90 percent of the game, then the Indians were only 60'6" away from another ninety victories last year.

General Manager Hank Peters brought in a new manager, Doc Edwards, and a new pitching coach, Mark Wiley, and the emotionally shell-shocked starters began to take on a new confidence, a new aggressive approach, going after the hitters, throwing strikes, not wasting pitches.

Greg Swindell, whose arm injury left his career flapping in 1987, came charging back to become the first in the majors to win ten games. Wiley has been getting Candiotti and John Farrell to pitch smarter, better, easier, to vary their pitches. For Farrell it was simply shifting gears from a high-strung fastball to off-speed. Candiotti now spins variations on his curve. Scott Bailes and injured Rick Yett have been erratic, but each has a winning season in his arm. Hopefully that season is 1988.

Doug Jones, your average pitcher, average surname, unremarkable in recent years except for a past life as Zeno the Stoic which bleeds through to the present, has been reincarnated as the feared reliever, Special Delivery Jones, with more saves than a circuit breaker at Three Mile Island.

The wild surmise of an '87 pennant, and the stick-and-stick routine of managerial drill sergeant Pat Corrales had the team cracking and losing. The operative word was CHOKE. The pressure is on in '88 but the response of the team is laid back, like Alfred E. Neuman chilling out at Catalina. The operative word is RELAX. The Indians publicly exhort each other against yielding to pressure the same way F.D.R. warned against fear of fear.

Andy Allanson hit a grand slam to beat the Yankees. When asked how it felt, he told the Plain Dealer's Paul Hoynes, "It feels red." Is Allanson into creative visualization? Does Swindell play Cyber Vision tapes, or what? Is Wiley showing David Carradine movies in the locker room? Are the Indians playing Kung-Fu ball? What if someone would have asked the Reagans a few years ago if they had any feelings about Scorpio conjuncting Mars?

This season is really different and I think it's about time the people of Cleveland were given some answers. The people have a right to know.

BROOKLYN AUGUST

Stephen King

for Jim Bishop

In Ebbets Field the crab-grass grows
(where Alston managed)
row on row
                in a somehow sad twilight
                I still see them, with the green smell
                of just-mown infield grass heavy
                in the dark channels of my nose:
                picked out by the right-field floods, just
                turned on and already assaulted by circling moths
                and bugs on the night shift—
                below, the old men and offduty taxi drivers
                drinking big cups of Schlitz in the 75¢ seats,
                this Flatbush as real as velvet Harlem streets
                where jive hangs suspended in the streets of '56
In Ebbets Field the infield's slow
and seats are empty, row on row
                Hodges crouched over first, glove stretched
                to touch the throw from Robinson at third
                the batters' boxes white as mist against

the glowing sky-filled evening
(Mantle homered early, Flatbush is down by 2);
Newcombe trudged past first to a silent shower
Carl Erskine is in now and chucking hard but
Johnny Podres and Clem Labine are heating
in case it goes haywire in the late going
In Ebbets Field they come and go
and play their innings, blow by blow
time's called in the dimness of the 5th
someone threw a bottle at Sandy Amoros in right
he spears it in wordless ballet, hands it
to the groundskeeper;
the faceless fans cry down juicy Brooklyn vowels
on both, who ignore them beautifully
Pee Wee Reese leans on his knees west of second
Campanella gives the sign
with my eyes closed I can see it all
smell eight pm dirt and steamed franks
in crenellated cardboard troughs;
can see the purple evening above the stadium dish
as Erskine winds and throws low-inside:

THE MINDS REEL IN DREAM AT-BAT

Peter Richmond

What goes through their heads when the best meet the best? With the pennant on the line?

We devised a dream at-bat: Dwight Gooden of the Mets on the mound, Tony Gwynn of the Padres at the plate, bases loaded, two out, bottom of the ninth, pennant at stake.

"Sounds good to me," Gwynn said from Yuma, Arizona. "Let's do it."

First, each offers some observations about the other.

Gooden, speaking at the Mets camp in Port St. Lucie, on Gwynn: "He gets his hits off me. But I've done well against him. You have to pitch him the opposite of everyone else because he anticipates what you're doing so well.

"I won't throw him any change-ups or off-speed curves because his reactions are too good. Also, he has some power, so I have to be extra careful. Every now and then he'll straighten up a little at the plate, and then I'll know he's going to try to hit for power."

Gwynn on Gooden: "I've seen every pitch he throws. He's one heck of a competitor. He knows how to attack a hitter. When I go up against him I realize he's got a game plan. He's not going to just be throwing the ball.

"Against Gooden I just want to get my bat on the ball. I don't want him to strike me out. His fastball is an overpowering fastball, and very rarely will I catch up with it. I might foul off a few down the left-field line. I know from experience he won't throw me off-speed stuff."

All right. Gwynn steps to the plate.

Gooden: "I'd start him off with a high fastball inside. Letter-high."

Gwynn: "I'm going to take it."

It's inside. The count is 1-0.

Gooden: "Same pitch again."

Gwynn: "Yeah—that makes plenty of sense to me. On the first pitch, I'm taking, and if it's a ball he knows I'm taking again. So he comes right back for a fastball."

This one slices the black on the rear inside corner of the plate: 1-1.

Gooden: "I throw him a hard curve. Hard breaking stuff."

Gwynn: "Taking it back to previous at-bats, I bet he comes back with a hard, snapping breaking ball. Not the slow overhand hook, but one that's got some snap."

Gwynn fouls it off: 1-2.

Gooden: "I'll paint him a fastball away. A half-inch off the plate. Hopefully, he goes for it."

Gwynn: "You betcha! That makes plenty of sense. With two strikes as a hitter I'm trying to protect the plate."

For the sake of drama, the pitch sails a foot outside. Gwynn holds off: 2-2.

Gooden: "Then I come back with the fastball up and in."

Gwynn: "Yep, I'm going to be looking for that."

But it's high. The count is loaded. The runners are going. The season is on the line.

Gooden: "I throw him the hard hook."

Gwynn: "There it is. Yes, sir. I was going to say it before you said it. He's going to come back with the hard overhand curveball. There have been times he's thrown me fastballs—three, four in a row, and after the first two you say to yourself, 'Sooner or later he's going to come with the hard overhand curve,' but you can't look for it. You have to look for the fastball."

Gwynn fouls it off. Still 3-2.

Gooden: "Then I just hump it up and reach for the extra fastball. The best fastball I can throw."

Gwynn: "Let's do it."

For the sake of fairness, let's leave it right there. The Gooden fastball is sailing in. The runners are going. Gwynn sets. He explodes out of his crouch . . .

REDS, YANKS, AND O'S

Dwight Allen

Baseball is a long game," my mother said to me one night this summer. We were in Cincinnati, outside the pile known as Riverfront Stadium, where we'd just seen the Reds play the division-leading San Francisco Giants. We'd sat in the left-field corner, high above the synthetic blue-green sward, behind a guy who wore a Red Man chewing tobacco cap and said things like "Aw, shoot" and "You big sissy" (when a San Francisco pitcher intentionally walked Eric Davis, the Reds' bony cleanup hitter). My mother read Thomas Merton on prayer between innings and sometimes during innings, and I and the white-haired gent next to me (my father, the only person within sight wearing a tie and a seersucker suit) studied Pete Rose, who hardly budged from his foxhole in the dugout, and livelier, less celebrated folk, such as Rick Mahler. (Marge Schott, the Reds' principal owner and a person who dearly loves the limelight, made a pregame appearance to salute the state high school Triple A baseball champs; her two St. Bernards, who get a fair amount of ink in the Reds' official literature, didn't appear.) Mahler, a rubber-armed right-hander who labored for Atlanta and its farm teams for fourteen years before ascending to Cincinnati last winter, regularly leads the league in hits allowed, and tonight he permitted the visitors an even ten. He also surrendered five runs, but the three San Francisco pitchers were more generous: the Redlegs scored twelve times, four of them on a Paul O'Neill homer that followed the free pass to Davis. "Woo-hoo, mama," shouted the guy in the Red Man cap.

My parents live in Kentucky, about two hours from Cincinnati, and my mother may have been thinking about the drive home when she made that comment about baseball being a long game. We were walking across a footbridge that links the ballpark to downtown. The western sky featured a half-moon. I looked back at the stadium, which sits on the bank of the muddy Ohio and in the glare of day resembles an industrial-belt eyesore (a vat, a holding tank), and thought that, awash in lights, it looked pretty good. I was feeling pretty good myself, having abstained from drinking the local beer, Hudepohl, and from eating the local fried meats which, as Satchel Paige pointed out, "angry up the blood," and my father, his tie loosened, was walking like a man who had just seen his team rout the black hats. I thought about my mother's comment. She wasn't wrong, of course. The baseball season—six months, 2,106 games—is flat-out long, and it is a rare one of those games that doesn't ramble or sputter or digress or somehow (as they say in lit class) violate the rules of dramatic narrative. Baseball takes its own sweet time reaching its conclusions, or, to put it another way, it gives *you* time (while the pitcher lollygags and the batter idles outside the box, adjusting his gloves and 24-karat neckwear), to nap or meditate or consider the swell bubble-gum bubble that Will Clark, the Giants' strong-jawed first baseman, has just produced.

Baseball yields its pleasures erratically and sometimes, it seems, almost aimlessly. Nothing much happens, and then a little cloud of dust rises from around second base; Todd Benzinger, the Reds' unswift first sacker, has just surprised the Giants' pitcher by stealing. Moments later, more dust is stirred up around second; Benzinger, overexcited perhaps by his theft, has wandered too far from the bag and been picked off. As it turned out, none of this mattered; the Reds were ahead, 8-4, when Benzinger ran, and they would not have got him home anyway. But this sequence—the kind of unserious thing that sets baseball apart from compact, clock-driven games—is stuck in my memory, next to socko stuff like Paul O'Neill's grand slam.

In 1961, when the Reds played the Yankees in the World Series, my father won two tickets in an office lottery and took me to Cincinnati to see Game Five. We sat in folding chairs at the very top of airy, rickety Crosley Field (razed in 1972 after the Redlegs moved to Riverfront) and watched the Yankee *reserves* (Mantle and Berra were on the bench, Maris was worn out) pound our boys. I was ten, and for a little while after this show of force I was a Yankee fan.

The major-league ballpark nearest to where I live now is Yankee Stadium—a long way from Cincinnati. Yankee Stadium is the kind of place where, I imagine, my mother would find it hard to concentrate on Thomas Merton. It's the kind of place where people tend not to say "Aw, shoot" or "Dadgummit" when they express displeasure. It's the kind of place that employs enough security guards and trenchcoated crowd-control experts to make you wonder if General Steinbrenner and his lieutenants are preparing for a siege. It's the kind of place where the game sometimes appears to be a sideshow to whatever is happening on the jumbo video screen—commercials, blooper films, replays, live footage of the "Bud Fan of the Game" and other telegenic people. It's possible to imagine a person going to Yankee Stadium and deciding that baseball, at least as it's practiced in that garden spot, is *too* long a game.

I have friends who, for their own reasons, are lifetime Yankee fans, and I went with one of them early in the season to watch the Bombers play the Texas Rangers. My friend, a building contractor who had decided to skip an appearance in small-claims court that evening so that he could see his team, grew up in southeastern Pennsylvania, territory that the Philadelphia Phillies and the Baltimore Orioles shared. (His father rooted for the Phillies, up to, during, and even beyond the Great Collapse of 1964.) But it was the Yankees who took hold of him, in the fifties and early sixties, when they were mighty and he was young and impressionable.

It's not easy being a Yankee fan nowadays, if for no other reason than that it takes some effort to keep up with the roster changes. Most Yankee players seem to be on temporary leaves of absence from other clubs. The Yankee pitching mound is a place that many people wearing pinstripes visit and few return to with any frequency. The night my friend and I went to the Stadium, the hill was occupied by Andy Hawkins, a recent import from San Diego. Hawkins has a peculiar lazybones sort of pitching motion, in which he pauses at the hindmost point in his windup, as if to consider his options, and then seems to flip the ball toward the plate. He managed to keep the potent Ranger offense at bay until the fourth, when Ruben Sierra hit a long and distinguished triple to left center. A group of Latinos sitting in front of us made a joyful noise. "Aieee, Sierra!" One in a group of crabby Anglos sitting behind us said, "Why dontcha shud-dup?" Twenty-six Rangers followed Sierra to the plate during the fourth, fifth, and sixth, and twelve of them took a tour of the bases. My friend muttered unkind things about Hawkins and his successor, an ex-Ranger named Dale Mohorcic, who hit three batters (two of them *dos-à-dos*) in a brief, inglorious stint. By the eighth, the Stadium had nearly emptied out. The video screen continued to flash and boom, and the organist continued to noodle away, but the loudest sound was the quiet in the stands.

I came back a couple of weeks later, to see the American League champion Oakland A's, in their white shoes and yellow stockings and green hats, hoping that the Stadium would be, well, a happier place than usual. I sat in a twelve-dollar seat in the loge, in the general vicinity of the left-field foul pole. Everybody in my section stood up for the national anthem (it was canned, and was introduced by Bob Sheppard, the stadium P.A. man and elocution master, with terrific solemnity), and many people in my section stood up again to watch a fight in another part of the stands or to make a beer run or to howl at the Yankee pitcher (Hawkins again, strangely enough). It was another night at the Stadium, except that the Oakland pitchers—the firm of Burns, Honeycutt & Plunk—threw a perfect one-hitter. (Only Rickey Henderson reached base, and he was instantly erased on a double play.) Though this performance seemed to take place behind a scrim, in between distractions, I found it possible to admire in a distant sort of way. An hour or so later, when I and some sullen Yankee customers were trying to exit Lot 13 and make our way onto the Major Deegan, I was still admiring it. It—the unlikely game—was the only thing about the night that I was able to remember with any pleasure.

A week before the A's game, I drove down to Baltimore. This was shortly before the Oriole players and coaches started saying things like "Yes, we have been pretty amazing, but remember, it's only June." The Orioles lost 107 games last year, surpassing by seven the franchise high set in 1954 by the newly renamed and replanted (but not rehabilitated) St. Louis Browns. Last season the O's, who had the best record in baseball between 1957 and 1987, won one game in April (out of twenty-three) and ten in May (out of twenty-seven). When I arrived in Baltimore, the club was hovering near the .500 mark, which was close to the top in the wan American League East. Those perennial non-contenders the Cleveland Indians, the Orioles' weekend opponents, were just ahead of them, in second place.

Fifteen summers ago, when the Orioles won their fifth division title in six years, I lived within shouting distance of Memorial Stadium, in a green working-class neighborhood, across the street from a convent. I suppose I didn't really appreciate my situation, since I went to only two games and have retained only odd bits of them: Don Baylor making a shoetop catch, Mickey Rivers (then with the Angels) streaking from home to third (he hit a pair of triples), my girl-friend's sunburned knees. When I came back this spring, I wondered if my wife and child would consider relocating—if not to within shouting distance of the ballpark (the O's are planning to move downtown in 1992), then to within the Baltimore area code. I walked to the stadium from my parking spot over near Calvert Street, past row houses that had gliders or swings on their front porches and flowers in their yards. I heard a mother say to a child hiding in some bushes, "Time for supper." I got to the stadium early, so I circled it—a horseshoe-shaped concrete struc-ture built in the fifties—listening to the sounds of batting practice (*tock*-pause-*tock*-pause) and looking for an entrance marked Early Birds & Fannish Fans. I read the inscription to the Baltimore war dead above the main entrance, and then went inside—with kids equipped with mitts and moms and pops and some people wearing Cleveland caps. The non–New York atmosphere made me giddy, and before I got to my seat I'd bought a program, a Media Guide, deep-fried crab cakes, a Coke, an orange O's T-shirt for my son, and a team cap for myself (the 1989 black model, which is emblazoned with a regulation *Icterus galbula* instead of the grinning jokebird of old). My seat was a dozen rows or so behind the home dugout, on the third-base side, and for a few moments I just sat there with my stuff, smiling in gratitude.

A local a cappella group called the Sweet Adelines sang the national anthem. (Oriole fans tend to hum and mumble and clear their throats until the second instance of "Oh, say," which they render, fortissimo, as "O's.") And then all the Ripkens—Cal, Jr., the shortstop, who was playing in his 1,126th consecutive game; his frisky younger brother Bill, who took over at second base in mid-1987; and their white-haired father, Cal, Sr., who has been an Oriole hand for thirty-three years and now serves as third-base coach, following an unhappy year and a week as manager—covered their heads. Jeff Ballard, the O's starting pitcher and the only player on the field with a degree in geophysics, covered his head, too, and went to work on Oddibe McDowell, the Tribe's flyweight leadoff man, who laid down a neat bunt between third and home. But it wasn't neat enough. Ballard, whose follow-through (he's a lefty) carried him in the direction of the bunt, threw out the fleet McDowell. Ballard and his mates sparkled in the field all night (good defense is an Oriole trademark), and the Oriole offense (built, in untraditional Oriole fashion, around speed and gumption) scuffled for a handful of runs off John Farrell and hulking former Oriole Tim Stoddard. "Love them ex-Orioles," a Southern gentleman sitting next to me said when Brady Anderson, the Baltimore center fielder, touched Stoddard for a single.

The game was in the seventh. It was raining a little, and there was thunder in the distance, and I was trying to decide whether to stay or go. The Orioles were up, 5-0, Ballard had retired fourteen Indians in a row, a few restless citizens in the upper deck were trying to make a Wave, I was coming back for the Sunday afternoon game—and then the Baltimore batter, Phil Bradley, swung mightily and hit a dribbler up the third-base line. Stoddard reached it just as a base runner, Craig Worthington, was about to reach him. Stoddard ran Worthington back toward third, where another Oriole, Brady Anderson, who had stolen second a moment ago, was about to perch. (There were two outs, which was why everybody was on the move.) Anderson retraced his steps, pursued by Felix Fermin, the Cleveland shortstop, who, when Worthington tried to head for home again, threw to his third baseman, Brook Jacoby, who was taking it easy down near the plate. Jacoby got on his horse and tagged out the re-retreating Worthington. All this took about ten seconds to accomplish, and when it was over, I said to myself, "Gee, I'd be crazy to leave."

FROM FATHER, WITH LOVE

Doris Kearns Goodwin

The game of baseball has always been linked in my mind with the mystic texture of childhood, with the sounds and smells of summer nights and with the memories of my father.

My love for baseball was born on the first day my father took me to Ebbets Field in Brooklyn. Riding in the trolley car, he seemed as excited as I was, and he never stopped talking; now describing for me the street in Brooklyn where he had grown up, now recalling the first game he had been taken to by his own father, now recapturing for me his favorite memories from the Dodgers of his youth—the Dodgers of Casey Stengel, Zack Wheat, and Jimmy Johnston.

In the evenings, when my dad came home from work, we would sit together on our porch and relive the events of that afternoon's game which I had so carefully preserved in the large, red scorebook I'd been given for my seventh birthday. I can still remember how proud I was to have mastered all those strange and wonderful symbols that permitted me to recapture, in miniature form, the every movement of Jackie Robinson and Pee Wee Reese, Duke Snider and Gil Hodges. But the real power of that scorebook lay in the responsibility it entailed. For all through my childhood, my father kept from me the knowledge that the daily papers printed daily box scores, allowing me to believe that without my personal renderings of all those games he missed while he was at work, he would be unable to follow our team in the only proper way a team should be followed, day by day, inning by inning. In other words, without me, his love for baseball would be forever incomplete.

To be sure, there were risks involved in making a commitment as boundless as mine. For me, as for all too many Brooklyn fans, the presiding memory of "the boys of summer" was the memory of the final playoff game in 1951 against the Giants. Going into the ninth, the Dodgers held a 4-1 lead. Then came two singles and a double, placing the winning run at the plate with Bobby Thomson at bat. As Dressen replaced Erskine with Branca, my older sister, with maddening foresight, predicted the forever famous Thomson homer—a prediction that left me so angry with her, imagining that with her words she had somehow brought it about, that I would not speak to her for days.

So the seasons of my childhood passed until that miserable summer when the Dodgers were taken away to Los Angeles by the unforgivable O'Malley, leaving all our rash hopes and dreams of glory behind. And then came a summer of still deeper sadness when my father died. Suddenly my feelings for baseball seemed an aspect of my departing youth, along with my child-hood freckles and my favorite childhood haunts, to be left behind when I went away to college and never came back.

Then one September day, having settled into teaching at Harvard, I agreed, half reluc-tantly, to go to Fenway Park. There it was again: the cozy ballfield scaled to human dimensions so that every word of encouragement and every scornful yell could be heard on the field; the fervent crowd that could, with equal passion, curse a player for today's failures after cheering his heroics the day before; the team that always seemed to break your heart in the last week of the season. It took only a matter of minutes before I found myself directing all my old intensities toward my new team—the Boston Red Sox.

I am often teased by my women friends about my obsession, but just as often, in the most unexpected places—in academic conferences, in literary discussions, at the most elegant dinner parties—I find other women just as crazily committed to baseball as I am, and the discovery creates an instant bond between us. All at once we are deep in conversation, mingling together the past and the present, as if the history of the Red Sox had been our history too.

There we stand, one moment recollecting the unparalleled performance of Yaz in '67, the next sharing ideas on how the present lineup should be changed; one moment recapturing the splendid career of "the Splendid Splinter," the next complaining about the manager's decision to pull the pitcher the night before. And then, invariably, comes the most vivid memory of all, the frozen image of Carlton Fisk as he rounded first in the sixth game of the '75 World Series, an image as intense in its evocation of triumph as the image of Ralph Branca weeping in the dugout is in its portrayal of heartache.

There is another, more personal memory associated with Carlton Fisk, for he was, after all the years I had followed baseball, the first player I actually met in person. Apparently, he had read the biography I had written on Lyndon Johnson and wanted to meet me. Yet when the meeting took place, I found myself reduced to the shyness of childhood. There I was, a professor at Harvard, accustomed to speaking with presidents of the United States, and yet, standing beside this young man in a baseball uniform, I was speechless.

Finally Fisk said that it must have been an awesome experience to work with a man of such immense power as President Johnson—and with that, I was at last able to stammer out, with a laugh, "Not as awesome as the thought that I am really standing here talking with you."

Perhaps I have circled back to my childhood, but if this is so, I am certain that my journey through time is connected in some fundamental way to the fact that I am now a parent myself, anxious to share with my three sons the same ritual I once shared with my father.

For in this linkage between the generations rests the magic of baseball, a game that has defied the ravages of modern life, a game that is still played today by the same basic rules and at the same pace as it was played one hundred years ago. There is something deeply satisfying in the knowledge of this continuity.

And there is something else as well which I have experienced sitting in Fenway Park with my small boys on a warm summer's day. If I close my eyes against the sun, all at once I am back at Ebbets Field, a young girl once more in the presence of my father, watching the players of my youth on the grassy field below. There is magic in this moment, for when I open my eyes and see my sons in the place where my father once sat, I feel an invisible bond between our three generations, an anchor of loyalty linking my sons to the grandfather whose face they never saw but whose person they have already come to know through this most timeless of all sports, the game of baseball.

"IT'S DONE"—WILL CLARK
—a poem for Bobby Stanley
Thom Ross

I sit here tonite (Oct. 9, 1989)
on a date which is important
now
to baseball fans
and will become some trivia question
soon;
and I re-read your poems
of Giants and your grandfather
and the tears came again to my eyes
as they did when Ryno grounded to Thompson and
after I turned off the television
I wept then;
both phones unplugged so as not to disturb this
DO NOT DISTURB
room.

Images came to mind I had not seen
nor thought of
for two decades . . .
the loud tock
of the clock in your house
when I spent the nights there as a child
and we burned Joe Nuxhall baseball cards (God knows what

they might be worth NOW)
and listened to Davenport pinch-hit in the ninth:
". . . . Bocabella chases it into the corner"
a triple in a win that would lead . . .
no where.

and your grandfather (who knew my grandfather)
took us to Candlestick in his Corvette;
Photo Day
with Duke Snider now wearing the orange and black,
Cepeda still here,
you talking to McCovey
and Ron Herbel beating the Reds
with Jim Ray and Orlando hitting home runs
over a fence which still revealed the Bay
(before the 49ers built up the walls)
and that strange red and white striped ENORMOUS
tripod
a mile away over the right field fence which we called
"McCovey's Foul Pole."

We had our own league formed of plastic and
car floor mats,
and named after our heroes. . . .
and if the call went against me I could always say
"Oh, yeah!! then I'm goin' home!!!"
and the call would swing my way
(and never did I do THAT unless I was so sure
in my mind
that I had been robbed and my threat of exit
was justice served. . . . I would not have argued
otherwise).

Del Cranberry driving a home run over Doug's play pen
in deep (55') right.
and the
Willie Mercury grand slam
over the high oleanders in centerfield and
Ron Search getting hit above the eye
at Planet Stadium (22' to right)
and we all huddled and agreed, even me who was, in fact,
Ron Search, that he could not play for 2 weeks

(22 stitches is what we ruled; above the left eye; 21
day DL. . . . and it stood!)

Scooter McDowell, Mij Kidney, Max Climax, Lobster Thermometer,
Will Power (did you see the sign the fan held up?)
and the boys with the swinging bats:
Richard Nowlan, Pierre Rouzier, Seth Roberts, Peter Gealy,
Devin Mahr, Ray Blacow (who I talked into a game of whiffle
ball on the day Joe Namath and the JETS beat the COLTS
in Super Bowl III), R.J. Krajeski & his brother Jan, &
you, me & Hunter
with Roy's "home movie" lights strung up to the top of
the tennis court fence so we could play
ALL NIGHT LONG!!
and the neighborhood kids lay in their beds and watched
our games!

Year in and year out we measured the year
(it's summer)
by the northward migration of the geese and the Giants . . . maybe
that's one reason why baseball is the great game it is . . .
we play it at the time of year that is the best
for everyone.

So as I sat here this afternoon
with the phones unplugged
and cried
I thought of you, Bobby;
of how we are so   intwined with
the black and orange
and how far back it goes
to a time when Kennedy was President,
Roger Maris had just broken Babe's record
and every game
was THE game.

NOTES ON THE 1986 PLAYOFFS AND WORLD SERIES

Richard Grossinger

*"It's a bit hard to realize that the only time you were a
real poet in your life was when you were only 25 years
old, sprawled out in right center field at Shea Stadium,
praying that you'd catch a line drive off Brooks
Robinson's bat. In everything I've done in my life
since then, I've tried to recapture that feeling, that
sense of true poetry. But perhaps it only happens
once."*
Ron Swoboda

Jesse Orosco heaves his glove into the night sky and kneels on the mound in a jubilation that
is also spontaneous prayer. He is burning an indelible moment onto thousands of highlight
films that will proceed into the future cloning one another until no one will remember how
we got to it or feel any longer the emotions of two embattled teams. Its future is to become stale
newsreel iconography. But in its present this moment is like a hot log crashing to the ground,
releasing thousands of embers, flashbacks in baseball time. No amount of replays or recalls can
ever bring that phenomenon back.

The most recent of the embers is barely hours old: trailing 3-0, the Mets went down
quietly in the bottom of the fifth inning in their twenty-second shot at an insoluble Bruce Hurst.
"Is it for real this time, or are we being led on again?" I asked my friend Nick with feigned
optimism.

"I am *sure* we are being led on," he said.

At that moment I had little hope; it seemed the Mets' miracle sixth-game comebacks had
merely postponed an inevitable Boston victory (made inevitable by Dave Henderson's destiny-
changing home run in the fifth game of the American League playoffs). Then suddenly, sparked
for the second straight night by a Lee Mazzili pinch single, New York rallied to tie the score; an
inning later they took the lead. The bottom of the sixth began a charge to the end of the season
reminiscent only (among "seventh games") of the back-and-forth reversals of the Yankees-
Pirates finale in 1960. For a brief duration the Mets and the Red Sox each seemed to have the
momentum to overcome whatever the other did. Against Roger McDowell, who mowed them
down an inning before, the Sox rallied for two runs on three hits in the top of the eighth and had

the tying run on second with no one out when Orosco entered the game—shades of Dale Long and Mickey Mantle in the bottom of the ninth in Pittsburgh. But suddenly the revels ended; the 1986 post-season goblin had played his last trick.

Most baseball games are simply ordinary; even with a few remarkable moments, most seasons in a team's history are humdrum and equalizing. For a franchise only twenty-five years old, however, the Mets have found themselves in a couple of centuries' worth of both bizarre games and unlikely seasons. Before the 1986 playoffs even began, they could supply a full résumé of marathons—twenty-five innings against the Cardinals in 1974, twenty-four against the Astros in 1968 (ending 1-0), twenty-three against the Giants in the second game of a doubleheader in 1964 (they lost all three). Other Met sagas played right into "The Twilight Zone." For instance, in their nineteen-inning battle in Atlanta in '85 the Mets tied the score against Bruce Sutter in the ninth; they took the lead twice in extra innings only to have the Braves retie it each time on home runs. The second such homer, with two outs in the seventeenth, was hit by pitcher Rick Camp (because the Braves had run out of pinch hitters). Camp came to the plate with virtually no chance even of getting a hit let alone hitting a home run; he had one of the worst batting averages in the history of baseball. (Are we being led on . . . indeed?) (It seemed almost part of the bewitching that Tom Gorman, the victim of both home runs, thought he was pitching to Gene Garber at the time.) The Mets did finally win, 16-13, but not before Camp came to the plate again as the tying run and made the final out.

The Mets' 1962 season was a classic of blown ballgames and unlucky losses defying the law of averages. Then in 1969, against 100-1 odds, the Mets won the first Eastern Division Championship of the National League in a charmed late-season run that included a doubleheader of 1-0 wins over Pittsburgh (with the pitcher driving in the only run in both games) and a victory over Steve Carlton in which nineteen Mets struck out but Ron Swoboda hit two two-run homers. Players like Wayne Garrett and Al Weis then rose from ordinary careers to get clutch hits off all-star pitchers and lead the team to the pennant and the World Championship.

In 1973, behind Tug McGraw, the Mets came from under .500 and just out of last place in September to win the Division. In one improbable game they outlasted the Expos (who repeatedly loaded the bases with less than two outs in extra innings); they rallied from two runs down in the ninth inning against Dave Giusti and the Pirates, winning on a single by Ron Hodges; they beat the Pirates two days later on an extra-inning "non–home run" that bounced off the railing into Cleon Jones's glove (the base runner was thrown out at home). They then survived the Big Red Machine in an intense five-game playoff and, on the heels of a Koosman gem, took a 3-2 lead in the World Series out to Oakland. But it was not until thirteen years later that the franchise won its next Series game.

Do teams have their own individual myth cycles? The notion seems romantic and far-fetched at first glance; certainly players vehemently deny any jinx from earlier seasons (especially ones played before they were on the team or, in some cases, even born). Yet there are curious recurrences: the Red Sox of the supposed "Harry Frazee" curse are the franchise that sold Babe Ruth and other stars to the Yankees (creating the great American League dynasty of the 1920s and 1930s if not of all time); they are the team that was paralyzed by Enos Slaughter's inspired dash in the eighth inning of the seventh game in 1946, that lost the seventh game to the Cardinals again, behind Bob Gibson in '67, that blew a one-game lead to the Yankees with two games left in '49 (giving Casey Stengel his first pennant and initiating an incredible string of World Series appearances over the next sixteen years), that was turned back again in the seventh game of the '75 Series by Tony Perez, Pete Rose, and the Reds *immediately after* their own miraculous sixth-game win (New England's entry for the greatest game ever played); and then they were the victims of the Yankees' late-season dash of 1978 culminating in the unlikely Bucky Dent home run in the one-game playoff (New England's singlemost game of infamy). Many a Boston fan considered their own team legitimately the one with soul, the Mets another New York ogre—a sign at Fenway during the third game expressed the mood well: Red Sox 2, Mets 0; Yankees: No Game Today.

The Yankees have their own distinctive Ugly American/carpetbagger heritage (their very name resounds through Latin America in "Yanquis Go Home"); the legacy is so deliberate and conscious that George Steinbrenner was able to resurrect it merely by buying the franchise and then Catfish Hunter and Reggie Jackson (just as Babe Ruth, Lou Gehrig, Joe Dimaggio, Mickey Mantle, and Yogi Berra were purchased before them—I mean these guys weren't draft picks). The Cubs have a sentimental downbeat tradition, from early World Series folds, to the fade of '69, to Leon Durham's error in the '84 playoffs—highlighting the collapse of what seemed an unstoppable pennant surge at Wrigley just days earlier. (How did Sutcliffe, Dernier, and company all turn into pumpkins at precisely the bewitching hour?)

The Cardinals of 1984, with Willie McGee and Vince Coleman, were a true Gashouse Gang throwback, streamlined and funked up for the eighties. The Dodgers of Valenzuela and company recall the interregnum of Drysdale and Koufax who recall the Brooklyn duo of Erskine and Labine. (On the other hand, the Pirates and Phillies of the seventies seem quantum breaks in the tradition of their franchises.)

The 1986 postseason played itself out within the established destinies of the teams involved. The Angels blew the big game and then self-destructed. It was an all-time frustrating miss for a franchise whose most heroic identity remains the expansion team of Ken McBride, Leon Wagner, and George and LeRoy Thomas.

The Red Sox saw the ghosts of 1946, 1949, 1967, 1975, and 1978. How often can you miss from *that* close?

The Astros enacted their own unique tradition with exquisite precision. From the time they were born simultaneously with the New York Mets in 1962 (as the Houston Colt .45s), they have been locked in a transcendental pitching duel with their twin, supplying the likes of Dick Farrell and Mike Cuellar, Don Wilson and Larry Dierker, James Rodney Richard and Bob Knepper (remember the historic twenty-four-inning 1-0 game at the Astrodome). The Mets were at a definite disadvantage until the era of Seaver, Koosman, and Gentry, reenacted now by Gooden, Darling, and company. (Ironically enough, the two most dominating pitchers on the '86 Astros were ex-Mets Mike Scott and Nolan Ryan.)

Insofar as the 1986 National League Championship Series was enacted by two teams locked in a millennial pitching duel, single, almost incidental plays took on ultracritical significance. The Met pennant was the result only of a conspiracy of dozens of infinitesimal episodes, any *one* of which going the other way could have tilted the series to the Astros. As the winning team, the Mets entered twenty-nine of the sixty-four innings tied, another twenty-nine behind, and only six ahead. All of those six were in the second game! They never entered an inning ahead during the three games at their home ballpark yet won two of them!

How many times do we hear that a team is presently 40-1 or 85-2 when they hold the lead going into the ninth inning? Yet three times in twelve *regular-season* games the Astros were tied by the Mets in the ninth or tenth (though they recovered to win the last two of those in Houston). Darryl Strawberry's ninth-inning homer off Dave Smith tying the eleventh game of the regular season between the two teams was exactly prescient of Len Dykstra's dramatic home run off Smith turning defeat into victory in the third game of the playoffs.

Home runs by Strawberry and Knight respectively tied and then won a July game in the tenth inning at Shea—much in the fateful way the Mets would come from behind late in the third and sixth games of the playoffs. In the fifth playoff game only one well-timed swing by Darryl Strawberry prevented Nolan Ryan from shutting the Mets out and sending the series back to Houston with the Astros ahead. That homer kept New York in the game until Gary Carter could punch his tension-breaking grounder through Charlie Kerfeld's legs in the twelfth. (Meanwhile, detractors of Strawberry's post-season play tend to overlook not only that home run off Ryan but the three-run shot that tied Knepper in the Dykstra game and then the solo homer off Al Nipper that clinched the seventh game of the World Series. Strawberry could have struck out every single other at-bat—and almost did—and still have had one of the great clutch postseasons of all time. His first two homers were game-transforming shots off pitchers in absolute grooves.)

As unusual as the '86 playoffs were, the Astros must have had the feeling they had been there before. For Mike Schmidt, it was déjà vu 1980, fourth and fifth games (under the old five-game format). The Phillies won the first game of that series at home and almost took the second too: as Astro pitcher Frank LaCorte walked dejectedly off the mound, Bake McBride, carrying the winning run, was inexplicably held at third by coach Lee Elia. Houston eventually won, setting the stage for everything that would follow.

The Astros also took the third game, typically 1-0 in eleven innings, and, when they carried a 2-0 lead forged against Steve Carleton into the eighth inning at the Dome, it looked like curtains for the Phillies.

No! The Phils scored three runs to take the lead; then the Astros countered with one in the ninth to send the game into extra innings. In the tenth, pinch hitter Greg Luzinski doubled to left, and Pete Rose scored all the way from first with a forearm to Bruce Bochy's face.

The next day the Phillies found themselves in an even worse position—down 5-2 going into the eighth inning against Nolan Ryan in his prime. Then, keyed by Del Unser's critical pinch hit, they exploded for five runs; the Astros miraculously answered with two in the bottom of the inning. In the tenth, Gary Maddox doubled in Unser with the pennant-winner.

After watching the Mets and Astros carry their monumental battle into extra innings (and evening) at the Astrodome, Schmidt recalled the desperation of the 1980 Phillies. To paraphrase him from memory: "It was the Astrodome, where they believed they were unbeatable; it was Nolan Ryan; they had us by three runs; we had two shots left; there was no way they could lose.

Same thing today; only it was Bob Knepper and he had the Mets beat through eight innings. Yes, the Mets won it, but the Astros once again lacked something extra needed to close it out."

Dramatic turnaround at the point of victory (or defeat) was the hallmark of the 1986 post-season. (It actually began with the Kansas City Royals' stunning reversals over the Blue Jays and Cardinals in 1985. The sixth game of the 1985 World Series was the only time all season the Cardinals' bull pen blew a lead in the last inning.) How many times during the regular season does a good team carry a *two-* or *three-*run lead into the last inning and lose? Yet it happened four times in twenty postseason games in 1986, including twice with two out. Perhaps these post-season dramatics reflect a level of intensity missing during the regular season. Players enter an almost psychic state, pushing their abilities to the limit to try individually to wrest the outcome. Some players anyway. . . . Or maybe an undiagnosed archetype prevails.

Let's review that epic ninth-inning rally in Houston: The Mets had gone down meekly that afternoon without even threatening for eight innings (and for essentially the preceding twenty-one in New York); they opened the ninth with Lenny Dykstra, a left-handed pinch hitter (because there were no viable right-handed ones left) against a dominating left-handed pitcher. Dykstra drove a triple to right center field. Perhaps Billy Hatcher should have caught it, but he certainly wasn't playing Dykstra to pull Knepper. Billy Doran *could* have caught Mookie Wilson's soft liner if he had judged his leap properly. When Hernandez hit a shot to center one out later, the tying run was on second. Dave Smith came in again and painstakingly walked both Carter and Strawberry; now the flow of energy had turned in the Mets' direction. Ray Knight's ensuing at-bat was the key. First Knight almost walked and was furious at the umpire's call; then he almost struck out. When Astro catcher Alan Ashby challenged this second call, Knight turned and started yelling at *him*. It was no more big salaries, primetime showbiz bullshit; these guys were playing hardball. Knight muscled a shot deep enough to right to bring in Hernandez. Danny Heep could have ended it all by taking four balls, but he fidgeted through customary half-swings and struck out.

Now the game marched off into never-never land, freezing baseball fans in a trance for almost the duration of a second entire sudden-death game. It was the whole of what baseball is, all at once. The background intensity—from game to game, season to season—had come forward into a single contest and burst from the stadium into the world, freezing entire cities for hours.

When Wally Backman singled home a run in the fourteenth inning, a Met pennant was almost tastable. I hung before the TV, just waiting. Orosco struck out Billy Doran to open the bottom of the inning. But suddenly and without warning, Billy Hatcher hit a tremendous home run just fair down the left-field line. There was no way out of this game. Exhausted players were on the roller coaster and they had to ride it to the end.

Although Keith Hernandez confided to a number of Astros on the base paths, "Isn't this a great game?", there was no way for the teams to declare it a tie, shake hands, and walk off the field. The ancient ballcourt had two different exits, and eventually everyone on that field, and every fan following the two teams, would take one or the other. Yet it *was* a collaboration, and the teams honored each other merely by being in it together.

The way Houston (and Mike Scott) finished the regular season, the Mets were walking open-eyed into a buzz saw. The Astros could have been heavy betting favorites over even the '27

Yankees. By making it through the buzz saw, the Mets defined themselves as a team. Then a softer version of the same curious puzzle was thrown at them in the Series (with Bruce Hurst replacing Mike Scott), and in solving that, they completed a mythic season.

When the Mets went to the well for the pennant against the Astros in the extra innings of that sixth game, I was transfixed in the tension; their whole team history passed before me. It was such a sinuous many-season path to this climax that the ordinary events of a baseball game couldn't contain the nuances of it. The real energy existed in an aura that surrounded the field of play and submerged it in the realm of epic and legend. Otherwise, it was just a bunch of men playing baseball on television, or, at best, a crucial playoff game. (George Leonard refers accurately to the aikido black belt exam, or the World Series game "during which every last spectator realizes at some level that what is happening out on the field is more than a game, but rather something achingly beautiful and inevitable, an enactment in space and time of how the universe works, how things are.")

Seasons upon seasons are played in order to come to moments like these; so when you participate in the millennial game, you are reliving the memory of such seasons, the subtle textures of their innings and players. To the fan of a team, such a game is a hologram reflecting hundreds of other games.

Likewise, the true follower observes unrequited seasons through the imagined crystal of this moment of truth (whether or not it ever happens), for it is the potential of winning the pennant and Series that gives each season its taut boundaries and keeps the games meaningful. As in any ceremony, the significators are hidden and the deeper image is concealed in the simple sequence on the surface. Finally, a game this big cannot contain itself.

Thus, Jesse Orosco pitching for the Mets at the moment of truth was also the Jesse Orosco of 1979 and 1982, who failed as a rookie after coming over in a trade for Jerry Koosman, who worked his way back through the minors and then ran off a marvellous skein of saves and wins in 1983. It was the same Jesse Orosco who gave up several game-tying and winning home runs over the years, but who also regularly got the game-ending strikeout with the tying or winning runs on base. He would never again be as good as he was in '83, but by the time he took the mound in Houston he had a complex history, he had individuated—and, in the end, he was good enough. Mike Scott may have been better, but the game wasn't in Mike Scott's hands. Jesse Orosco in the Astrodome (and in the ninth inning of the seventh Series game at Shea) was also John Pacella and Scott Holman. All of those images of pitchers on the mound in Met uniforms flow together. Likewise, hundreds of shadow Wally Backmans and Mookie Wilsons combine in memory to frame the single narrative stream of an afternoon.

The Mets were not born contending in 1984; they do not take their identity from only the successful season of 1986. All of the players who didn't make it to Houston are still present. Steve Henderson and Hubie Brooks are there; how could Hubie not be a part of it? Though long gone, Henderson struck a franchise-changing three-run homer off the Giants' Alan Ripley one June night in New York. Recalled from exile, Lee Mazzili represents Doug Flynn and Frank Taveras. But also everyone else participates, from Leon Brown to Craig Swan, from Charlie Puleo to young erratic Mike Scott and Jeff Reardon. If they weren't there, it wouldn't be the Mets; it would just be some good team winning the pennant, the same thing some good team does every year. Most of all, John Stearns is there, kneeling in the dust by home plate, his fist clenched while runs pour across, never losing the fire or dignity. That image was waiting five, eight years, to be redeemed in this game. No matter how physical these games are, their real truth lies in the spirits not the bodies of those that play. (Do you doubt that if the New Jersey Nets ever win the championship, however many decades in the future, Buck Williams will be there rebounding . . . for all his leaps from beyond exhaustion in the fourth quarter, for all the hopeless games and meaningless seasons in which he refused to give up?)

I think you must look inward, because "inside" is where it's coming from; otherwise, what would the game mean but tin soldiers on a toy field, or data pouring through computer terminals? Yes, we are in an era of "acting out" and externalities, from jihads and nuclear bombs to heavy metal, venture capital, and quick sex, but it is the human experience of those things that gives them texture and power over us. Throughout those extra innings I kept asking myself— Why? Why does this (which means nothing at all) mean so much I can barely breathe?

Familiar insights replayed themselves—the joy of collective participation with all the other people identifying with the Mets . . . projection of my psyche into a certified mythic event . . . transference of my paralyzed sympathy for everyone to just these players (as I wrote in *The Temple of Baseball*). Those thoughts, after interviewing players in the visiting clubhouse at Candlestick (August, 1984), were still my yardstick for explaining the confusion of pop culture, neurosis, and myth:

Looking at Ron Darling sitting there with his glove I picture the players of the fifties disappearing back into the men of the forties, and then look back to the old-time uniforms and small gloves at the turn of the century, the bases laid out on the Civil War battlefield, then, before that, club-ball in England, field games with bean-filled balls between Indian groups to mark the equinox, an opening in the ancient North American wilderness. The diamond within the circle of baseball summarizes thousands of ancient games and extinct tribes, people who have disappeared by becoming us, pitchers who threw before there were balls and fielders who caught according to the rules of nondecimal systems. There is something about Ron Darling as a half-Chinese, half-Irish pitcher from Hawaii that is both nineteenth-century and pre-Columbian. Modern baseball cheapens its own largeness through its ambition and self-promotion, but the overdrop of history is still there and gives it the texture that the media then hammers out into its own hysterical season. The myths may be a threatened resource in 1984, but they have not yet run out. The pretense of empty records and fake history is overshadowed by the old fields and decades of grassroots players who carried out this game.

Looking around the locker room of the Mets one last time, I am saddened by the media event, though it's the only reason I'm permitted to be here. Despite the proprieties the confusion of public and private is a confusion of *our* identity with *their* identities, and underlying that is the almost epochal confusion of our compassion for each other. We are overwhelmed by news of famine in Africa and slaughter of boat people at sea by Asian pirates. We hear about new brutalities and abuses of the innocent every day. We have almost lost our authentic emotions for each other, and we have turned the possibility for true comradeship and empathy into star-creation and hero-worship; the media has exploited our weakness into its own billion-dollar industry—

in the process, making it a collective trance. Instead of looking for humanity in everyone, we seek it in these players because they are already universalized and particular, and it is easier to locate their public personae than the terrifying blank wall of millions of starving Ethiopians. When we find the ballplayer's supposed humanity it is like discovering our connection to the root. But it is a dangerous lapse in modern life, and its consequences are not determined because we do not know yet what will be required of us in this century. The result is a profound and hollow cavity in the clubhouse and in the game itself, a loneliness in the midst of crowds. The pennant can still bring a wave of euphoria to a city, but it would take the spirit of a Papago ballgame to carry that fire through the winter and transform it into a new harvest of brotherhood and sisterhood in the spring.

But I don't want to dwell on metaphors and symbols. My participation in the Mets is finally unconscious, or semiconscious at best, and only secondarily intellectual. During the play-offs my wife Lindy remarked that the intensity of me and my son were absurd to her. "Who cares?" she said. "This doesn't affect or interest me, and it's an intrusion on my life." One night she added in exasperation: "I don't get it. Are we involved in professional baseball? I didn't get married to have professional baseball imposed on me." I was mortified; it *did* look ridiculous.

Put under the gun by her as much as myself, I couldn't just watch passively. At least if I was going to be there, I needed to answer some of the questions. Given the world situation, given the existential life situation, how important could this game be?

This time I wanted to go even deeper. I wanted to expose not only the myth of baseball but the game in which *I* was a player:

Watching myself watch the game is like the meditation required of life itself. Although a game isn't real in the way it seems to be, neither is life, and yet you are called upon to participate in it at the most profound level possible. The ballgame shadows life and gives it a sort of counterweight. Baseball generates an intrinsic significance to disguise the fact that the world itself is mysterious and open-ended. Our need for some ultimate confirmation falls on the field of play, especially during the playoffs and Series, because it can never fall on us for a resolution. How strange! Creatures in a dream invent a tournament with an ultimate prize to relieve themselves of the terror of the dream itself. In that sense, baseball gives symptomatic relief from the tyranny of time by creating its own alternative cyclical universe. It is far more than a rite of spring. It is a complete meditational calendar, a mnemonic device for keeping track of events in a hollow and secular culture. (Sometimes, in thinking of death, one of the things I find it hardest to imagine is that the Mets will go on playing games the results of which I will never know with players I have never heard of.)

But baseball is not only a practice of life; it is a practice of practice, and we have to probe it not for the obvious symbols baseball philosophers are fond of pointing out in the American frontier psyche but for the nature of our attachment to those symbols.

Deep in extra innings against Houston I perceive a new level: I experience that I am fragmented and contracted, never a whole coherent organism. The part of me that is locked into the game is isolated from real hungers and desires, so it thrives on the exercise of strong emotion bound in this event. Not capable somehow of the full tenderness of the life itself, "I" prefer some hit from outside that's at least also real, i.e., not a story or a fantasy. (The reason it can't be movie stars or rock singers is that they "win" every time, whatever they do; their mere persona is a display of triumph.) The advantage of the game is that its unfolding occurs apart from anything I can intervene to change, like geology or astronomy—which is why rotisserie leagues seem sterile to me: who cares about imposing the aggrandizing manipulative self on an event that has its own integrity.

It's not just that baseball involves a fragment of my personality. The game brings together two fragmented selves I spend much of my life trying to meld on an unconscious level. There is the positive visionary self, that writes, that seeks spiritual discipline, that communicates from the heart not the mind, that is capable of unquestioning love. The part of me that has not attained this level but is addicted to its poignancy tries to get a "rush" out of the game. Real transformation doesn't happen, but, at the moment it doesn't matter, the semblance of it does. Just because it's baseball is no reason to trash it; we little enough understand the sources and accessibility of the tremendous energy we each contain.

At the same time, there exists the dreading anxious part of me, the self that is overwhelmed by the danger of the streets, the threat of nuclear war, the ever-nearness of disaster and loss. That being has occupied as much of my inner life as the visionary. Its basic style is to move from one dread to another, to be satisfied only when some imagined catastrophe doesn't happen—the hysteria of continually postponed air raid sirens.

The "sudden death" of the sixth playoff game is an opportunity for both selves. Each time the Astros come up I "practice" my anxiety and observe it. Each time the Mets come up I yearn for my visionary high in the form of the pennant. I go back and forth between the two and experience their nearness. And I realize that it has always been this way. The two intensities are the polar boundaries of my emotional life and the game allows me to project them and enjoy their pure oscillations without dilution or distraction. However I get there, this deeply charged state is crucial to me.

For my teenage son Robin it is not quite the same. He enjoys the mere fact that the Mets are in this game, and though he will be depressed and teary if they lose, he is not negative during it. In fact, I drive him crazy through the eleventh, the twelfth, thirteenth, fourteenth innings, kicking the ground, drumming with my leg, hitting the chair every time a pitch doesn't go right. I am unconscious of these gestures, but he tells me, so I leave the garage and go to the TV inside, where my twelve-year-old daughter Miranda is reading a book and cares only insofar that if the Mets win, I have promised a walk to the bakery for a victory cake.

When the Knight singles in Strawberry in the top of the sixteenth, I go back outside for the rest of the three-run rally, but I flee when the Astros begin scoring in the bottom half. The game is the epitome of no control, with the history of baseball at stake: The Astros are within one hit of an all-time miracle comeback recalling Bobbie Thomson's home run, and I can do nothing but pace in stunned silence.

Later we learn that, at that dangerous moment, Keith Hernandez came to the mound and jokingly told Carter, "No more fastballs, or you'll have to fight me right here." (Carter denied this and attributed it to Hernandez's buoyant postgame mood when he talked fast and loose, as one is inclined to in the giddiness of such a time. When reality has transcended myth, it has become myth, and one is tempted to create an archetypal version of what happened because it alone seems true.) But the point is: Hernandez is thinking all the time about the game situation. He is never paralyzed. There are very few players who are so present in the game that they become the game. Hernandez is the baseball equivalent of an aikido master. His intelligence does not require self-consciousness. That's why he went to second to nip Hatcher on Walling's grounder in the hole that inning. If he had taken the easier play at first—which is what most infielders in the history of the game would have done—Glenn Davis's ensuing single would have tied the score (. . . another of those intricate subsets of possibility that propelled the Mets rather than the Astros into the World Series!).

In another sense, that "game intelligence" is why Hernandez got the key ninth-inning double off Knepper after not hitting him all day; it's also why he was the one who broke the ice off Bruce Hurst in the seventh game of the Series with a bases-loaded single, precisely the deed he performed for the Cardinals against the Brewers, seventh game, 1982—essentially the identical hit (off another difficult lefty, Bob McClure). When games and whole seasons come down to infinitesimal points, it is these bits of disciplined mentality on which the result turns. Of course, Hernandez would perceive all curveballs to Kevin Bass (Bass would finally swing and miss strike three—pandemonium, release at last from this game!).

Afterwards, Mike Schmidt's first observation was about Bass. "Only by failing in that situation," he said, "do you learn how to succeed the next time. When you succeed, it's not some out-of-the blue thing. You reach back inside yourself into the previous failure and that's the place you succeed from." He was telling us a secret. When he struck out with the tying run on third in the fifth game of the 1980 playoffs, that was the spot from which hundreds of clutch hits would later come.

The Mets started the World Series the same way they started the playoffs, losing 1-0, although in a lower-energy game, decided not by a home run but a ground ball through Tim Teufel's legs. They lost the second game, too, when Dwight Gooden was soundly thumped. The forces at large seemed profoundly opposed to a Met victory; in the fourth inning, tremendous shots to right field by both Strawberry and Howard Johnson simply died against a cushion of air. It was as though the Sox were swinging against the moon's gravity, the Mets against Neptune's.

To many observers, including ones who had predicted a Met sweep, it was all over. But not to Mike Schmidt, who said that if he were the manager, he would tell the players, "All you have to do is win two in a row. How many times have you done that this year? Forty maybe."

The Mets went up to Boston and did precisely that. They didn't even wait for a chance to fall behind again. As the first batter in game three, Len Dykstra, a self-activating spark, stroked a home run; then the Mets scorched Oil Can Boyd for three more first-inning runs, and though he held them off from there till the seventh, it was enough.

The following day Gary Carter found a left-field screen clearly made for his stroke, twice. The Green Monster, like the wind at Shea, became the ally of the visitors (Mookie Wilson played it like a lifelong New Englander, nailing Rich Gedman at second base). Carter, Ojeda, and Darling had come home victoriously (I am counting the Kid's years in Quebec). The Series was tied. But the biggest hurdles for the Mets were actually ahead.

"It's not Darling on three days' rest that worries me," said Schmidt. "It's Gooden on three days' rest. If I were Dave Johnson, I'd give the ball to Rick Aguilera or Sid Fernandez and say, 'Son, go out there and make a name for yourself.'"

Johnson, though, had lost his patience with the gopher balls. Fernandez wasn't as notorious as Aguilera (and Rick still had to pitch to a guy named Henderson in the tenth inning at Shea), but El Sid had thrown an unnecessary one to Alan Ashby in the fourth game against Houston, and he had been no mystery to the Red Sox in Game Two. So Gooden returned from his shelling on short rest. Ironically, Fernandez was to appear twice more during the Series (not in a starting role), and the Red Sox were to find him nothing short of the second coming of Sidd Finch, or the myth of the old Gooden.

That original Gooden, though, was everything Schmidt feared. Here was someone who, for two whole seasons, controlled the universe of baseball from the pitching mound. He went back and forth between raw heat and Lord Charles, allowing little more than a run per nine innings and striking out ten or so along the way; as games went on, he simply got stronger. If a runner should reach third with no one out, Dwight had the awesome focus of power to throw nine strikes by the next three hitters (as the Dodgers learned many times). He even taught himself to hit and probably could have gone to the minors and returned in two years as an outfielder with power. He was the prototype of the guy who came down from a higher league. The fact that he didn't get to pitch in the playoffs or World Series was one of the main unfulfilled fantasies of 1984 and 1985.

But in 1986 Gooden was not the same pitcher, or even the same batter. Despite Met denials that anything had changed, he was erratic and, at times, hit extremely hard. He seemed confused on the mound. He tired late in games and, on a number of occasions, yielded ninth-inning tying homers. He became a raw rookie struggling for even the inklings of mastery more often than at any time previously in his career (except maybe for a few innings at Kingsport and Little Falls in 1982).

During his first two years in the majors, Gooden was a virtual Zen master. He hardly spoke, and what he did say was pragmatic, appropriate, and modest. He had no news; he simply fulfilled the requirements of public speech. For all the effect of his words, he might as well have taken a vow of silence; he was a "silent" teacher.

Who needed Sidd Finch or Bill Lee's yogic relief pitcher making the baseball disappear and reappear? Gooden was the eye of the storm.

In 1985 at Candlestick I sat among his family. His father was as impassive as Doc, but the young cousins or brothers must have thought Dwight was supposed to be Michael Jackson. They wanted a strikeout on every batter, and when anybody put the ball in play, that was an outrage, a "shuck." A hit was a mistake—"You can't do that; no one can hit Doc!"

At one point a friend or relative came down with a few baseballs that needed autographing. The family member sitting beside me acted as though he were expected to haul them out to the mound on the spot. "Didn't I tell you never to bother the Doc when he's at work. Can't you see, man. Doc's operatin'. He's conductin' business; he can't sign no baseballs."

Doc emerged from an underbelly of American black culture, and he transformed its chaos in himself into a functional veneer of calm. As a ballplayer he was dignified, gallant, and spare.

These Goodens didn't even know their kin was playing baseball; they wanted cartoon-like domination, triumph of the *nouveau riche*; Dwight even did a rap record of their voice in him.

The explanations for what happened to Gooden in '86 ranged from the banal to the supernatural: the hitters adjusted to him; he didn't have control of the curve anymore; he ruined his motion trying to cut down on his leg kick; drugs and other personal-life distractions drained him; he lost motivation with the Mets not needing him to win every time; he had a physical injury (the mysterious ankle?), an undiagnosed disease; or it was simply (Bob Gibson) that no one's that good.

Perhaps no single thing caused the change. After all, Gooden's mastery was not some iron domination of strength; it was a subtle combination of speed, rhythm, and control. Other pitchers threw harder; other pitchers had as good a curveball. Dwight put it all together in a dance.

Even before word of Gooden's cocaine use came out, some people knew. Apparently the kids in the playgrounds of Tampa got the word, but those playgrounds are a long way from corporate headquarters, and there are very few commuters between them to carry the word. A local friend whose job involves working with athletes who have cocaine problems told me he was certain that was Gooden's problem after watching the Giants bomb him one afternoon at Candlestick. He saw a slight distraction of timing and rhythm, a laboring that wasn't there before, a familiar mild bewilderment in Doc's eyes—because he had never fallen so out of sync before. "What chance did he have, really?" my friend asked me. "He was young, black, wealthy, uneducated, suddenly famous, and he lived in Tampa." But Dwight protested such accusations all season, and even had a drug-testing clause put into his contract.

It makes you wonder if the disease is the drug—or the denial. It also casts a different light on Vida Blue: maybe he never had a chance either. If the great Bob Gibson closed out an era, then Vida unknowingly opened another.

But it will be many a season before we close this one out, for American baseball is merely a fifteen-minute-old puppet show up against the millennial games now being played in Iran, Afghanistan, and Colombia. And most ballplayers are simply grown children, educated by a pop culture for which they are heroes. They are given mentally draining jobs with lots of hollow, meaningless time, and plenty of money. Surely they are set up to be the victims of every big-time global scam; after all, how are they going to outwit poor South American and Southeast Asian farmers or urban drug lords in the battle for the planet's resources; they are mainly worried about "Cardinals" and "Cubs" and how to spend the cash. By the time cocaine reaches suburban Tampa, it is already dressed like the next-door neighbor, and it speaks in whatever street language it needs to get in. Ballplayers might read the papers, but they're the first ones to distrust the information there. They read right through the warnings.

In any case, drugs are not their own answer, nor are they a psychological monolith, transcending all the idiosyncratic events of personal history and culture. Whatever the proximate cause of his struggle (cocaine or some other malaise), an aspect of his unresolved past must have engulfed Doc. He couldn't transform chaos into mastery indefinitely. Every act casts a shadow, and Dwight's first two seasons required some compensation, psychological and physical. That he did as well as he did under the circumstances merely contributes to his myth as a superplayer. The first two seasons he coasted on raw talent and the blessings of both Athena and Zeus; in

1986 the gods opposed him and look what he accomplished! Destiny prescribed that he would lose not only the All-Star Game but two World Series games; sheer guts and ability won seventeen games during the regular season and dueled both Mike Scott and Nolan Ryan by the hair's breadth of a run in the playoffs. If Doc hadn't summoned every ounce of remaining energy and skill he had to force Ryan into extra innings in the fifth game of the playoffs, the Mets never would have made it to the World Series.

I don't believe it for a moment when the Red Sox said after the fifth game, "No one beats us with two pitches." The Dwight Gooden of 1984 and '85 beats them with *either* the curve or the fast ball. The Dwight Gooden of 1986 was on a mission to the Underworld; he was thrashing through the chaos he magically suppressed for two seasons (the same chaos Oil Can struggles with, less successfully). Dwight was a wounded pitcher in the World Series, although we could not see the wounds or know the degrees to which they were physical, psychological, and spiritual. He was pitching with the gods against him, and hits rattled all over Fenway. He was on the most perilous leg of a pilgrimage, far more serious than the game; I mean, two months later he could have been shot dead or had his right arm broken on the streets of Tampa. We don't put much stock in celestial interference these days, but archetypally that was still the work Zeus, in partnership with a malefic Saturn. No wonder he couldn't pitch. That he even survived is a statement of his charisma. ("The sudden fame and fortune he achieved is nice," Frank Cashen would say six months later. "But we sort of robbed him of his youth.")

So, the Mets had to overcome not only their exhaustion and lethargy, and the Sox' two-game lead, they had to play through the deflation of Gooden's invulnerability, a myth so central to the new Mets that it had become almost their team identity. They had to win the big one without him.

To what degree was the World Series uphill for the Mets? Although they did not trail in runs within individual games quite as often as they did during the playoffs, they were behind the Red Sox in the Series itself entering 50 of the 64 innings (all except the first seven innings of the first game, the first two innings of the fifth game, and the first two and last three innings of the seventh game). They actually led in the whole Series for only its final three innings. Several times in the bottom of the tenth of the sixth game they came within one strike of losing it all.

Mike Cieslinski, the inventor of a statistical board game called Pursue the Pennant, tried to recreate the Met comeback in the tenth inning of the sixth game. Using cards representing actual players and dice to randomize outcomes, he sent Carter up to bat against Schiraldi with two outs and no one on. He played all night, but the Red Sox won the Series every time. In his own words, "With two outs—even if you get one or two baserunners—you usually get an out. That's what kept happening: I kept getting an out. Actually, I had thoughts of this never happening." But he went back at it the next morning: he rolled the dice 100 times, 200 times, until finally, on his 279th try, the Mets rallied and won. That puts the odds against a Met comeback informally at 278 to 1. Which means you watch the game from that point 279 times (more than a season and a half) and the Red Sox win 278 times. Why did we get the 279th game on our only try?

Even the one Met who truly walked on water in '69, Ron Swoboda, was astonished. Asked to compare World Series teams, he did some philosophizing and reminiscing: "The champagne dried a little bit and the years went by, but I really enjoyed watching these guys do it because they put their own signature on this one. I can't believe it. They almost killed me. . . . When it was two outs in the bottom of the tenth, my heart was down there in my shoes. I'm trying to figure out some kind of fallback position. I'm thinking, 'Geez, if they don't win it, well at least we're the only ones who did'—all kinds of rationalizations—and all of a sudden you get three base hits, a wild pitch, an error, and I'm screaming, you know, I'm screaming."

When the Mets had two outs and no one on, I stood up and approached the TV, ready to turn it off because I didn't want to watch the Red Sox celebrating. Apparently Keith Hernandez felt the same way, because he went back to the manager's office—where he watched the most miraculous World Series comeback of all time. In normal circumstances no one comes back from there; in the sixth game of the World Series, definitely not. But all along Robin was telling me no, not to worry, that they couldn't lose. Hit after hit proved his faith. He kept saying, "Rich, sit down. Don't even think of it." So much positive energy in such a hopeless cause. Then, as Kevin Mitchell scored the tying run, I yelled myself hoarse; I had watched baseball all my life trying unsuccessfully to root a wild pitch with the tying run on third. Why now, when it mattered most?

This was clearly the same Twilight Zone into which Rick Camp had hit his home run. Mookie Wilson was so faint afterwards he could barely talk. This was hardball too, but it seemed more like a UFO descended on New York City. And the fans just stayed and cheered the visitation. On an evening begun by Paul Simon singing the national anthem, and punctuated by a comet-colored second-inning sky-plunger, the inevitable ending had been written.

Too often, in the months afterwards, Mookie has been cheated out of the wonder of that at-bat. In a batting slump, with the whole season on the line and no strikes to give, he fouled off two biting Bob Stanley sinkers, dodged the game-tying wild pitch, and made contact with another sinker, sending it toward first. All that work, plus his intimidating speed, led to Buckner's error. "Mookie the whiff," said a Red Sox fan in typical contempt for both the batter and the pitcher, in an attempt to minimize what happened and make it tolerable. But Wilson well described the drama and intensity inside himself: "When I was up there, I felt like everything was happening in slow motion. I didn't hear the crowd. That was the most I concentrated in one at-bat in my whole career. That at-bat was my career. When it was over, I was drained. That's what I've played all these years for. You dream about that situation, being up with the game on the line. Everything went down to one at-bat. It was the difference between winning and losing. It was perfect."

The parallels between seventh games of two World Series eleven years apart run so spookily close that they suggest the synchronicities of the Lincoln and Kennedy assassinations. Both games followed historic extra-inning contests of sudden reversals of fortune. In both seventh games the Red Sox had a 3-0 lead entering the sixth inning, with a rare left-handed pitcher seemingly in command (in '75 Bill Lee threw the Moon Curve to Tony Perez and suddenly it was 3-2). In 1975 the losing pitcher was Jim Burton, who finished his career on the Mets' Tidewater farm club; in 1986 the losing pitcher was Calvin Schiraldi who spent much of the previous season on Tidewater. (In fact, it seemed a particularly bad omen for the Sox that in a tight seventh game of a World Series they should twice go to the bullpen in late innings and come up with two of their opponent's least effective hurlers in a 26-7 loss to the Phillies the season before, not only Schiraldi but Joe Sambito.)

For my final insight on the close of 1986, I am again drawn back to the less satisfying (but equally vital) 1984 season:

Because baseball is a game, one forgets it is also a play; the players are actors; otherwise they would be baseball players year-round all of their lives, like worker ants. The illusion is that they play only the game, the ancient game with its linear rules and precise boundaries, but they play also themselves—they play themselves playing baseball. How well they play is a function of how they communicate the cyclical dramas of baseball.

A game is different from a play or a dance, for its outcome is unknown; its moves are not scripted by any playwright or choreographer. It is a play caught in elemental probability theory, unfolding as the universe of matter does, giving shape to itself instant by instant according to rules. But a game is also a myth, so it repeats its themes by variations: new players occur in pre-existing roles, even as Osiris was transformed into Horus, and Mars replaced Ares millennia later.

On the 1984 Mets Darryl Strawberry played Darryl Strawberry, not exactly as the media and fans expected him to play it, but he did it well and transformed the role. Hubie Brooks also transformed the character of Hubie Brooks. Ed Lynch found weaknesses in his character, so his position in the game is in jeopardy. There is also no way to explain why one season Danny Heep plays Danny Heep with four pinch homers, the next season with none. There is no way to foresee the sudden arrival of Dwight Gooden with such *tour de force*. But since these are only people playing roles in a game, they must go home, live, dream, change, survive, and come back to the myth, which will also change with the constellations of the night sky. In the meantime the collective mythical being constituted by the Mets rests at a turning-point moment in its existence, with the possibility of making something more lasting than 1969.

But when Herm Winningham flies out to end the season, this is the moment of the longest wait till the next game. There is an unexplored sorrow in this, but it is the way everything is: darkness lies between night and morning, consciousness and unconsciousness, and fills interstellar space between epochs and suns. Baseball is wonderfully ordinary and we don't usually think about it in cosmic terms. We want to find a gentle thread of continuity waiting for us again in some form next spring. If life on Earth survives, the players will be reincarnated by their ka-souls on sunny practice diamonds in the spring, and, within this episode of American life, the ceremony will go on.

Or, as Gary Carter put it later, "In a corner of my mind I will stand forever with my bat cocked, waiting for the two-one pitch from Calvin Schiraldi. It is the bottom of the tenth inning, two out, nobody on base."

With acknowledgment and thanks to the following sources for quoted material: *Mets Inside Pitch* (Ron Swoboda epigraph and Mookie Wilson), *Baseball America* (Mike Cieslinski), *The Silent Pulse* (George Leonard), *A Dream Season* by Gary Carter and John Hough, Jr. (Gary Carter), and Sportschannel/New York (Mike Schmidt and Ron Swoboda).

O FOR A MUSE OF FIRE!

Jonathan Williams

Date: Tuesday, May 13, 1958—
a date previously memorable in history for the birth of
Joe Lewis (1914),
the Empress Maria Theresa (1717),
and the beheading of
Johan Van Olden Barnveldt (1619)
Place: Wrigley Field, Chicago, Illinois
Time: 3:06 P.M.; warm and sunny; breeze steady, right to left
Attendance: 5,692 (paid)
Situation: top of the sixth; Cardinals trailing the Cubs, 3-1;
one out; Gene Green on 2nd
Public Address: "Batting for Jones, #6, Stan Musial!"

The Muse muscles up; Stan the Man stands in . . . and
O, Hosanna, Hosanna, Ozanna's boy, Moe Drabowsky comes in

2 and 2
"a curve ball, outside corner, higher
than intended—
I figured he'd hit it in the ground"

("it felt fine!")

a line shot to left, down the line,
rolling deep for a double . . .

("it felt fine!")

Say, Stan, baby, how's it feel to hit 3000?

"Uh, it feels fine"

Only six major-league players in baseball history had hit safely 3000 times prior to this occasion. The density of the information surrounding the event continues to surprise me, rather belies Tocqueville's assertion that Americans cannot concentrate.

From **GROWING UP BRONX**
Gerald Rosen

Sometimes, after school, on a day when the Yankees were playing a night game, I would remain on the train for two additional stops, journeying to Yankee Stadium to talk to the players as they arrived. This always seemed unbelievable to me: that you could, simply by loitering outside the stadium, get to talk to the players—Mickey Mantle, Whitey Ford, Billy Martin. The same players whom the men at Ha-Ya Bungalows discussed for hours. The same players who appeared on TV and in the newspapers every day, the players thousands of people paid money to see at a distance. You could walk with them and talk to them for free.

It was like getting in touch with Real Life.

Of course, things didn't always go smoothly. One afternoon I ran over to greet Yankee pitcher Allie Reynolds, called "The Big Chief." I had seen so many photos of him, had watched him pitch so many times, that he seemed like an old friend. I ran right up to him and said, "Whaddya say, Big Chief?" I expected a warm response. He grunted and shoved me roughly out of the way. Well, perhaps he'd had a hard day. For all I knew maybe he blamed me for stealing this country from his people three hundred years ago. If the kids at Sacred Heart School could spit on us for "killing the Savior" when the Philadelphians played basketball in their gym, anything was possible.

In May of 1955, I became batboy for the Cincinnati Reds at the Polo Grounds. I got the job for a day—a doubleheader on a Sunday—through my friend Midge Waxenthal, the Giants' batboy. Midge had been the batboy for the Giants during their miracle world championship year of 1954 and it was during that season that my association with the Giants had begun. Midge and I journeyed to the Polo Grounds after school to sign baseballs in the clubhouse for the veterans in hospitals. We each practiced imitating the players' signatures and we specialized in half the team apiece.

In a way, I guess you could say this was my first experience in writing fiction. I took on the identity of other characters, imitating them and writing words for them. People believed it was true, and it made these people happy. No one was hurt by it.

On the day of the game, I went to the park early and put on my Cincinnati uniform, number 99. I went out onto the field for the Giants' batting practice. Not sure where to go, I wandered into the outfield.

When I reached my position in center field, a muscular man, about my height, perhaps a little shorter, trotted my way and stopped a few feet to my right. When I looked at his face, I saw he was Willie Mays.

Just then, the batter hit a fly ball toward deep right center field. I took off after it. Willie Mays took off after it, too, but I was closer. Before I realized what I was doing, I shouted, "I got it, Willie!" He pulled up and stood back as I caught the ball and threw it into the infield. He went back to his position.

And suddenly it occurred to me what I had done. I, Danny Schwartz of Nelson Avenue, had waved off Willie Mays, arguably the best all-around baseball player that has ever lived, and I had caught a ball in his territory, center field at the Polo Grounds, a huge pasture which he *owned*, which, in its immensity, seemed almost to have been built just for him to have the space to show off his amazing talents in front of millions of people. I had shouted, "I got it, Willie," and I had caught the ball just like that.

I didn't know what to make of it. On the one hand, I feared that I was in the wrong place, taking Willie's space; on the other hand, there was Willie, back at his position over to my right, not complaining, acting like I had done just what I should have by calling for a ball that was mine.

And I did catch it. And as I stood there, I began to feel very good about what had happened. Nothing else that happened that day or for years afterward quite touched that catch.

BLUES FOR A LOST OCTOBER

John Krich

The possibility of leading a normal life—at best, a problematic affair—has long eluded me during the month of October. What does this tenth flip of each calendar year augur for me and millions like me? Thanks to the expanded playoff system, it offers up to twenty-one—count 'em, twenty-one—nationally televised showcases for our favorite game's seemingly infinite penchant for suspense, controversy, and the revelation of human personality under pressure. October signals a classy class reunion for the boys of summer, a chance to catch up on the gossip and assess how time and booze and general managers have been treating the nation's perennial playmates. October means living close to the tube and the radio, trying to run businesses, errands, and even romances in those odd hours between late-morning and early-evening assignations with the game. October is always about trying to fit this archaic and delectably slow rite within the tightly scheduled grid of modern life, then finding it can't be done—to our immediate frustration and secret delight. Every fan has a story: how he left a blowout game with an inning to go, then drove halfway to Sacramento before that inning could be completed. This time, witnessing in person the Giants' pennant-clincher at the 'Stick produced a personal best in keeping the rest of life at bay. I calculated that the noontime start would give me plenty of time to make my psychiatric appointment at five. Instead I got to the couch with just enough time left in my hour to make excuses for my tardiness. This time my shrink dared not suggest that I was displaying resistance. He knew his patient well enough to know that baseball was the best therapy.

For me the most remarkable date in this remarkable month was not the sunny, shaky 17th, but that previous Monday afternoon, October 9th. Talk about an intersection of interplanetary forces, an astrological doppelgänger, a convergence of karma, a tsunami of pseudo-events! On that day the Bay Area was treated to a full harvest moon, causing the year's highest tides; a visit from the Dalai Lama; the observance of Yom Kippur, the Jewish day of atonement; the contrasting start-up of carnal Fleet Week; and, out at unblessed Candlestick Park, I was among the screaming thousands who witnessed Will Clark—that eternal archetype of a ballplayer, who'd be just another scrawny, soft-spoken, prematurely balding bigot pumping gas in Mississippi were it not for an archangelic hitting stroke—strike a positively anointed bases-loaded single that guaranteed the first Bay Area series, producing on cue the scripted ending dreamed by every kid who ever wanted to be a bat-wielding hero. Perhaps none of this meant anything beyond blind coincidence. Yet in California we've become disposed to put stock in such things. Our advanced high-tech consciousness has led us back to that lowest of low-tech beliefs in creating a meaning out of the uncontrollable turning of celestial gears. Reading in what we want in order to read ourselves: that's what religion is all about. Baseball, too.

The World Series is best read as a convergence of franchises, an interlocking of fortunate fates, a simultaneous cresting of two waves straining to reach a final shore. And in baseball, preeminently a game of patience, the long view is the only view worth taking. The last time that the San Francisco Giants could boast champion rights was back in 1954, before they were even the San Francisco Giants. In the interim, those galling, gauchely clad interlopers across the Bay had proved to be the most successful outfit in the game's history: eight divisional crowns, five Series appearances in only twenty-one years of operation. While the Giants pouted or praised Jesus or considered leaving town, the A's had gone through at least five flamboyant phases: Reggie's Raiders ('68–'71), Mustache Gang ('72–'75), Finley's Fire Sale ('76–'79), Billy Ball ('80–'84), Bruise Brothers ('85–?). Given such a historical imbalance, could anyone doubt the outcome of this first-ever get-acquainted session? It was I.B.M. versus Pop's Computers, it was the Temperance Union against the Vietcong. There was hope for parity only in the fact that the two clubs' recent development had been so remarkably parallel. Both had been rescued for the Bay Area by local, old-money Jewish families (Haas and Lurie) who even belonged to the same synagogue; both had begun their turnaround through the hiring of a pair of savvy managers (LaRussa and Craig) and general managers (Alderson and Rosen) who went out and drafted future stars off U.S. Olympic teams (McGwire, Walt Weiss, and Will Clark). As I watched the first pregame introductions on television, that collective doffing of caps that makes for one of baseball's most pleasing spectacles, I could not help commenting to a group of fellow party-goers in San Francisco caps, "When I see the Giants on the same field with the A's, I can't help being overwhelmed with a feeling of pity."

This remark hardly increased my popularity. In all honesty, it had just slipped out of me, with no premeditation or premature desire to rub any unspecified substance in anyone's specified face. It was more that I had never understood how anyone could choose, consciously, so masochistic a mission as putting your heart in the hands of the Giants. It wasn't a matter of winning or losing. As a fan of those talented Dodger teams who always finished a heartbreaking second to the soulless, swaggering Yankees, I could empathize with longtime adherents of the Red Sox or the Cubs. Now those were teams whose time-tested knack for squandering ability and good will were truly epic, downright Sophoclean. But there was nothing grand enough about the Giants' persistent mediocrity. They weren't tragic, just luckless. The timing of the earthquake, just when the city finally appeared poised to deliver a new stadium, seemed to me a perfect illustration of a Giant-style jinx. If the Lord was on the Giants' side, as the team's many "God squadders" claimed in postgame interviews, then Satan had to be the clubhouse manager. Now Dave Dravecky, a former John Bircher, was at the apex of Giants' iconography. The only appealing components in this year's edition were the sallow, laconic, and unshaven vets like Rick Reuschel and Don Robinson, guys whose guts—both psychic and protruding—offered confirmation of my democratic belief that anyone could indeed become a ballplayer. And then there was something about those Giant colors: vaguely menacing, Halloween ghoulish.

Of course my feelings were entirely irrational. That is the whole point of fandom. To give in to subconscious subjectivities and let them frame your world view, for once to get positively Daliesque! One of the great pleasures of the World Series turned out to be tuning in to KNBR's Ralph Barbieri, that weasel-voiced shill for the Giants' company station. Live and before a vast listenership, he had to eat crow after each defeat. There had to be easier ways to make a living. Eventually the line that emerged from Barbieri went something like this: "Yes, the A's are a stronger club, but unlike the Giants, they're unlovable. They lack charm because they're just *too* good." Yes, the greatest skill learned by the fanatic is an ability to rationalize anything—even optioning out your own mother to the minor leagues. It isn't a skill that stands you in good stead when it comes to real life.

During the playoffs, I'd promised myself to root for a Bay Area Series. But the closer I got to Candlestick for the contests against the Cubs, the more I felt the old hostility level rising. This response was partly encouraged by the stadium itself. I have never been a great admirer of the Oakland Coliseum. A's captain Sal Bando got it right when he dubbed that too-symmetric, no-frills, basic-concrete ring "the Mausoleum." It could be said, however, that at least the place (in contrast to the 'Stick) has real parking lots instead of muddy automotive Maginot Lines littered with moon rocks; the bathrooms are negotiable without nose-holding; the refreshment lines don't extend to Palo Alto; the bleacher seats are actually within a stone's throw of the outfield grass. And those bleachers are packed with the rowdy, redneck crowd you'd expect from working-class Oakland. A Candlestick crowd is more racially diverse—drawing far more Latins and Asians than appear at the Coliseum—but is conspicuous for its groups of raging, drunken, unaccompanied white male bozos. It's a nine-inning episode of "Animal House," in which the food fights and fist fights prove far more compelling than anything happening on the field. Compared to Oaklanders, San Franciscans appear to know a lot more about baseball but much less about winning. The Candlestick bleachers presented me with the side of sports I customarily work hard not to see.

Fortunately, there is one social virtue inculcated by sporting passion and that is patience. Dave Stewart's methodical domination of the Giants in Game One gave me plenty of time to chart the gradual ripening of this fall's bountiful harvest. I eulogized, in a roll call of ignominy, some of the players who'd filled the roster first inherited by the Haas family: Mack "Shooty" Babbitt, Dave "Buddha" Heaverlo, Mitchell "Rage" Page, Rob "The Peach" Picciolo (whose wife kept a running chart of how many homers her husband needed to surpass Babe Ruth), Mickey "No Nickname Necessary" Klutts. The only link between the club purchased from Finley and the club of today was Oakland's own Rickey Henderson—and he'd been mercifully sent off to enjoy the Big Apple for awhile while the rest of us had to suffer through the team's agonizing remake.

I realized that I'd been there on the exact day that this Series victory had been made possible. It was two Januarys back, when I'd talked my way into the press conference held in an unused hofbrau, full of empty steam tables, deep within the Coliseum's gray intestines, where the team introduced its six off-season acquisitions, including rambunctious, recovered alcoholic Bob Welch, asking Tony LaRussa to just "give me the ball"; green-eyed, carnivorous Dave "Cobra" Parker, exuding confidence and swearing off his former allegiance to Dick Gregory's dietary schemes; and a journeyman outfielder released by the Giants named Dave Henderson, who abruptly quit his infectious gap-toothed grinning when asked about his backup role, answering, "When April rolls around, I plan to be starting in center field." Standing about afterward, a modest Tony LaRussa admitted to the gathered journalists, "Any team with McGwire and Canseco should win ninety games." And it looked like he now had the troops to nab him those critical ten more victories which distinguish league champ from chump. The only other player who bothered to show up for that press conference was Dave Stewart. After all, he'd just had to bop over from his Emeryville condo. Dave kindly agreed to meet me for lunch at the Ice Creamery on Lakeshore—when he could have suggested Trader Vic's—so I could write the first of many "local boy makes good" pieces to follow. Rescued from the scrap heap by his hometown club, saved by strong family values from youthful flirtations with drugs and sin, Stewart has become the storybook symbol of the A's resurgence. But I'm sure he's still happy to have lunch at the Ice Creamery, a place where he can shoot the shit with old pals and the waiters. Dave Stewart was, and is, for real.

Unfortunately for the American League, so is Sandy Alderson. This team, this World Series victory, belongs to him more than any other recent victory has belonged to a general manager. His acquisitions of Mike Moore and Rickey Henderson were the cappers in a well-considered master plan. Yet no one in the history of the game has taken a more unlikely route to his position. During the spring training of '87, when T-shirts boasted that the A's were baseball's "most improved," I took a couple of early-morning runs through the disheartening sprawl of Phoenix with the game's leading "baby boomer" executive. I found the man accessible and honest, just as casual and unaffected as the jogging outfits he wears to work. Yet the biggest scoop I got from my pantings in the desert was the fact that, yes, the man did occasionally break a sweat. This bespectacled, articulate, trained lawyer, whose big break in life came when he clerked in a

San Francisco firm along with future A's president Roy Eisenhardt, struck me as equal parts attorney and ex–Marine drill sergeant. You have to wonder if he pops open a beer once he gets home, smacks his kids around, or gets out his back-issue *Playboys*. Given the chance that millions of ball fans dream of getting—namely, to run a rotisserie-league team in earnest—there was no way Sandy Alderson was going to blow it. He's too methodical and too smart, especially smart enough to keep his smarts to himself. These A's are not a Big Green Machine; they are junior partners in the law firm of Alderson, LaRussa and Eisenhardt.

But my exercise in patience proved to be shortlived. The Series was taking place just too nearby for me to resist. Despite the three-hundred-dollar markups being asked by newspaper advertisers, I couldn't restrain myself from at least trying to pick up a last-minute ticket for the second game. By the time I got to East Oakland, word was out on the street. None of the ghetto kids trying to make a quick buck by peddling souvenirs near the alternate lots could pretend to impartiality. They were all cooing, "Sweep! Sweep!" A few had even brought along their whisk brooms. I didn't mind this Third World profusion of hawkers and hustlers. This was just more proof, in case anyone needed it, that Oakland qualifies as a "developing" city, as in dirt poor. What bothered me were all those white-collar hooligans working out of the classified pages. Men and women who were trying to make the most out of some child's desire to root for his favorite team were truly the lowest of the low. The spectacular greed of defense contractors or stock speculators has always been around in one form or another—but this widespread, unquestioned, automatic reflex to take advantage of one's fellows at every turn is truly America's unique contribution to the organized, civilized descent into barbarism. The few scalpers dumb enough to be too obvious about their dirty work on the grounds of the Coliseum were being led away in handcuffs, but as usual this two-strike swing at justice was total hypocrisy. The big fish were getting away. But how could I blame these profiteers? As with their brethren in the Medellin drug cartel, they were only servicing a heightened demand. And I was doing the demanding.

Actually I was looking for one honest man. What a setup! I did spy one anonymous good samaritan emerging from some office party in a parking lot tent to hand over two tickets, gratis, to a stunned ten-year-old carrying a placard that read, "Two seats needed for kid and his pop." I thought I'd found my sugar daddy on the rampway leading to the BART station. The suspect was a prosperous looking Latino, mid-thirties, with mustache and razor-cut hairdo, clad in a tan windbreaker. He looked thoroughly like a fan, not a dealer in stolen goods. But he braked a little too quickly at the sight of my hand-lettered request for one ticket. Though he laughed off my first offer of eighty bucks, he kept coming back to bargain. He dropped his asking price by half in a matter of moments and got me up to a hundred and ten. He handed me the precious slip of paper and was gone. Apparently we would not be sitting together.

Still, I suspected nothing. I was confident that I'd found my exception to the rule. I called friends in gloating triumph before being dispatched to my seatless meandering through the park. Now, it was tough to concentrate on Mike Moore's mesmerizing slider and remarkable country-boy composure when I was calculating how long it would take before some usher tried to shoo me along from my place with some other high-priced hobos at the top of the aisle behind home plate. This new challenge heightened my sense of strategy and guile. I experienced a bracing kinship with all those practitioners over the years of that time-honored baseball tradition that goes by the name of "The Knothole Gang." Of course, I could have spent the whole game standing in a variety of refreshment lines. Second inning: frozen yogurt. Fourth inning: stuffed baked potatoes. Fortunately there was no cover charge, no consumption of comestibles required. But I had more than mustard, I had egg on face.

Why did I feel I had to be here at any cost? Would this Series really be something I could tell my grandchildren about, when I put so much more effort into getting here than I ever had into producing descendants? I found no amusement when the game was delayed briefly by the appearance in right field of a sauntering peacock. The only comfort was that there seemed to be hundreds of others in the same ill-defined boat. Every aisle had a few homeless fans camped at the top. Dozens more stood where they could along the rafters. When Terry Steinbach calmly put lumber to horsehide for the three-run homer that set the rout going, I rose as one with the crowd. I'd forgotten that I wasn't sitting in a proper seat, but squatting on the low-overhead stairway at the back of the field level. Just when I'd begun to feel once more like another ordinary fan, I bashed my head on the low concrete cantilever of the upper deck. No more "Bash Brothers" for me.

Maybe the two teams didn't really need a travel day in order to recover, but I did. By the afternoon of Game Three, I'd regained my enthusiasm sufficiently to host a dinner party. A last-second possibility of a ticket to Candlestick had fallen through, and after my experience at the Coliseum I was just as happy to be at home, frying up some Italian sausages and peppers. The pregame show was flashing aerial views of the City That Waits to Die on this perfect cloudless California day. Tears welled up in my eyes. I did some more of the personal stock-taking that the Series always provokes in me: yes, I had made it through another year intact in body and soul; yes, despite occasional heartaches and increasing traffic, I still loved the place where I'd chosen to live. My first guest arrived in an equally buoyant mood, uncharacteristically expressing much the same civic pride. I was just opening the jug of wine that he'd brought when the postcard images on the tube fritzed out, bookshelves went askew, wall hangings plummeted, my stove and sausages slid. Still, things didn't seem that bad until we joined a street full of panicked neighbors, heard wild radio flashes about the destruction of SFO's airport tower, saw the plume of smoke from the Marina fire. The earthquake, as I'd once predicted in a novel, was proving to be a great social opportunity. I even got to assess the emotional stability of one attractive neighbor who I'd been angling to meet for months. My pal and I didn't have a flashlight, candles, or a wrench to turn off the gas. We got through the big event the same way we got through most of life. We sat in the car and listened to A's announcers Bill King and Lon Simmons. To hell with the emergency broadcast system! Why don't they just let the play-by-play men take over the world? There was nobody I could have trusted more at that moment than these fatherly, familiar, and philosophical voices who'd already talked me through the minor disasters of a dozen summers. Lon and Bill were magnificent. They proved they could joke their way through the apocalypse and also that baseball had taught them well about how to sort fact from conjecture. I didn't even mind when Lon admitted that he'd felt the last five Bay Area tremors while sitting on the toilet.

They also kept all piousness at a minimum. Unfortunately, that's about all we'd hear over the next ten days in which the Series was delayed. One moment, the Bay Bridge Series was functioning beautifully as the great social distraction, meant to enthrall the masses and keep them in their place. The next moment, all good and decent men could agree that there were so many things in the world more important than baseball. Did all these pundits need an earthquake to make them come to that brilliant realization? Personally, I didn't particularly want there to be anything more important at the moment. I'd worked very hard to get to the place where more painful preoccupations could fade away for a time. And I didn't see baseball as being mutually exclusive with volunteerism, mourning, or social justice. In a society brilliantly designed to keep people apart, we were all suddenly exhorted to "pull together." I didn't really care if the Series continued so long as the do-gooding rhetoric ceased.

By the time the third game rolled around once more, we decided to hold our dinner party elsewhere. My friends were a little spooked about recreating the scene of the quake and I couldn't blame them. An added last-minute arrival was a skeptical Uruguayan exile who said he wanted to see "how the real baseball fans behave." He saw us rising from our couches in unison to exult at the mighty blows struck by "Hendoo." He heard us predict that a miffed Jose Canseco just might be due to produce his own monstrous shot—and got to witness the generalized self-satisfaction that smothered our mood better than the hot sauce smothered our take-out meal of short ribs. He got to hear us debate, *ad nauseum*, whether the delay had served the A's by allowing them to use their two best pitchers over again, or the Giants, who at least got to see them for a second time. The outcome soon made our debate moot. And the Uruguayan kept muttering, "I don't get this game. Isn't it very e-slow? Isn't it a little e-stupid?"

I could hardly have turned down the offer made to me just a couple of hours before the clinching Game Four. By then, I couldn't have cared less about the Series. Just when I wanted it the least, I had a ticket dropped in my lap. Doesn't life always work that way? I picked up the requisite monster sandwiches and *frittata* and made my way out to the game as though preparing for a dreaded elementary-school field trip. Once I got to my terrific seats among a section of fervent Giant boosters, and Rickey Henderson's leadoff homer set the evening's monotonous tone, I figured this was my big chance to strut, gloat, take credit for the deeds of others, and generally make myself obnoxious. My countdown to the championship was stalled briefly by LaRussa's perverse choice to put a laboring Gene Nelson back on the mound. In the end my confidence was rewarded by Tony Phillips, a charming fellow I'd once sat beside as he merrily gambled away his winter-league pay at the gaming tables of Santo Domingo, whose fielding exploits would have been celebrated throughout the nation if this had been a normal Series. Thanks to his lunging dives, I soon witnessed my second A's championship clinching. Back in 1974, I'd gone on the field to wander about with the rest of the stupefied Coliseum mob. This time, the game didn't even end with a proper latently homosexual piling-on of teammates on the mound. Since Dennis Eckersley sealed the victory with a putout at first, the Series ended as it had been played: off-line and out of whack. I thought of Roger Angell's poignant description of Red Sox fans, enraptured even in defeat, simply refusing to leave Fenway Park at the end of 1967's wondrous campaign. Now the 'Stick emptied with incredible rapidity. The Giants fans didn't seem disgusted so much as exhausted. I lingered to watch the scoreboard transmission of Dave Stewart meeting reporters, his mom at his side. The good son's falsetto and un-macho homilies rattled via P.A. around the silent stadium.

After fifteen years, we—the East Bay—are champs again. But never has it seemed less urgent to possess that championship. Never has it been tougher to say just who "we" are. Fifteen years ago, the A's rode through downtown in a procession of antique cars that was both sweeping and rinky-tink. This time, there would be no parade in respect for the victims of the Nimitz overpass debacle. Or was it for the demise of Capwell's? No cars this time: in an act of supreme civic consciousness, I took BART and the A's came by ferry. In typical Oakland fashion, the crowd that gathered at Jack London Square was relatively meagre and well behaved. There seemed to be one souvenir peddler along Lower Broadway for every five fans. One woman close to me did manage to faint. In general, the most excitement was generated by the bargains on "Bay Series" T-shirts. The players stepped forward in turn to offer their two-sentence valedictories. Nothing quotable or memorable here like former A's captain Sal Bando's contention that his manager Alvin Dark "couldn't manage a meat market." Just Dave Henderson declaring, "Look for me next year, I'm having a blast!" So what if Rickey Henderson managed to mangle his syntax instantly, declaring, "You all are one of best fans I ever played for"? The kick was seeing how Stew or Steiny looked in three-piece suit or cashmere sweater and confirming that, even in their civvies, these boys were broader and taller and somehow more forthright, ruddier, well oxygenated, or just downright better than you or I.

Were these A's really so "hard to love"? Perhaps they were a little easier to love with the hulking José characteristically absent. Yet even without Canseco, Parker, Phillips and others who'd been excused to their homes after the unusually long season, I was astonished at how much talent and heart had been assembled on one platform. There was soft-spoken Carney Lansford from San Jose, almost unnoticed as the second-best hitter in the American League, who'd overcome the death of his infant son. There was Dennis Eckersley, Fremont's own, who'd turned his life away from partying and madness just in time. There was blustery Bob Welch, who'd put aside alcoholism and the recent death of his mother. And how about that tough little bantam Mike Gallego, whose cancer was in remission? For once I had to agree with Tony LaRussa's managerial hyperbole about how no team in history ever had to overcome what this team overcame. The A's exemplified real heroism over the long haul—not the one-shot variety of slinging hash for a day at a Red Cross shelter. Why should these guys play second-fiddle to an earthquake?

Compared to Oakland's last champions, that aggregate of militant blacks and mellow country boys bridling under the yoke of Charlie Finley's authority, these A's were certainly far more a reflection of their community. They weren't just a bunch of carpetbaggers who'd accidentally landed on this shore. They had local ownership and boasted homegrown players galore. One image from up on the platform seemed to say it all: Sandy Alderson, casual as always in his newly minted Champion's cap, holding the small child of one of the black players in his arms through the entire ceremony. If Charlie Finley had been there, he'd have kept the babe at arm's length or fed him a big slice of watermelon. In its own way, this A's squad is as much a reflection of its time as the fiery A's of old. In place of yesterday's anger, there is quiet compassion; in place of poised rebellion, there is psychic "recovery"; in place of color and tumult, there is a touch of blandness but also a modicum of decency. These A's are, like the late eighties, more conformist than the preceding epoch but perhaps more caring.

Wandering off through Oakland, that zero-ground to which I always seem to return, I tried to assess the changes of the last fifteen years. The Welfare Department looked busy as ever, as did police headquarters and the spiffy new city jail. The "New Rose Room" still offered taxi-dancing, at a quarter a turn. The cracked facades and many condemned brick buildings attested to quake damage that was far worse than San Francisco's, yet, like the A's, had been under-reported. Yet downtown Oakland looked better than ever, at least to middle-class eyes. There were real bookstores finally, spiffy restaurants and hotels, a pleasant "City Square" mall where office-workers could scarf down lunch-hour pasta salads and *espresso*. "Cappuccinos? In Oakland?" As a place, it certainly gives a greater sense of integrity and cohesion. But what of the picture beyond all this heavy investment in image-building? The last time the A's won, we were talking about Bobby Seale and Watergate and East Oakland's infant mortality rates; this time, we had the demise of Huey Newton and the remnants of Irangate, a rotting infrastructure and crack. The problems don't change as quickly as the faces in our team yearbooks.

Baseball is history condensed, a crude primer of American society that provides grand confirmations for a nation of "little men." But how long can I follow it without being made littler myself? How much of a sucker do I have to become to understand this country of come-ons and con jobs? For all the satisfaction of seeing my standard-bearers perform to the heights of their capabilities, the memory that I'll carry of the 1989 season will always be of those moments when I roamed bereft of enthusiasm, ticket, context. It's astounding how all-encompassing and all-satisfying is American prosperity, American spectacle, American urgency when you're on the inside—and how quickly you can find yourself on the outside. Our national obsession with celebration and self-congratulation may be little more than a backhanded admission of how fragile this culture of ours really is, how tenuous are the connections we have to one another. For me, the image that will remain emblematic of the Earthquake Series is the rubber ticket which guaranteed my sudden exile from the realm of rah-rah. In those shaky seconds when I roamed the Coliseum periphery, squinting after familiar pleasures rudely eclipsed by crisis, a personal temblor struck—rocking the assumptions beneath our golden age of champions as the quake would jolt the illusions built into our golden cities. In that terrific moment, baseball's rich welter of meanings faded to black, and I went looking for my seat in a world where America itself had disappeared.

"There are three ways to get rid of a slump.
One is to drink and change the feeling you are walking around with.
Another one is to get involved in some sort of hobby so you can forget for a while.
The third is just to practice and practice again.
In order to get rid of the uneasiness, the first two
should always be considered."

SECOND BASE:

THE

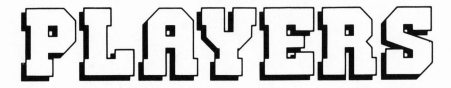

THE LANGUAGE OF SCOUTING
Kevin Kerrane

*Language is not an abstract construction of the
learned, of the dictionary-makers, but is something
arising out of the work, needs, ties, joys, affections,
tastes of long generations of humanity, and has its
bases broad and low, close to the ground.*
Walt Whitman, *"Slang in America"*

The language of scouting is really several vocabularies. Numbers or letter grades project a player's skills into a possible future; psychological catchwords describe his makeup; and a money code expresses an ultimate evaluation, the dollar sign on the muscle. But most basic is a vocabulary sharpened by slang, superlative, and metaphor—a descriptive catalogue of tools and talents, bodies and body parts.

Quickie, anesthesia ballplayer, quiet bat, wrist wrapper (what Howie Haak calls a "hooker"): these were some of Branch Rickey's contributions to the word-hoard of scouting. In the 1980s many scouts still use these coinages and others that go back just as far. On a spring Sunday in Lakeland, Florida, as I watched a player touted as the best amateur pitcher in America in 1981, I listened to the language of scouting and caught a sense of the oral tradition behind it.

BOY: ANY AMATEUR PLAYER

At the age of twenty years and seven months Ron Darling was six foot three, 205 pounds, strong, poised, articulate—all in all, "a mature-looking prospect." But until he signed his first professional contract, he would remain a *boy* or even a *lad*.

Pitching for Yale in the first game of a doubleheader against Purdue on Charlie Gehringer Field at Tigertown, Darling had an audience of twenty-four, of whom twenty were major-league scouts. Ed Katalinas, who had helped to design this training complex, held court next to the small observation tower behind the backstop. Dick Gernert of the Rangers was there, and so were Al LaMacchia of the Blue Jays, Frank DeMoss of the Cubs, Tony Stiel of the Braves, Dick Teed and Regie Otero of the Dodgers. Three Phillies' scouts were sitting off by themselves instead of socializing with their colleagues.

"They sent three? I'd call that *over*-scoutin'."

"Nah, one's there just to check up on the other two, to make sure they don't say hello. Loose lips sink ships."

"Loose lips sink draft picks."

"Hey, how ya been? Feelin' better now?"

"Oh, fine, fine. It wasn't serious. I'm rested up and ready."

"Well, you know, at your age you got to start cuttin' down on pussy. No more than once a day from now on."

"Hey, that's a prescription I can follow. Every Saturday night my wife and I hold it up and bet which way it's gonna fall."

Over near the Yale bench Bill Kearns of the Mariners was studying Ron Darling's warm-up pitches. Seattle would have first pick in the June draft and would almost certainly choose a pitcher. On the basis of Kearns's reports they might make Ron Darling the number one boy in the country.

SNOWBIRD: A NORTHERN SCOUT ASSIGNED TO FLORIDA IN EARLY SPRING

While baseball lies dormant in the north, the snowbird flies south where there are too many games for local scouts to cover. Florida is patched with baseball fields, more per square mile than in any other state, and in the spring every one of them seems to be in use every day. Dozens of northern colleges come down for early season games, so the snowbird may be able to get a line on players to follow next month, back home.

Dick Lawlor, the Phillies' scout for New England, had already followed Darling for a year. He had watched through the spring of 1980 as Darling, in his first season as a pitcher, compiled a record of 11-2 with two saves and a 1.31 earned run average. And he had watched through that summer as Darling competed against top amateur talent in the Cape Cod League, where he was named Most Valuable Player. Now Lawlor sat on the observation tower steps with two other Philadelphia scouts, Joe Reilly and Randy Waddill. He was easy to identify as a snowbird, because his face was newly sunburned.

"I sunburn easy. My father's Irish and my mother's Italian, born in Florence. I got his coloring and her features. But look at Ronny. His father's Irish and his mother's Chinese-Hawaiian, and he got the Irish features and the darker coloring. Handsome kid. And just a *great* body."

Whenever possible, Lawlor said, he tried to "project bodies into the future." And sometimes that meant taking account of "ethnic factors"—like the tendency of Italian boys to gain weight in their twenties, at the very time that Polish boys tend to shed the last of their baby fat. But Lawlor knew of no ethnic factor, other than hybrid vigor in general, to help project an Irish and Chinese-Hawaiian body. Instead, he relied on "power, proportion, and energy. Especially energy. Ronny's quick, agile, . . . springy. He's wound tight."

WOUND-TIGHTNESS: THE POTENTIAL ENERGY VISIBLY PRESENT IN AN ATHLETIC BODY

Wound tight doesn't mean nervous. It may mean high-strung, but only in the way that race-horses are high-strung—the long hamstring muscles tapering to high gluteals, the whole body at rest still vibrating with power. This scouting metaphor may have originated, in fact, at the racetrack rather than the ballpark: sometimes a horse is said to be "wound tight" when in the starting gate it seems doubly poised, both relaxed and cocked.

Ultimately the comparison is either to the coils in the armature of a motor or (more likely) to a spring mechanism like a watch. Either way, the scout is talking about potential energy, in firm control but ready to become kinetic in an instant. "If a boy is wound tight, he lets you imagine him running when he's just walking. He has a live body."

DEAD BODY: ATHLETIC INERTIA, AS MANIFESTED BY SLOW REFLEXES, HEAVY FEET, OR BAD HANDS

Scouts associate one kind of dead body specifically with football, and many of them resent the sport for beefing up, and then banging up, baseball talent. After football season, they say, the player is less likely to be loose or extended than to be short-muscled, literally muscle-*bound*. "Bulk as in hulk" is Brandy Davis's contribution to this lore of dead bodies.

Rich Diana, the Yale first baseman, was also a star running back in football. In the first inning, with a big stride and an uppercut swing, he struck out on a fastball. In the third he lifted a long fly to left field. In the language of scouting Diana looked like a "good uppercutter," who tends to meet the ball at an upward angle and thus loft it for fence power—as opposed to a "bad uppercutter," who collapses his back elbow in toward the chest and fails to extend his arms. But some scouts surmised that Diana was a "one-tool player," with little baseball potential beyond the power swing.

At first base, for example, Diana seemed to lack "the soft hands." Soft hands are good; they are, in fact, prerequisites for a catcher or infielder at the professional level, allowing their owner to accept the ball rather than fearing it or fighting it. Of a fielder without soft hands it's sometimes said: "He couldn't catch a two-hopper eye-high."

In the sixth inning, when Diana hit a ground ball and was slow getting out of the box, the scouts began to sort out their impressions of his body.

"This boy runs like he's waitin' for his blockers."

"I got 4.6 on the watch."

"I got 4.7. Horseshit either way."

"It's only a *slightly* dead body. You know he has good athletic ability. Another week in Florida, he gets those muscles stretched out, he won't be so sluggish."

"Looks like Tarzan. Runs like Jane."

HORSESHIT: UNIVERSAL TERM OF DISPARAGEMENT IN BASEBALL

Any baseball talent, body, body part, effort, action, player, team, city, or scouting assignment can be *horseshit*. The term covers everything but the world of words—the world of stories, explanations, and scouting reports—at which point *bullshit* takes over.

A real sentence spoken by a scout discussing a former colleague: "His written report was all bullshit, and that's when I knew he was a horseshit guy."

Bullshit can be a verb; *horseshit* can't. (A sentence like "Don't horseshit me" would make no more sense to a scout than to a nonscout.) Novices sometimes elide the word into *horshit*, but the veterans get the first *s* down deep in the throat, with the tongue at the back of the palate, lots of air whistling past the lower teeth, and then they follow through for full emphasis. *Horsseshit!*

The word is popular throughout baseball—with players, managers, umpires, and executives. And it's clear enough why scouts, whose business is evaluation, would find it a handy label for anything deserving a low grade. What remains unclear, though, is the *horse*, which is far more prevalent here than in the lingo of any other subculture or occupational group in America, even cowboys. It's absent from baseball talk in Latin America: scouts down there rely on the all-purpose *mierda*, with no animal prefix.

Is *horseshit* an image from the country days of baseball, like *bull pen* or *outfield pastures*? Probably not. Only a generation ago any American living in a city could see horseshit every day, and older scouts say that the word's baseball popularity is relatively recent. It might be that *horseshit* is really a modern scouting term that has the merit of *sounding* old-fashioned, allowing its user to think of himself as a traditional baseball man rather than an investment analyst constrained by bureaucratic procedures.

NEGATIVE SCOUTING: BEING RIGHT 92 PERCENT OF THE TIME

"If you just focus on a boy's faults," Al LaMacchia said, "you'll become certain that he's not a major-league prospect—and you'll almost always be right. But negative scouting can kill you, because you'll write off some boys who are *gonna* be great. Positive scouting means projecting a player into the future, and that means when you go to a game you focus more on tools than performance. Skills can be taught; talents can't.

"You see Ron Darling pitch a weak first inning. His delivery and follow-through are too straight up. He chokes the curveball. But those are just *skills*. And right away you see that he's blessed with the *talents*: the good live arm, the good low fastball, control on the mound, control on his pitches. So already you say 'prospect.' And then he retires the next twelve men in a row, and strikes out six of 'em."

CHOKING THE CURVEBALL: GRIPPING THE BALL TOO TIGHTLY OR TOO FAR BACK IN THE HAND

If you choke the curveball, your pitch will lack "bite." Instead of breaking sharply downward ("falling off the table"), it will usually be flat and slow, and easier to hit. Ron Darling's curve was a "lollipop," according to Dick Lawlor. "It needs less choke and faster arm action. As is, professional hitters could tee off on it."

But the Purdue hitters couldn't tee off, because Darling disrupted their timing by using his curve like a change-up, mixing it effectively with the fastball and slider. Purdue's few fair balls were either grounders or pop-ups. In the first inning Darling gave up two runs on a walk, two ground singles, and a key error by the shortstop. Hanging or breaking, the curves were out of the strike zone, and he fell behind hitters on the count. But from the second inning on, Darling threw the curveball for good slow strikes, even a few strike-threes, while establishing the fastball as his real out pitch.

ADDING A FOOT TO THE FASTBALL:
GAINING PHYSICAL MATURITY AND THUS GREATER VELOCITY

Darling had filled out a little since last season, Lawlor said, and had become "that much" faster. (He held out his hands as if describing a prize trout.) The extra foot was a translation of velocity into distance, a way of saying how it might *feel* to bat against a good pitcher if the mound were moved closer.

Darling's fastball did not look overpowering. The scouts weren't disappointed, though, because they knew he had pitched an inning in relief the day before and a complete game three days before that, and because his pitch had such good "life" or "run." He threw it from a high three-quarter arm angle, instead of straight over the top, and the result was a sinking fastball that tailed in sharply to right-handed batters. In order to describe this pitch some scouts abandoned words in favor of shorthand (——), but my own notes incorporated one of Moose Johnson's coinages—"wicky fastball."

I also wrote down this idle computation: if a boy really added a foot to his fastball, it would be roughly equivalent to an extra 1.5 miles per hour. An 86 fastball, for example, would become 87.44. "In that case," one scout said, "I can tell you that I've seen high-school pitchers add *five* feet to their fastball between junior and senior year."

86 FASTBALL: THE AVERAGE MAJOR-LEAGUE FASTBALL,
AS CLOCKED BY RADAR GUN

Darling's fastball hovered right around 86, and in the middle innings a half dozen scouts hovered right around the gun, looking over shoulders to see if Darling might be slowing down. If anything, he was getting stronger.

Most scouts consider radar guns awkward to carry around and use, useless at gauging what they really want to see ("life"), untrustworthy in making fine discriminations of speed, and truly valuable only in night games when the fastball is harder to read. Nevertheless, they don't mind craning their necks to check the numbers on somebody else's gun. As a result, the scouts who do carry guns sometimes have them adjusted to give phony readings, so that an 86 fastball might flash up as 80. But if the distortion is more than a couple of miles per hour, it usually takes less than an inning for the magpies behind the gun to begin muttering "Bullshit" or "Add six."

Ed Katalinas, a big teddy bear of a man, was amused by the radar game and its pseudoscientific language. "The old-fashioned scouts, like me, we used to say: 'He can throw hard.' That meant he could throw hard. 'He's got smoke,' we used that expression. The eye sees it; the brain tells you. Ability is naked to the eye. But some of these scouts don't trust their own eyes, and the modern way is: 'He throws 86,' or 'He has a 76 curve.' It's a number thing, just like scoutin' is a number game now.

"You only get one out of twenty-six in the draft, and you don't get the boys you want, because everybody's seen them and the big number-wheel turns around. Or you're a scout director, like me, and you tell your area guy: 'Offer George eight thousand dollars, and if he don't want it to hell with him.' Because of the number that he got.

"Back when Billy Pierre was on his last legs as a Tigers' scout, he used to call me up and say, 'Ed, I got a boy who can play.' I'd say, 'What's his name? Where's he from?'—address and all that, and we'd do everything on the phone—and then Billy'd go out and sign him. Or I'd call him and say, 'I hear Johnny Jones is pretty good.' 'Ed, he can't play.' That was it—that was the old-time way.

"But you wanta hear a story about a fastball? Okay. Back in 1962 I happened to be in Clinton, Iowa, one day. I'm scoutin' the Midwest League to look at other clubs' first-year players, and when I arrive in Clinton I run into a guy name of Rich Kolsch. He says, 'Ed, I know why you're here. *He's* gonna pitch tonight.' I say, 'Right, that's why I came.' And meanwhile I'm wonderin' who the hell *he* is.

"Turns out it's Denny McLain, who the White Sox had signed that June, and I've never seen him. In Clinton the bull pen was up on a sort of hill, and if you sat near home plate and looked up you could see the pitcher warm up in the distance. So here's this McLain before the game throwin' with a beautiful delivery, and here's the catcher bobbin' up from his crouch whenever McLain throws the fastball. I say to myself: 'He must have a *riser!*' Then the game starts, and McLain throws what today you'd call maybe a 90 fastball, and besides that his ball just *jumps*, and he strikes out about twelve guys. Now my wheels are turnin'. Are the White Sox gonna protect McLain in the minor-league draft? And then I figure it out—they can't.

"That year the Sox had signed four pitchers, McLain and . . . I need three names. De-Busschere, the great basketball player—they gave him seventy thousand and put him on the major-league roster, so he was frozen. Then a boy name of Mike Joyce out of the University of Michigan—they gave him thirty-five thousand. Then a boy out of Villanova—can't remember his name, but he was a right-hander with a good slider. So I realized there's no way the Sox can protect four first-year men on their roster. And at the end of that season here comes McLain through waivers, and the Tigers claim him for eight thousand.

"Now that's what you call bein' in the right place at the right time. And it was luck. Because to add to the story: I wound up in Clinton because I'd come to this fork in the road, and a sign said Burlington this way and Clinton that way, and it didn't matter which one because I had to see all eight clubs in the league, and I just said, 'Oh, what the hell, I'll go to Clinton.' No reason. . . . So who sent me there to see that catcher bobbin' up for those risin' fastballs? My guardian angel!"

TWO-WAY SHOT: A PLAYER WITH MAJOR-LEAGUE POTENTIAL BOTH AS A PITCHER AND A HITTER

Dave Winfield, Fred Lynn, and Cal Ripken, Jr. were once two-way shots, but shortly after each turned pro he abandoned pitching to become an everyday player. It was conceivable that Ron Darling would do the same. As a college hitter he averaged about .380 with home-run power, and he usually played center field when he wasn't pitching. He had intelligence, baseball instincts, catlike reflexes, and that arm.

Throughout the game Darling showed all-around baseball talent. In the bottom of the sixth, with the score tied 2-2, one out, and Purdue runners on first and third, Darling foiled a suicide squeeze by pouncing off the mound to snare the bunt just before it hit the ground. The runner from third was still moving toward home—still sure, even after the bunt was caught, that it was uncatchable. Darling glanced at him, then trotted easily to third for the final out.

The score was still tied after the regulation seven innings, but Yale rallied in the top of the eighth. With a man on third, no outs, Rich Diana hit a sacrifice fly to left for a 3-2 lead. Then Darling came to bat for the last time. In three previous at-bats he had shown good whip in his swing, and in the third inning he had lined a ground-rule double to left. Now in the eighth he stepped into an outside curveball: his stride was long and maybe a tenth of a second early, but he kept his hands back and then used his hips to spring a swing worthy of a major-league hitter—head down, arms extended, front leg straightened into a fulcrum, and back leg bent into a perfect *L* with the toe-spike still dug in and pushing for power. The ball carried deep to right center, between the fielders, and Darling was in high gear before he'd turned first base. He made third base standing up, and some of the scouts were panting harder than he was.

As the very next pitch became a ground ball toward shortstop, Darling broke for home. He slid in head first, twisting away from the bat near the plate while shoving his right arm ahead of the tag and between the catcher's feet. Breaths were sucked in all around me.

"Holy shit!"

"No, he's okay."

"Yeah, look at him bounce back up."

"Holy shit . . . he coulda broke that arm."

"And lost himself a hundred and fifty thousand."

"Only a hundred thousand if Seattle drafts him. Right, Bill?"

Bill Kearns said nothing. Signability was no joke.

LOUNGE HITTER: LATE-NIGHT BAR CRUISER
(WORDPLAY ON *LUNGE HITTER*)

In the bottom of the eighth inning, working with a two-run lead, Darling struck out the first Purdue hitter on a low and wicky fastball, maybe his best pitch of the day. The second hitter lined out to the second baseman. The third hitter looked at three killer pitches: another beautiful low fastball, a curve with real bite, and then a *high* fastball—the only one Darling threw all afternoon—that sailed in on the fists to end the game.

In eight innings Darling had given up three walks and four hits, none big, and had struck out ten. And his command and composure had been at least as impressive as his physical performance. Dick Lawlor said that wasn't all, that Darling was "a good boy off the field, too—serious, earnest, well behaved." But the consensus among the scouts was that if Darling wanted to be a lounge hitter, just for tonight, he deserved it . . . as long as he kept Casey Stengel's adage in mind: "It ain't sex that's troublesome; it's stayin' up all night lookin' for it."

SIGNABILITY PROBLEM: THE GAP BETWEEN
(A) WHAT A BOY THINKS HE'S WORTH AND (B) THE SCOUT'S EVALUATION

At the water fountain near the observation tower Tony Stiel introduced himself and gave Ron Darling a business card.

"I enjoyed watchin' you pitch today."

"Thank you. I didn't have the good heater."

"Well, when was the last time you pitched?"

"I did an inning yesterday."

"Yeah? Well, you looked fine today. You know when you might pitch again?"

"Right now I'm scheduled against East Carolina on Thursday."

"I'll try and catch that game. Anyhow, you got my card—Tony Stiel of the Braves. Real nice to meet you. And take it easy now."

Once upon a time Tony Stiel would have tried to ingratiate himself with a prospect like Darling, jockeying for position among the other scouts. Now, because of the amateur draft system, Stiel simply had to put the dollar sign on the muscle and check to see if the boy had "unrealistic" bonus expectations beyond that figure. And since the Braves would have the twelfth selection in the June draft, and since Darling was almost certain to be chosen before that, there was really not much point in romancing him.

Some boys create signability problems by hiring an agent. Ron Darling would later exercise that option on the eve of the draft. But right now he was less interested in money than in proving his abilities to the scouts.

"No, I don't mind this many at a game. I think it helps me bear down, because I want to show them. Of course, I don't *know* many of them, except for Dick Lawlor, and I don't have any preference about ballclubs. It doesn't matter; it doesn't matter to me. I just want to *get there*, you know? Sometimes people say if you get drafted by a lower club, you have a better chance of gettin' to the majors, but I'm not sure that's true. If you have good talent, and you're in a good system, they'll get you up there somehow—or trade you to someone that's gonna get you up there. I want to get drafted as high as I can. Not just for the money, but because the ballclub would be givin' me a high priority, and they'd have a big stake in my progress."

Up close Darling was even more strikingly tall, dark, handsome, and wound tight. In a relaxed voice he spoke modestly about his repertoire of pitches. "I've been workin' on my curveball, and I've worked so much on my curveball that now my slider's dropped off a little, because I had a good slider last year. So I've gotta make sure I work on each pitch the same and not give one a preference over the others."

MILEAGE: MILES PER HOUR, AS EXPLAINED BY REGIE OTERO

"For me," Regie Otero said, "I consider that this boy throws a curveball. And in the minors he can really improve that curveball to become a real curveball. If I had anything to do with him, I would tell him: 'Stop throwing the slider! You keep on throwing the slider, you will lose your curveball.' Because the slider is thrown with the, what do you call, stiff wrist, and then the curveball with the break of the wrist.

"Now, his fastball. He's gonna strike out many people because it *moves*—see? Sails, sinks, tails—see? With my experience and knowledge to see a boy, and I don't care the mileage that he throws or anything like that, because if today we didn't have the radar gun or anything like that and you see a Steve Ho pitch, and I get behind the plate, I say, 'I think that boy's right on,' and no questions asked. See, so the radar gun doesn't mean anything."

Somewhere in there was a bias, or insight, typical of Dodger scouting—distrust of the slider. It was another of Branch Rickey's precepts, by way of Al Campanis. But if you looked at Ron Darling through that lens, wouldn't you then have to project a third pitch for him?

"Exactly. The chonge! The straight chonge is the most dongerous pitch in baseball, because the hitter's timing throws it off. Andy Messersmith had the best. Messersmith had a pretty good curveball, pretty good fastball, and an *outstanding* chonge, and the Do-yer coaches teach it right on. So when Mr. Darling gets all three pitches, he is in the big leagues.

"If the boss says, 'How much you give this kid?' I would have to said, 'Sixty thousand.' If he says, 'They don't want sixty: they want eighty,' I would said, 'Give it to them!' Because if I'm gonna give sixty, I give eighty. Otherwise, why draft him? You might say, 'Ron Darling, no way will he be available when the Do-yers' turn to draft comes.' But you could say the same thing two years ago about Steve Ho."

Steve Ho was Steve Howe, who had been drafted by the Dodgers in June of 1979, as the sixteeenth player selected in the first round, and who had become the National League Rookie of the Year in 1980. And Regie Otero was Casey Stengel, as performed by Desi Arnaz. He had come to the States thirty-five years earlier, after being signed out of Havana as part of Joe Cambria's first wave of Latin talent, but he still handled the English language as if playing a tricky bunt. He remembered Cambria as "Papa Joe, a man with a big cigar in a white linen suit—a good scout, and could see the tools, the five talents."

"And did Cambria tutor you as a scout?"

"What?"

"Who broke you in? Who taught you to scout?"

"God. He was my teacher. He give me the grace to see the diamond in the raw. To *see* the talents is as much a gift as to *have* the talents. I do not say as great a gift, but is as much a gift. Like this boy today, the way he plays there is a light shining through him. Every scout might tell you something different about how bright or how long's gonna burn. But Darling has it. Mark Fidrych had it; Willie Mays had it: the grace, the heart, the what they let you see. Fidrych was a meteor—blazes, comes down, hits the ground. But then here comes along a new boy with a gift from God. Same as we had Caruso and then Mario Lanza and now we have Pavarotti."

THE FIVE TALENTS:
RUNNING, THROWING, FIELDING, HITTING, HITTING WITH POWER

These are the five talents for position players. For pitchers the five talents are usually stated as fastball, breaking pitch, delivery, control, and poise. Control and poise are two sides of the same talent, and most scouts would say that with pitchers you have to forget about distinguishing sharply between tools and makeup, the physical and the psychical—if you ever really separate them in the first place.

Because whatever else the language of scouting is, it is not scientific. Baseball scouts are men who think they're being technical when they describe a pitch in terms of miles per hour. That the ball also travels in feet per second, or that key reaction times like bat speed can be computed in tenths or hundredths of a second, simply does not interest most of them. Their language is impressionistic, based on four generations of oral tradition. Regie Otero's "Darling has it" echoed one of Sinister Dick Kinsella's scouting reports from 1928: "Hubbell has it." And now, just as then and always, the *it* names a mystery beyond the reach of technology.

The business of baseball scouts is to describe the future, and, despite occasional exceptions like Steve Howe, that future is generally four years away. Consequently, their vocabulary emphasizes energies—the live fastball, the live arm, the live body (wound tight)—rather than static quantities. This is Al LaMacchia's "positive scouting," genial in spirit, more vitally expressed by "holy shit" than "horseshit." Sometimes it's even aesthetic scouting, because in the modern era scouts are able to look at a player like Ron Darling without plotting how to steal him from other scouts; they have to be resigned, as a fact of life and as a basis of pure appreciation, to losing him in the draft. "Will never be there when we pick," read one of Dick Lawlor's many reports on Darling—and yet there Lawlor was: enjoying this great performance, proud of it, and oddly protective of a boy his organization would have no chance to acquire.

The language of scouting is also religious. To have a talent is to be "blessed" with it—and scouting itineraries can sometimes be planned by guardian angels. And if you really want to know about the five talents, there are scouts who will tell you to read the Gospel of Matthew, chapter 25, where *talent* means a unit of wealth. After receiving talents from their master, two servants invest the money and double it, but one servant just buries his talent in the ground. As a moral parable, the story ends with weeping and the gnashing of teeth. As a baseball parable, it ends with some scout telling you about a lounge hitter who never developed his God-given potential.

At the end of the spring I talked with Al Campanis, the Dodger's general manager. He was a Rickey man and thus more of a rationalist in scouting. It was Campanis who had refined number grades as the new language of evaluation, and his 60-to-80 scale was the most popular grading system outside the Major League Scouting Bureau.

"Regie told you that God taught him to scout? Well, I'll just say that he wasn't speaking for the Dodger organization on that point. Scouting's a lot more than intuition. . . . It does take *some* intuition in baseball, though—more than in football and basketball—because you have to look further ahead. You watch a boy and you try to see him as a pro. Can he make the transition? Will he quit on you?

"You ever hear of 'the good face'? Well, I never used to sign a boy unless I could look in his face and see what I wanted to see: drive, determination, maturity, whatever. And when I was the Dodgers' scouting director, we used to have a real thing about that. Some scout would give me a report on a boy, and I'd say 'Tell me about his face,' or 'Does he have the good face?'"

The good face? What the hell could that mean? Certainly nothing you could define in one snappy entry. It was the strangest way I could imagine of judging major-league potential, aside from Cy Slapnicka's clubhouse inspection of Lefty Gomez. But it was also one of the most resonant terms in the language of scouting. And as it turned out, I would spend much of the scouting year learning what "the good face" was all about.

JAPANESE HOME-RUN KING GIVES TRUE STORY ON FAMOUS HAIKU

Jim Cohn

When he was 39, Sadaharu Oh
Had 800 homeruns & still
Took batting practice for a half-hour before every game
He ran with the rookies & roomed with a young player
                                 on the road.
Fans stood in line outside the park.
& they waited at his house
For he always made time to sign autographs.
On one kid's cast he wrote—
    That pond was smaller than a heart
    The old frog no bigger than a tear
    & the splash that broke the stillness
    Couldn't startle the moon.

From **A ZEN WAY OF BASEBALL**

Sadaharu Oh (with David Falkner)

*And so we resumed our work on a daily basis. I could
no longer say it was fear or love of the game or even
the presence of Nagashima-san, but I seemed to put
more and more of myself into what I was doing. It
was not so much a question of hours but of feeling. I
wanted to swing the bat, I wanted what standing on
one foot brought to me. More and more I came to see
that when I stood on one foot, my sense of things
changed. On one foot, I became hungry for hitting.
On two feet, I was just another hitter. I loved the
contest between myself and the pitcher, the struggle of
wills that, miraculously, could be resolved in this unity
of movement that was the home run.*

AS A YOUNG BALLPLAYER

My uniform number was One—all the years I was in high school and all the years I was a major-league ballplayer. Number One. People made something of that. BIG ONE the press blurbs read. Big One! What is a "big one"? I don't put that down. I enjoyed it too much. But I know who I am—or who I have been. I am ordinary. No larger, no smaller than life-size. But my number matters to me. In my mind's eye, I see my number on my uniform jersey in the only way that it has ever been important—showing toward the pitcher as I assume my batting stance. When I was at my best, I turned my back almost ninety degrees toward the pitcher. I felt like a rough Japanese sea. My number suddenly rose toward the pitcher like a dark wave just before I struck.

In the middle of all this was baseball. Baseball was everywhere in those years following the war. You could no more avoid baseball as a boy in Japan than a Canadian child could avoid skates. Even though we had no real fields to play on, though our equipment was handmade and very crude—balls fashioned from wound string and strips of cloth, bats made from tree limbs and discarded sticks—baseball seemed to grow from the very rubble itself, like some mysterious blossom of renewal. There were pickup teams from the neighborhoods, sandlot teams, school teams, and the reemergence of the pro teams. Baseball had always been popular in Japan (an American missionary, so the story goes, introduced the game here in 1873; pro baseball began in Japan in 1936, although it was suspended during the war). But now, in the ruins of the Occupation, streets and alleyways became meeting places for sudden games of catch, eruptions of ground ball, and pop-fly drills. I was a very typical Japanese boy. From the earliest time, I simply loved baseball. The country was baseball crazy, and so was I!

Don Larsen *did* serve as an inspiration for me—but not in the way it was reported. The real story is far more curious. On New Year's Day that winter, Mr. Kubota said that he wanted me to watch a film of Larsen's perfect game. I went to a house in Toshima Ward to see it. There was nothing special about the house. It was small, unpretentious, typical of many in that area of Tokyo. But it belonged to Arakawa-san!

I could scarcely believe it when I saw this shadowy figure of my boyhood dreams standing there in the doorway to greet us. What did this mean? Did he remember who I was? Was this only the wildest coincidence, or had Arakawa-san all the while remembered me and been keeping tabs on me at Waseda? I bowed to him and shook his hand.

"We meet again," he said with a smile.

No coincidence at all!

But I could not bring myself to speak or to ask questions. I was there because it was determined that I should see this film, and that was all I permitted myself. The film, obviously, confirmed the correctness of what I had been working on. I saw what was possible at the highest level of professional play using this style of delivery, and it immediately compelled my attention. I watched Larsen's motion very carefully, making notes as I went. I studied the position of hand and glove at the waist, the way in which the turn of his body helped hide the ball till the last moment before the whip of the arm, how the stride forward left him balanced and in perfect fielding position. All the while I tried to see this in a kind of reverse mirror, checking each of these points against the movements I made as a left-hander. Yes, of course, it could be done. More than that, just because it eliminated so much excess motion, it might be the ideal counterfoil to the destructive effects of my nervous system. I was full of hope for the new year and the new season, which was shortly to begin.

I felt tremendous gratitude to Mr. Miyai and Mr. Kubota for helping me. But toward Arakawa-san I felt something I could not begin to explain. It was as though, in reentering my life at this point, he had all along been a kind of invisible helping spirit, watching me from afar, interceding just at those moments when I needed help the most. I wanted to say some of this to him, but it was all too confusing.

I bowed deeply to him when I said goodbye. I wondered if he saw what was in my heart. I did not want to embarrass him, and yet I wanted to convey some sense of this powerful upsurge of thankfulness. He smiled and nodded, and the glint in his eye, whether a glimmer of recognition or the simplest light of good feeling, was enough to send my spirits soaring.

At any rate, it was my impression then that this meeting was a kind of circle closing on a magical story. I knew I would be all right now. But I still had no idea that the story had not yet even begun.

One night I woke up and wrote this: "There are three ways to get rid of a slump. One is to drink and change the feeling you are walking around with. Another one is to get involved in some sort of hobby so you can forget for a while. The third is just to practice and practice again. In order to get rid of uneasiness, the first two ways should be considered. The last way sometimes deepens the feeling of uneasiness. However, the first two have nothing to do with progress. If the monster called slump requires improvement in technique and skill then there is only the road of practice and practice and practice. . . ."

THE TRAINING

Arakawa-san and I, as any other students, sat at the far edges of the room, on our heels in the proper position, toe touching toe. All of the fledgling warriors wore combinations of white or white and black blouses with *hakama*. Ueshiba Sensei alone was dressed in a full-flowing black kimono. The time I first saw him, he was approaching eighty. His appearance and manner, though, were vigorous. He had a long, wispy, snow-white beard and mustache along with bushy white eyebrows. Severity and kindliness both seemed etched into his features. He looked more like a fifteenth-century village elder than a master of the martial arts—that is, until he began to perform the movements he had perfected over a lifetime. The beauty and power of these movements were astonishing. Trained athletes or dancers could not easily have duplicated them. They were the fruits of unparalleled accomplishment. When he finished his session, we spoke to him. It was Arakawa-san's turn to play the straight man.

"What is *ma*?" he asked, deliberately echoing Kikugoro. But the Sensei answered him differently.

"*Ma* exists because there is an opponent."

"I understand," Arakawa-san said. This seemed to jibe with something he was thinking. He took me by the elbow.

"You see," he said to me, "in the case of baseball it would be the pitcher and the batter. The one exists for the other; they are caught, both, in the *ma* of the moment. The pitcher tries in that instant of time and space to throw off a batter's timing; the batter tries to outwit the pitcher. The two are struggling to take advantage of the *ma* that exists between them. That's what makes baseball so extraordinarily difficult."

As long as I live, I'll never forget how lovely that day was. The sun on the sidewalk was like the first sun of the world. I have never seen such a sight! I stared like a man who has taken leave of his senses. My mother certainly was startled, because she prodded me to get a move on. I was late for the game! But I wanted nothing more than to drink in this sudden perfect beauty. There was a particular way the pavements shone with the rain of the night before; the color of the sky was so pure. I wondered, if Fortune had first put me in the way of Arakawa-san, was it not Fortune also at work in this moment? Not Fortune in any sense I had known before, but Fortune as a trickster, glazing my eyes and soul with the romance of things, so that I would be blind to the certain sorrows that awaited me. What was my answer?

The rain glistened on the pavements. The noon sun warmed the world. The sky was a painter's curve of blue.

"Get a move on, don't be so lazy! Move!"

Yes, I had to move. I had to leave, what choice had I? The beautiful aftermath of a storm. But you see, if it had rained that day, I would never have become a top batsman. For it was out there, under that lovely blue sky, just an hour or two away, that the idea of hitting on one foot came about.

———————

"Look," he said, "it's time we faced up to something. That hitch of yours looks like it's here to stay. We are going to have to get a little extreme, I think."

"Extreme?"

"Very," he said. "Remember one day in Miyazaki we returned from camp and I had you take different poses with the bat in your hands? Do you remember?"

I vaguely remembered trying to experiment with different batting poses as a way of getting myself to stop hitching, but I didn't remember specifically what Arakawa-san was referring to.

"The one-legged one, remember that? The one where you bring your right foot up and hold it there?"

"Yes, yes." It came back to me.

I was at first not sure Arakawa-san was really being serious. Perhaps this was just another bit of shock therapy to make a point. But, no, he was quite in earnest. He picked up a bat and coiled himself into the pose to demonstrate.

It looked *so* peculiar. I could not imagine how a batter could survive more than a few seconds in such a position, let alone react to any kind of pitch. But what I saw in front of me was a man standing on one foot, who told me, as he stood there, that the time had now come for me to try that in a game.

I didn't know whether to laugh or cry. I sat there bewildered. Arakawa-san winked and smiled. And continued standing on one foot.

I was miserable. Why was he playing with me? What was he trying to do? I finally decided that all this was just an attempt to psych me up for the game, so I tried as politely as I could to shrug it off and gear my thoughts to the afternoon's work. But Arakawa-san did not budge. Only now the smile left his face. I turned, finally, and began to go off toward my locker.

"*Oh!*" he called; his voice snapped like a whip. I turned around. He was glaring at me.

"I order you to do it."

I stood frozen for a moment, terrified. All I could do was bow my head.

And thus commenced the biggest gamble of my life. The tens of thousands of fans in Kawasaki Stadium witnessed my first attempts at "flamingo batting" in the game that followed. I had no chance to try it beforehand, because the team had omitted batting practice; even in the on-deck circle before my first at-bat in the game there was no chance to do anything but kneel and wait.

"Batting for the Giants, number one, Sadaharu Oh," boomed the loudspeaker. I approached the plate, stepped into the batter's box, and then assumed my pose. The crowd buzzed, then chattered, then hooted and roared as the first pitches to me were thrown. With the count two and two, I flicked out my bat and hit a clean single into center field. The roaring of the crowd suddenly dropped away. I was standing on first. The first trial was done.

I came up again two innings later, and this time the crowd was ready for me. They whistled and stomped and called out to me as I moved to the plate. When I coiled myself into the flamingo position, they roared—I didn't know whether they were enjoying this or viewing it as an insult of some sort. I tried to concentrate. I held my leg as steady as I could. I took one pitch. Then on the next pitch, an inside fastball, I stepped forward, bringing my curled leg forward and toward the mound, snapping my bat through in the shortest possible arc. I hit the ball on the sweetest part of the bat. It rose on a low trajectory and kept going, far over the right-field wall. I circled the bases, wondering how in the world I could ever have done that standing in that position. But who was I to argue with Fortune, who had indeed smiled on us that day?

"Yes," Arakawa-san said, beaming with satisfaction, "yes. You have passed the 'dog-lifting-his-leg-at-the-hydrant' test. Now all that remains is for you to become what you secretly are."

"Look," Ueshiba Sensei said, "the ball comes flying in whether you like it or not, doesn't it? Then all you can do is wait for it to come to you. To wait, this is the traditional Japanese style. Wait. Teach him to wait."

"This business of standing on one leg," Arakawa-san purred, "we discover is a matter of life and death. Accordingly, when you step into the batter's box, you may never do it casually. Too much is at stake. The center in your lower abdomen prepares you for any contingency just as if you were a warrior awaiting the moves of a deadly opponent. Likewise, when you are good enough to have mastered *ma*, you bring your opponent into your own space; his energy is then part of yours. Together you are one. This is what concentration can bring, why it is so crucial. So you must locate it properly, in the one point, and be conscious of it at all times, even when you're walking down the street or sitting at a meal. Once your concentration is thus focused, you automatically begin to see things better. In a state of proper concentration, one is ready for anything that comes along. Even a baseball hurtling toward you at ninety miles an hour!"

As I have mentioned, you cannot be "merely technical" when you swing a sword. If it is possible to fall into the habit of a harmless game when you repeatedly swing a baseball bat, that can never happen with a sword. The feel of a sword in your hands will prevent this; the knowledge of what gleams on the edge of the blade compels your attention. It is also impossible to swing a sword without in some way risking injury to yourself. A slip, an off-balance move, going too far in a follow-through, and you run the very real risk of slashing yourself. Practice with the sword demands intensity. As your mind must be concentrated when you face an opponent, so, too, your practice must include this mental effort.

Because Arakawa-san forbade me any kind of combat in my training, he was forced to find other means to challenge me. The challenge of an opponent is, of course, the ultimate test in any martial arts practice. In baseball, just as much as in Aikido, success against an opponent is fundamentally bound up with timing. Our goal, "acquiring the Body of a Rock," literally meant having the discipline to wait. This implied far more than balance. To train one's entire being to hold back from the tricks and feints of a pitcher, no less than from an enemy with a sword, is finally the single most important step in harmonizing one's *ki* with the opponent's. *Ma*, the interval or distance between you, is eventually that which you rather than the other create by the strength of your waiting.

Arakawa-san and I had reached the point where there were no tricks in what I was doing. And consequently no tricks used against us would get in our way. Nothing could stop me from hitting. I longed to hit as a starving man longs for food. The ball coming toward me was a rabbit, and I was a wolf waiting to devour it. I attacked a baseball as though it were no longer a question of hitting it but of crushing it totally. The home runs rocketed off my bat almost as though a power beyond my own was responsible. I was fascinated by the runs I got all by myself. My head, my mind—quite literally—became a void. I went to the plate with no thought other than this moment of hitting confronting me. It was everything. And in the midst of it, in the midst of chanting and cheering crowds, colors, noises, hot and cold weather, the glare of lights, or rain on my skin, there was only this noiseless, colorless, heatless void in which the pitcher and I together enacted our certain, preordained ritual of the home run.

BREAKING THE HOME-RUN RECORD

When I left my locker and headed for the field, I had no feeling of tiredness. I could feel in my bones that this indeed was the night. I came upon the lights and noise of Korakuen almost as if they didn't exist. The quietness my mother had brought me surrounded me like a spell. It was not going to be broken. I hit in the first inning and then in the third. The third inning. One out, no one on base. The pitcher's name, in this twenty-third game of the year against the Swallows, was Kojiro Suzuki. The goal, Arakawa-san had always said, was oneness of mind, body, and skill. You and the opponent together create the moment. The *ma* is the one you create but in which you are not at all separate from your opponent. The pitcher and I, the ball—and the silence my mother gave me—these were all one. In the midst of whatever was going on, there was only this emptiness in which I could do what I wanted to do. The count went full. Mr. Kojiro Suzuki threw a sinker on the outside part of the plate. I followed the ball perfectly. I could almost feel myself waiting for its precise break before I let myself come forward. When I made contact, I felt like I was scooping the ball upward and outward. The ball rose slowly and steadily in the night sky, lit by Korakuen's bright lights. I could follow it all the way, as it lazily reached its height and seemed to linger there in the haze, and then slowly began its descent into the right-field stands.

The crowd erupted, almost as a single voice. A huge banner was suddenly unfurled that read, "Congratulations, World Record!" Everywhere—but on the diamond—people were running and lights were flashing. For me, it was the moment of purest joy I had ever known as a baseball player.

No one can stop a home run. No one can understand what it really is unless you have felt it in your own hands and body. It is different from seeing it or trying to describe it. There is nothing I know quite like meeting a ball in exactly the right spot. As the ball makes its high, long arc beyond the playing field, the diamond and the stands suddenly belong to one man. In that brief, brief time, you are free of all demands and complications. There is no one behind you, no obstruction ahead, as you follow this clear path around all the bases. This is the batsman's center stage, the one time that he may allow himself to freely accept the limelight, to enjoy the sensation of every eye in the stadium fixed on him, waiting for the moment when his foot will touch home plate. In this moment he is free.

RETIREMENT OF THE MASTER

In our game, ever so team-oriented, there is a high moment of drama reserved for that contest that takes place between one strong batter and a strong opposing pitcher. We give the name *shobu* to this moment, and it is as if the struggle of one team with the other is narrowed and intensified in this desperate and decisive surrogate combat. It is the highest kind of individual struggle, but it bears with it the potential for victory or defeat for an entire team. Yes, I loved the *shobu*. The more intense the challenge, the more intense I was. I was just not up to this now. Whether I wanted it that way or not—and I certainly did—my performance on the field had direct bearing on my team. I had a certain pride as a professional player, which meant more to me than any record. And my pride, more than anything, revealed what it was I was facing. For the fact of the matter was that in this "slump"—as opposed to any other—I had lost all desire for combat. In my earlier days, when I had done badly, I had come back to the bench in a fury. I was already afire with desire for my next chance. Not now.

I struggled against this, of course. I did not want to admit that my spirit, which had served me for so long, had seemingly faded. Perhaps with renewed spirit, I thought, I would find enough in my body to return to some semblance of form. I began to sign my autographs with the word "spirit"—rather than, as earlier, with the words "patience" and "effort." I also went to my Sensei and, as I had done when I first began working with him, bowed before him, palms to the floor, and with all the yearning of my heart begged him to once more teach me.

Arakawa-san and I worked without letup for three days—just as we had in the past. Standing in my shorts, I swung bat and sword until my body was pouring sweat; I listened carefully for the low whistling sound of my sword; I measured carefully the kind of cuts I made through the swinging cards; in everything, in every motion I made, I concentrated *ki* in my one point and projected it downward into the ground and out through my forearms into the secret lengths of bat and sword.

"What shall I tell you?" Arakawa-san said at the end of our time. "You still can hit."

"But what has happened to me?" I asked.

Arakawa-san shook his head. "You still can hit," he repeated softly.

He knew what I was thinking without my having to spell out anything for him. There was no discussion of retirement or of my fears.

"I have no anger anymore," I said finally. He shrugged.

"Mastery in Aikido means loss of desire for combat. You have been a master for many years."

From **THE WRONG STUFF**
Bill Lee with Dick Lally

We were taught to fear sex as something that would rob us of our stamina. The word was, "Tiger, if you let women drain away your life's essence, you'll never be able to go nine." Some of that mythology has carried over to the pros. The Red Sox brass were always telling Sparky Lyle that if he kept screwing around he would lose his fastball. They claimed it would float right out of his dick. Later he told me they were right, but that they forgot to mention how it would add all sorts of movement to his slider and carry him to the Cy Young Award.

Strikeouts, from my perspective, are boring things. Nothing happens. They are fascist weapons. I prefer the ground-ball out and view it as the perfect symbol of democracy. It allows everybody a chance to get into the game, gives the crowds an opportunity to see some dazzling work in the infield, and has virtually the same effect as a strikeout. Only better. A ground ball can be converted into a double play, my idea of the ultimate two-for-one sale. Groundouts also take less of a toll on the arm than strikeouts. It's a far, far better thing to get a batter out with one pitch instead of three. I'd never pay to see a big whiff artist like Nolan Ryan pitch. I'd much rather watch Larry Gura or Tommy John. Those guys are artists, like Catfish Hunter and Mike Cuellar were.

Cuellar was the closest thing I had to a pitching idol. He was the great left-hander who played on those championship Baltimore clubs in the late sixties and early seventies. They used to bring him out to the mound in a sanitation truck and drop him out of a Glad Bag, looking like an Apache Indian chief in a baseball uniform. He was amazing. Once the game started he would begin serving up his garbage: "Here's a grapefruit for strike one. Take a swing at this toilet seat." You ever try to hit an empty beer can for distance? That's what hitting his screwball was like. It was awesome. He'd win twenty games every year. Just when the batters figured they had his slow stuff timed, he'd rip a 90 mph fastball at them and it would finish them for the rest of the game. That's what I call pitching.

The key to pitching at Fenway, whether you are right-handed or left-handed but especially if you're a lefty, is to keep the ball outside and away on right-handers and down and in on left-handers. Make that ball sink to left-handers. Your lefty hitter is going to try to shoot your pitch the other way so he can jack it against or over the wall. If he can't get the ball up he's going to hit a two-hopper to the second baseman. You can make the temptation of the wall work for you. The Monster giveth, but the Monster can also taketh away. You just have to know what to feed it. I had some success with it. When I started winning big for the Sox, the writers compared me to Mel Parnell, the lefty who pitched for Boston in the forties and fifties. I checked up on him and discovered that Parnell had a smashed middle finger that caused him to throw the ball off his index finger, making his pitches sink. That was interesting. I was always having the calluses shaved off my index finger. Obviously, we both threw off the same digit and were able to keep the ball on the ground, enabling us to win a lot of games in Boston.

Being on the mound puts me in a relaxed state of superconsciousness. The feeling is laid back, but still intense. Everything is slowed down, yet you are able to perceive things at an incredibly fast rate. Line drives shot up the middle may look hard to the observer in the stands, but they never seemed dangerous when they were hit back to me. They floated to the mound in slow motion. When your arm, mind, and body are in sync, you are able to work at peak perfor-mance level, while your brain remains relaxed. It's Zen-like when you're going good. You are the ball and the ball is you. It can do you no harm. A common bond forms between you and this white sphere, a bond based on mutual trust. The ball promises not to fly over too many walls after you have politely served it up to enemy hitters, and you assure it that you will not allow those same batters to treat the ball in a harsh or violent manner. Out of this trust comes a power that allows the pitcher to take control of what otherwise might be an uncontrollable situation. During those moments on the pitching rubber, when you have every pitch at your command working to its highest potential, you are your own universe. For hours after the game, this sense of completeness lingers. Then you sink back to what we humorously refer to as reality. Your body aches and your muscles cry out. You feel your mortality. That can be a difficult thing to handle. I believe pitchers come in touch with death a lot sooner than other players. We are more aware of the subtle changes taking place in our body and are unable to overlook the tell-tale hints that we are not going to last on this planet forever. Every pitcher has to be a little bit in love with death. There's a subconscious fatalism there. All baseball players attempt to suspend time, and the bitch of it is we're only partially successful.

I didn't like pitching to Kaline. Nothing against Al. He was a hell of a guy. I just hated the way umpires gave him the benefit of the doubt on almost every close pitch late in his career. I once threw him five straight strikes and walked him. He took a three-and-two slider that started on the outside corner and finished down the middle of the plate. The ump gave it to him. As Kaline made his way to first, I yelled at him, "Swing the bat, for Christ's sake. You're not a statue until you have pigeon shit on your shoulders." Al laughed at me. After the game I complained about the call to the home-plate umpire. He said, "Son, Mr. Kaline will let you know it's a strike by doubling off the wall."

I tried to be a technician on the mound; Eckersley was more of a manic dancing master. He was a pitching Reggie Jackson, putting pressure on himself and then coming through. He would go nuts between the lines, yelling at hitters and challenging them to hit his fastball. He'd tell batters on their way up to the plate that there was no way they were going to hit him, and then he'd strike them out. It was as if Dizzy Dean had been reincarnated. Dennis lived on a diet of prime steaks and Jack Daniels, and he threw severe heat. While he was still an Indian, he pitched a no-hitter against the California Angels. He had two men out in the ninth and the last hitter was taking his time getting to the batter's box. Eck came halfway in from the mound and shouted, "Stalling won't help. There's one more out to go and you're it." Then he reared back and blew the sucker away. I loved that confidence of his.

UNDERSTANDING ALVARADO

Max Apple

Castro thought it was no accident that Achilles "Archie" Alvarado held the world record for being hit in the head by a pitched ball.

"Because he was a hero even then," Fidel said, "because he stood like a hero with his neck proudly over the plate."

When people asked Mrs. Alvarado what she thought of her husband's career, she said, "Chisox OK, the rest of the league stinks. Archie, he liked to play every day, bench him and his knees ached, his fingers swelled, his tongue forgot English. He would say, 'Estelle, let's split, let's scram, *vámonos a* Cuba. What we owe to Chisox?'

"I'd calm him down. 'Arch,' I'd say, 'Arch, Chisox have been plenty good to us. Paid five gees more than Tribe, first-class hotels, white roomies on the road, good press.'

"'Estelle,' he would say, 'I can't take it no more. They got me down to clubbing in the pinch and only against southpaws. They cut Chico Carasquel and Sammy Esposito and Jungle Jim Rivera. What we owe to Chisox?'

"When it got like that, I would say, 'Talk to Zloto,' and Zloto would say, 'Man, you Latinos sure are hotheads. I once got nine hits in a row for the Birds, was Rookie of the Year for the Bosox. I have the largest hands in either league and what do you think I do? I sit on the bench and spit-shine my street shoes. Look there, you can see your greasy black mug in 'em.' Zloto always knew how to handle Alvarado."

Zloto came to Havana, showed Fidel his hands, talked about the fifties. Fidel said, "They took our good men and put them in Yankee uniforms, in Bosox, Chisox, Dodgers, Birds. They took our manhood, Zloto. They took our Achilles and called him 'Archie.' Hector Gonzalez they called 'Ramrod,' Jesús Ortiz they made a 'Jayo.' They treated Cuban manhood like a bowl of chicos and ricos. Yes, we have no bananas but we got vine-ripened Latinos who play good ball all year, stick their heads over the plate and wait for the Revolution. Fidel Castro gave it to them. It was three and two on me in Camagüey around November 1960. There were less than two dozen of us. Batista had all roads blocked and there was hardly enough ammunition left to kill some rabbits. He could have starved us out but he got greedy, he wanted the quick inning. When I saw that he was coming in with his best stuff with his dark one out over the middle, I said to Che and to Francisco Muniz, 'Habana for Christmas,' and I lined his fascist pitch up his capitalist ass."

"I'm not impressed," Zloto said. "When I heard about the Bay of Pigs I said to myself, 'Let's wipe those oinks right off the face of the earth.' You took Cuba, our best farm property, and went Commie with it. You took our best arms, Castro, our speed- and our curveball artists. You dried up our Cuban diamonds."

"Zloto, Zloto," Fidel said. "Look at this picture of your buddy, 'Archie' Alvarado. Don't you like him better as 'Achilles'? Look at his uniform, look at his AK 47 rifle."

"I liked him better when he was number twenty-three and used a thirty-six-inch Hillerich and Bradsby Louisville Slugger to pound out line drives in Comiskey Park."

"There's no more Comiskey Park," Fidel said. "No more Grace, no more Chuck Comiskey to come down after a tough extra-inning loss and buy a drink for the whole clubhouse. No more free Bulova watches. The Chisox are run by an insurance company now. You punch a time clock before batting practice and they charge for overtime in the whirlpool bath."

"That's goddamn pinko propaganda," Zloto said.

"You've been outta the game, big Victor," Fidel said. "You've been sitting too long out in Arizona being a dental assistant. You haven't been on the old diamonds, now astro-turfed, closed to the sun and air-conditioned. You have not seen the bleachers go to two-fifty. While you've been in Arizona the world changed, Zloto. Look at our Achilles, four fractured skulls, thirteen years in the big time. Played all over the outfield, played first and played third. A lifetime mark of two ninety-nine and RBIs in the thousands. He never got an Achilles Day from Chisox, Bosox, Tribe, or Birds. When he came home Fidel made him a day, made him a Reservist colonel. I did this because Achilles Alvarado is not chickenshit. You, Zloto, know this better than anyone.

"Achilles said to me the first time we met, 'Fidel, the big time is over for Archie Alvarado, but send me to the cane fields, give me a machete and I'll prove that Alvarado has enough arm left to do something for Cuba.' A hero, this Achilles 'Archie' Alvarado, but they sent him back to us a broken-down, used-up pinch hitter with no eye, no arm, and no speed.

"'Achilles, Archie,' I said, 'the Revolution was not made for Chisox, Bosox, Bengals, and Birds. We didn't take Habana for chicos and ricos. Cuba Libre doesn't give a flying fuck for RBIs. The clutch hit is every minute here, baby brother. Cuba loves you for your Cuban heart. I'll make you a colonel, a starter in the only game that counts. Your batting average will be counted in lives saved, in people educated, fed, and protected from capitalist exploitation.'"

"Cut the shit, Fidel," Zloto said, "I'm here because Archie will be eligible for his pension in September. He'll pull in a thousand a month for the rest of his days. That'll buy a lot of bananas down here, won't it?

"You may think that you understand Alvarado, Fidel, but I knew the man for eight years, roomed with him on the Chisox and the Bosox. I've seen him high, seen him in slumps you wouldn't believe. I've seen him in the dugout after being picked off first in a crucial situation. You wouldn't know what that's like, Castro. I'm talking about a man who has just met a fastball and stroked it over the infield. He has made the wide turn at first and watched the resin of his footprint settle around the bag. He has thrown off the batting helmet and pulled the soft, long-billed cap from his hip pocket. The coach has slapped his ass and twenty, thirty, maybe forty thousand Chisox fans start stomping their feet while the organ plays 'Charge,' and then he is picked off in a flash, caught scratching his crotch a foot from the bag. And it's all over. You hear eighty thousand feet stomping. The first baseman snickers behind his glove; even the ump smiles. I've seen Alvarado at times like that cry like a baby. He'd throw a towel over his head and say, 'Zloto, I'm a no-good dummy. Good hit and no head. We coulda won it all here in the top of the ninth. The Yankee pitcher is good for shit. My dumb-ass move ruined the Chisox chances.' He would sit in front of his locker taking it real hard until the GM or even Chuck Comiskey himself would come down and say, 'Archie, it's just one game that you blew with a dumb move. We're still in it, still in the thick of the race. You'll help these Sox plenty during the rest of the year. Now take your shower and get your ass over to a Mexican restaurant.' The Alvarado that I knew, Castro, that Alvarado could come back the next afternoon, sometimes the next inning, and change the complexion of a game."

Fidel laughed and lit a cigar. "Zloto, you've been away too long. The Archie you knew, this man went out of style with saddle shoes and hula hoops. Since the days you're talking about when Alvarado cried over a pickoff play, since then Che and Muniz are dead and two Kennedys assassinated. There have been wars in the Far East and Middle East and in Bangladesh. There have been campus shootings, a revolution of the Red Guard, an ouster of Khrushchev, a fascist massacre in Indonesia, two revolutions in Uruguay, fourteen additions to the U.N. There has been détente and Watergate and a Washington-Peking understanding and where have you been, Zloto? You've been in Tucson, Arizona, reading the newspaper on Sunday and cleaning teeth. Even dental techniques have changed. Look at your flourides and your gum brushing method."

"All right, boys," Mrs. Alvarado said, "enough is enough. What are we going to prove anyway by reminiscing about the good old days? Zloto means well. He came here as a friend. Twelve grand a year for life is not small potatoes to Archie and me. In the Windy City or in Beantown we could live in a nice integrated neighborhood on that kind of money and pick up a little extra by giving autographs at Chevy dealerships. Fidel, you know that Archie always wanted to stay in the game. In one interview he told Bill Fuller of the *Sun-Times* that he wanted to manage the Chisox someday. They didn't want any black Cuban managers in the American League, not then. But, like you say, Fidel, a lot of water has gone under the bridge since those last days when Archie was catching slivers for the Bosox, Chisox, and Birds. These days, there might even be some kind of front-office job to round off that pension. Who knows, it might be more than he made twenty years ago when he led the league in RBIs."

Castro said, "Estelle, apart from all ideological arguments, you are just dreaming. Achilles was never a U.S. citizen. After a dozen years as one of Castro's colonels, do you really think Uncle Sam is going to say, 'C'mon up here, Archie, take a front-office job and rake in the cash'? Do you really think America works that way, Estelle? I know Zloto thinks that, but you've been down here all this time, don't you understand capitalist exploitation by now?"

Estelle said, "Fidel, I'm not saying that we are going to give up the ideals of the Revolution and I'm not deluded by the easy capitalist life. I am thinking about only getting what's coming to us. Alvarado put in the time, he should get the pension."

"That's the whole reason I took a week off to come down here," Zloto said. "The commissioner called me up—he heard we were buddies—and said, 'Zloto, you might be in a position to do your old friend Alvarado some good, that is if you're willing to travel.' The commissioner absolutely guaranteed that Archie would get his pension if he came back up and established residence. The commissioner of baseball is not about to start mailing monthly checks through the Swiss embassy, and I don't blame him. The commissioner is not even saying you have to stay permanently in the U.S. He is just saying, 'Come up, get an apartment, make a few guest appearances, an interview or two, and then do whatever the hell you want."

Fidel said, "Yes, go up to America and tell them how mean Fidel is, how bad the sugar crop was, and how poor and hungry we Cubans are. Tell them what they want to hear and they'll pension you off. The Achilles I know would swallow poison before he'd kowtow to the memory of John Foster Dulles that way. They sent an Archie back home, but Cuba Libre reminded him he was really an Achilles."

"Fidel, let's not get sentimental," Mrs. Alvarado said. "Let's talk turkey. We want the twelve grand a year, right?"

"Right, but only because it is the fruit of Achilles' own labor."

"OK, in order to get the money we have to go back."

"I could take it up in the United Nations, I could put the pressure on. Kissinger is very shaky in Latin America. He knows we all know that he doesn't give a fuck about any country except Venezuela. I could do it through Waldheim, and nobody would have to know. Then we could threaten to go public if they hold out on what's coming to him."

Zloto said, "America doesn't hold out on anybody, Castro. Ask Joe Stalin's daughter, if you don't believe me. You guys are batting your heads against the wall by hating us. There's nothing to hate. We want a square deal for everyone. In this case, too. As for Kissinger, he might carry some weight with the Arabs, but the commissioner of baseball cannot be pressured. That damned fool Alvarado should have become a citizen while he was playing in the States. I didn't know he wasn't a citizen. It was just crazy not to become one. Every other Latin does."

"But our Achilles, he was always different," Castro said. "He always knew that the Chisox, Bosox, Birds, and Braves didn't own the real thing. The real Achilles Alvarado was in Camagüey with me, in Bolivia with Che, with Mao on the Long March."

"The real Achilles was just too lazy to do things right," Mrs. Alvarado said. "He didn't want to fill out complicated papers, so he stayed an alien. As long as he had a job, it didn't matter."

"Zloto," Fidel said, "you one-time Rookie of the Year, now a fat, tooth-cleaning capitalist, you want to settle this the way Achilles would settle this? I mean why should we bring in Kissinger and Waldheim and everyone else? I say if a man believes in the Revolution, what's a pension to him? You think I couldn't have been a Wall Street lawyer? And what about our Doctor Che? You don't think he would have made a big pension in the AMA? I say our Achilles has recovered his Cuban manhood. He won't want to go back. Estelle does not speak for him."

"Fidel is right," she said, "I do not speak for Archie Alvarado, I only write his English for him."

"If Estelle wants to go back and be exploited, let her go. Do you want those television announcers calling you Mrs. Archie again as if you had stepped from the squares of a comic strip? Does the wife of a colonel in the Cuban Army sound like a comic-strip girl to you, Zloto?"

"Fidel," Estelle said, "don't forget the issue is not so large. Only a trip to the Windy City or Beantown, maybe less than two weeks in all."

"You are forgetting," Fidel said, "what happened to Kid Gavilan when he went back to see an eye surgeon in New York. They put his picture in *Sepia* and in the *National Enquirer*; the news services showed him with his bulging eye, being hugged by a smooth-faced Sugar Ray Robinson. They wanted it to seem like this: here are two retired Negro fighters. One is a tap dancer in Las Vegas, the other has for ten years been working in the cane fields of Castro's Cuba. Look at how healthy the American Negro is. His teeth are white as ever, his step lithe in Stetson shoes, while our Kid Gavilan, once of the bolo punch that decked all welterweights, our Kid stumbles through the clinics of New York in worker's boots and his eye bulges from the excesses of the Revolution. They degraded the Kid and the Revolution and they sent him home with a red, white, and blue eye patch. That's how they treated Kid Gavilan, and they'll do the same to Achilles Alvarado."

"Well, goddamn," Zloto said, "I've had enough talk. I want to see Alvarado; whether he wants to do it is up to him."

"That," Castro said, "is typical bourgeois thinking. You would alienate the man from his fellows, let him think that his decision is personal and lonely, that it represents only the whims of an Alvarado and does not speak for the larger aspirations of all Cubans and all exploited peoples. The wants of an Alvarado are the wants of the people. He is not a Richard Nixon to hide out in Camp David surrounded by bodyguards while generals all over the world are ready to press the buttons of annihilation."

"No more bullshit, I want to see Alvarado."

Estelle said, "He is in Oriente Province on maneuvers with the army. He will be gone for . . . for how long, Fidel?"

"Achilles Alvarado's unit is scheduled for six months in Oriente. I could bring him back to see you, Zloto, but we don't operate that way. A man's duty to his country comes before all else."

"Then I'm going up to see him and deliver the commissioner's letter. I don't trust anybody else around here to do it for me."

"We'll all go," Fidel said. "In Cuba Libre, no man goes it alone."

ON MANEUVERS IN ORIENTE PROVINCE

The Ninth Infantry Unit of the Cuban Army is on spring maneuvers. Oriente is lush and hilly. There are villages every few miles in which happy farmers drink dark beer brewed with local hops. The Ninth Army bivouacs all over the province and assembles each morning at 6:00 A.M. to the sound of the bugle. The soldiers eat a leisurely breakfast and plan the next day's march. By 2:00 P.M. they are set up somewhere and ready for an afternoon of recreation. Colonel Alvarado is the only member of the Ninth Infantry with major-league experience, but there are a few older men who have played professional baseball in the minor leagues. Because there is no adequate protective equipment, army regulations prohibit hardball, but the Ninth Infantry plays fast-pitch softball, which is almost as grueling.

When Fidel, Zloto, and Estelle drive up to the Ninth Army's makeshift diamond, it is the seventh inning of a four-four game between the Reds and Whites. A former pitcher from Iowa City in the Three I League is on the mound for the Reds. Colonel Alvarado, without faceguard or chest protector, is the umpire behind the plate. His head, as in the old days, seems extremely vulnerable as it bobs behind the waving bat just inches from the arc of a powerful swing. He counts on luck and fast reflexes to save him from foul tips that could crush his Adam's apple.

When the jeep pulls up, Reds and Whites come to immediate attention, then raise their caps in an "Olé" for Fidel.

"These are liberated men, Zloto. The army does not own their lives. When their duties are completed they can do as they wish. We have no bedchecks, no passes, nobody is AWOL. If a man has a reason to leave, he tells his officer and leaves. With us, it is an honor to be a soldier."

When Zloto spots Alvarado behind the plate, he runs toward him and hugs his old friend. He rubs Alvarado's woolly black head with his oversize hands. Estelle is next to embrace her husband, a short businesslike kiss, and then Fidel embraces the umpire as enthusiastically as Zloto did. An army photographer catches the look of the umpire surprised by embraces from an old friend, a wife, and a prime minister in the seventh inning of a close game.

"Men of the Revolution." Fidel has advanced to the pitcher's mound, the highest ground. The congregated Reds and Whites gather around the makeshift infield. "Men of the Revolution, we are gathered here to test the resolve of your umpire, Colonel Alvarado. The Revolution is tested in many ways. This time it is the usual thing, the capitalist lure of money. Yet it is no simple issue. It is money that rightfully belongs to Colonel Alvarado, but they would degrade him by forcing him to claim it. To come there, so that the capitalist press can say, 'Look what the Revolution has done to one of the stars of the fifties. Look at his stooped, arthritic back, his gnarled hands, from years in the cane fields.' They never cared about his inadequate English when they used him, but now they will laugh at his accent and his paltry vocabulary. When they ask him about Cuba, he will stumble and they will deride us all with the smiles of their golden teeth.

"The commissioner of baseball has sent us this behemoth, this Polish-American veteran of eleven campaigns in the American League, Victor Zloto, who some of you may remember as Rookie of the Year in 1945. This Zloto is not an evil man, he is only a capitalist tool. They use his friendship for the colonel as a bait. Zloto speaks for free enterprise. He has two cars, a boat, and his own home. His province is represented by their hero of the right, Barry Goldwater, who wanted to bomb Hanoi to pieces. Zloto wants the colonel to come back, to go through the necessary charade to claim his rightful pension and then return to us if he wishes. Mrs. Alvarado shares this view. I say no Cuban man should become a pawn for even one hour."

"What does the colonel say?" someone yells from the infield. "Does the colonel want to go back?"

The umpire is standing behind Castro. He is holding his wife's hand while Zloto's long arm encircles both of them. Castro turns to his colonel. "What do you say, Achilles Alvarado?"

Zloto says, "It's twelve grand a year, Archie, and all you have to do is show up just once.

If you want to stay, you can. I know you don't like being a two-bit umpire and colonel down here. I know you don't give a shit about revolutions and things like that."

Castro says, "The colonel is thinking about his long career with the Chisox, Bosox, Tribe, and Birds. He is thinking about his four fractured skulls. He justifiably wants that pension. And I, his prime minister and his friend, I want him to have that pension, too. Believe me, soldiers, I want this long-suffering victim of exploitation to recover a small part of what they owe to him and to all victims of racism and oppression."

Colonel Alvarado grips tightly his wife's small hand. He looks down and kicks up clouds of dust with his army boots. He is silent. Zloto says, "It's not fair to do this, Castro. You damn well know it. You get him up here in front of the army and make a speech so it will look like he's a traitor if he puts in his pension claim. You staged all this because you are afraid that in a fair choice, Archie would listen to reason just like Estelle did. You can bet that I'm going to tell the commissioner how you put Archie on the spot out here. I'm going to tell him that Archie is a softball umpire. This is worse than Joe Louis being a wrestling referee."

"Think fast, Yankee," one of the ballplayers yells as he lobs a softball at Zloto's perspiring face. The big first baseman's hand closes over the ball as if it were a large mushroom. He tosses it to Castro. "I wish we could play it out, Fidel, just you and I, like a world series or a one-on-one basketball game. I wish all political stuff could work out like baseball, with everybody where they belong at the end of the season and only one champion of the world."

"Of course, you would like that, Zloto, so long as you Yankee capitalists were the champions."

"The best team would win. If you have the material and the management, you win; it's that simple."

"Not as simple as you are, Zloto. But why should we stand here and argue political philosophy? We are interrupting a game, no? You have accused Fidel of not giving Alvarado a fair opportunity. I will do this with you, Zloto, if Achilles agrees, I will do this. Fidel will pitch to you. If you get a clean hit, you can take Alvarado back on the first plane. If not, Alvarado stays. It will be more than fair. This gives you a great advantage. A former big-leaguer against an out-of-shape prime minister. My best pitch should be cake for you. You can go back and tell the commissioner that you got a hit off Castro. Barry Goldwater will kiss your fingertips for that."

Zloto smiles. "You're on, Castro, if it's okay with Archie and Estelle." Colonel Alvarado still eyes the soft dirt; he shrugs his shoulders. Castro says, "Do you think this is a just experience for you, Achilles Alvarado? This is like a medieval tournament, with you as the prize. This smacks of capitalism. But this once, Fidel will do it if you agree that your fate shall be so decided."

"What's all this about fate and justice," Estelle says. She takes the ball from Castro. "Archie had eleven brothers and sisters and hardly a good meal until he came up to the Chisox. He cracked his wrist in an all-star game and that cost him maybe four or five years in the big leagues because the bones didn't heal right. It's a mean, impersonal world with everything always up for grabs. Alvarado knows it, and he accepts it. He is a religious man." She throws the ball to her prime minister. "Get it over with."

The teams take their places, with Castro replacing the Three I League pitcher. Zloto removes his jacket, shirt, and necktie. He is six five and weighs over 250. His chest hairs are gray, but he swings three bats smoothly in a windmill motion as he loosens his muscles. Castro warms up with the catcher. The prime minister has a surprisingly good motion, more sidearm than underhand. The ball comes in and sinks to a right-handed batter like Zloto. Colonel Alvarado takes his place behind home plate, which is a large army canteen.

"Achilles Alvarado," says Castro, "you wish to be the umpire in this contest?"

"Why not?" Zloto says. "It's his pension, let him call the balls and strikes. If it's a walk or an error, we'll take it over. Otherwise, a hit I win, an out you win."

"Play ball!" the umpire says. Castro winds up twice, and his first pitch is so far outside that the catcher diving across the plate cannot even lay his glove on the ball. Fidel stamps his foot.

"Ball one," says the umpire.

The infield is alive with chatter: "The old dark one, Fidel," they are yelling. "Relax, pitcher, this ox is an easy out, he can't see your stuff, there's eight of us behind you, Fidel, let him hit."

Zloto grins at the prime minister. "Put it down the middle, Mr. Pink, I dare you."

Fidel winds and delivers. Zloto's big hands swing the bat so fast that the catcher doesn't have a chance to blink. He has connected and the ball soars a hundred feet over the head of the left fielder, who watches with astonishment the descending arc of the power-driven ball.

"Foul ball," says the umpire, eyeing the stretched clothesline which ended far short of where Zloto's fly ball dropped.

The power hitter grins again. "When I straighten one out, Castro, I'm gonna hit it clear out of Cuba. I never played in a little country before."

Castro removes his green army cap and runs his stubby fingers through his hair. He turns his back to the batter and looks toward his outfield. With a tired motion he orders his center fielder to move toward left center, then he signals all three outfielders to move deeper. Estelle Alvarado stands in foul territory down the first-base line, almost in the spot of her complimentary box seat at the Chisox home games.

Zloto is measuring the outside corner of the canteen with a calm, deliberate swing. He does not take his eyes off the pitcher. Castro winds and delivers another wild one, high and inside. Zloto leans away but the ball nicks his bat and dribbles into foul territory, where Estelle picks it up and throws it back to Castro.

"One ball, two strikes," says the umpire.

"Lucky again, Castro," the batter calls out, "but it only takes one, that's all I need from you."

The prime minister and the aging Rookie of the Year eye one another across the sixty feet from mound to plate. Castro rubs the imagined gloss from the ball and pulls at his army socks. With the tip of a thin Cuban softball bat, Zloto knocks the dirt from the soles of his Florsheim shoes. The infielders have grown silent. Castro looks again at his outfield and behind it at the green and gentle hills of Oriente Province. He winds and delivers a low fastball.

"Strike three," says the umpire. Zloto keeps his bat cocked. Estelle Alvarado rushes to her husband. She is crying hysterically. Fidel runs in at top speed to embrace both Alvarados at home plate. Zloto drops the bat. "It was a fair call, Archie," he says to the umpire. "I got caught looking."

"Like Uncle Sam," Castro says, as the soldiers stream in yelling, "Fidel, Fidel, the strike-out artist." Castro waves his arms for silence.

"Not Fidel, men, but Achilles Alvarado, a hero of the Cuban people. A light for the Third World."

"Third World for Alvarado. Third strike for Zloto," an infielder shouts, as the Ninth Army raises Fidel, Achilles, and Estelle to their shoulders in a joyful march down the first-base line. The prime minister, the umpire, and the lady gleam in the sun like captured weapons.

Zloto has put on his shirt and tie. He looks now like a businessman, tired after a long day at a convention. Fidel is jubilant among his men. The umpire tips his cap to the army and calms his wife, still tearful atop the bobbing shoulders of the Cuban Ninth.

"Alvarado," Estelle says, "you honest ump, you Latin patriot, you veteran of many a clutch situation. Are you happy, you fractured skull?"

"Actually," Alvarado whispers in her ear, "the pitch was a little inside. But what the hell, it's only a game."

BACKYARD

Rochelle Nameroff

for Larry

"There are two theories on hitting the knuckleball.
Unfortunately, neither of them works."

it was all so serious
as he taught me
digging the knees together

a deliberate hunkering
the back & forth wiggle
shifting the weight

it screws yr behind in the ground he said
protection I guess
or the secrecy of boys

he called it
The Stan Musial Crouch
& man how I practiced

getting it right to unwind
breathless exquisite & deadly
the permission to love

without going crazy
& o big brother
how much I remember

26 Feb 80

TIME LOVES A HAIRCUT
BERNIE CARBO, CLUTCH HITTER, RATES A WAVE
Bill Cardoso

All right, buddy, sit down and I'll see what I can do," said the old outfielder, now thirty-nine and twenty pounds heavier at 201 than he was when he left the game in 1981, playing for Vera Cruz in the Mexican League.

Bernie Carbo, the Cincinnati Reds' number one draft choice in 1965, chosen ahead of Johnny Bench. Bernie Carbo, clutch hitter, home-run hitter. Bernie Carbo, who kept the many visages of Buddha in his locker. Bernie Carbo, who, it is said, never knew what day it was, let alone where he was.

Well, we're in Wyandotte, Michigan, downriver from Detroit. Bernie's neck of the woods these days. We are in a brown two-story building where Bernie Carbo's We Are Family Hair Stylists shares space with Nunzio's Construction Services, Inc. The salon had been a real estate office until Bernie moved in with his clippers and his "family," Sonia and Dorothy, colleagues in the world of lock and tress.

"That tail, yeah," Bernie was saying of the single lock of hair starting to trail down the nape of my neck. "Extension, you call 'em? I like that. Ride 'em, cowboy. You see mine? I got a tail. I had mine new when I went to Saudi Arabia in, what? Three years ago. I went to Saudi Arabia to do a baseball clinic. I couldn't believe it. All these kids were running around, big gold necklaces and Mercedes-Benzes and everything like that. And they all had tails. Every one of them had a tail. And that's when I came back and said, those tails are pretty neat. And I started growing a tail.

"So, I've had it for a few years. And then I bleached it. Put some bleach in it. Back then I had my hair a little bit longer. Then I went shorter. I like it shorter, like yours. I'm gonna blow it a little bit." The blow-dryer purred.

"It looks all right. You're getting the works. I'm gonna give you what we used to call— remember the ducktail? The duck ass? Heh-heh. The DA? The *lively* DA! DA with a tail! The tail is really not off-center. But it's the way your hair grows. Oh, that tail looks good. You look like a movie star. Hah hah hah." Bernie was clipping away.

"Yeah, man, you know what? My first full year, in 1970. Sparky Anderson was my manager. I said, I'm going to get me a perm. I'll be the first white ballplayer to have an Afro. In 1970, in San Diego. Paid forty-five dollars. That was a lot of money then." Indeed.

"Went back to the ballpark. Sparky took one look at me and said, 'You ain't playing today. You ain't playing tomorrow. You ain't playing until you get that hair cut!'"

Now Sonia, who had been Bernie's instructor at Virginia Farrell's hair school before she joined the family, spoke. "Hey look, Bernie, Bill ain't got no stockings on!"

I'm stuck in the Hamptons, Sonia. Socks ain't legal there.

"Hey, you know what?" said Bernie. "You laugh about the no stockings. Sonia laughs. Listen to this. When I was in St. Louis, this lawyer came in to read a letter from Mr. Busch. Mr. Busch was going to give us a pep talk: 'Hey, you guys, you gotta go out there and win. You know, you don't win a championship playing like this.' And the lawyer that was reading it didn't have any socks on. I walked up to him and said, 'Hey, you don't got any socks on. Do you mind if I read that letter?' He says, 'Yeah, you can read it.' And the next day I got released. I got released for asking him about his no socks."

My word! How's my extension?

"Good. Don't touch it! I'll tell you what, though. Your hair is not the easiest to cut. Swirls all over the place. It's cra-zy! Strong hair. Your hair sticks out on the sides there. The tail is— see how that is right now? That's in the middle of your hair. But watch how your hair grows. See? Look at that. That's something, isn't it? It grows right into a circle."

I'll have to *mousse* it?

"Not *mousse* it! I'll *grease* that son of a gun. We'll grease it. Get it all nice and greased. But look how nice the neck is. I'll comb it to grow toward the middle, into that DA. And worn a little close to the neck like this. And let that tail grow down like this. And when it gets long enough, we can braid it. Let that tail start growing out.

"See, mine's a little bit longer than that. Mine was long, but Sonia cut it. When yours gets a little bit longer, braid it. Do you trim your mustache? Do you like it off your lip?"

I like it bandito-style. Zapata.

"Oh, wild and crazy, eh?"

Yup.

"I'll just trim it a little bit here. Relax. Close your lips." Bernie snipped away. "Looking good! Yeah, when I went to that fantasy camp the Red Sox have in Winter Haven I took my clippers with me. It was the worst thing I did the whole damn week. I was giving the whole fantasy camp haircuts. Shaving their beards. Bill Lee had a beard. And his wife wanted me to shave it off. Bill's over in Rome now, doing a clinic. So, I shaved it off. The whole thing. Gave him a haircut."

Clip clip. "I thought the '75 Boston Red Sox was the best team I ever played on. That's including the Big Red Machine in '70. We played the World Series in '75 without Jimmy Rice. He had a broken wrist. Who's to say, if he played, I probably wouldn't have hit my two pinch-hit home runs. Do you want this above the ears, or do you like it on the ears?"

A little over the top of the ears.

"Just a little bit over the top? That's the style, to show your ears a little bit. You like it to cover the ears a little?"

No. The new style, Bernie. I want to be with it, now that I'm finally in the eighties.

"I tell you, Bill, the extension doesn't look that bad. Yeah, I did the Red Sox fantasy camp with Dom DiMaggio. I did the Cincinnati Reds, too. There ain't too many I can't do. I played on enough teams. I'll tell you that.

"The most fun team, though, was the Boston Red Sox. See, I don't actually say I was a Cincinnati Reds man. Although I'd like to see Rose and those guys win. But I'm a Boston Red Sock. The only reason was Mr. Yawkey. He's the one who made my day. He was in the clubhouse one day. I walked in and said, "What'd we do? Hire another old man?' He had a pair of brown pants on. Old shoes. A work shirt. And he comes my way and says, 'Bernardo! How're you doing? I'm Mr. Yawkey.'

"And I went, 'Mr. Yawkey!' Wasn't he great? He really cared for his players, I'll tell you that. Too bad he had to go and pass away. Well, I'm almost done. You look like a movie star! All right now, I'll just clean you up a little bit. Well, what do you think? The tail's looking *good!* I wish it was longer. Then I could braid.

"Too bad the old man didn't live, eh? I'd probably still be playing for the Boston Red Sox if he was still living. You know what happened? In '75 I hit those two pinch-hit home runs. And that was the year my contract was up. And I had to sign, right? So, I got a 20 percent cut in pay after that World Series. That damn Haywood Sullivan and Buddy LeRoux took over the club in '77, and they gave me a 20 percent cut. And then they traded me to Milwau—who'd they trade me to, Cleveland? They traded me to Cleveland, didn't they? No, that was in 1977. No, they traded me to Milwaukee. I went to Milwaukee. That's when my wife was nine months pregnant and stuff like that. Took a 20 percent cut in pay. Couldn't believe they treated me like that. Mr. Yawkey probably would've given me a nice contract. Just like he did prior to that.

"But I think your tail really turned out nice. I don't know if these tails are gonna be in style that long, or what. What do you think? Three years? Three years. You know who started the tail? The Japanese. The Japanese!

"Yeah. Bill, you need to let this grow just a little bit longer. There you go, looking like a movie star! I told my father I was gonna be a haircutter when I grew up, and he said, 'No you're not. You're gonna be a ballplayer.' See, one side of the family had too many boys and no girls, and the other side—my father's—was all girls. So, I'd get together with the girls and try to straighten my hair, or I'd do their hair."

And then one day, his career at an end, it all came true. Bernie was tending bar at the Bump Shop in Lincoln Park, in the downriver area of Detroit, when a customer, Allison McKay, talked him into going to hair school with her.

"You know, Bill, the most fun I used to have, even when I was having trouble playing ball and stuff, you know what I'd do? I'd stop at the side of a ballpark, where there were kids playing, you know, throwing the ball all over the field and everything. And I'd stop and watch them because of all the fun they were having. And I just tried to realize, hey, I had a lot of fun when I played when I was a kid, too. If I could just get that frame of mind. You know what I mean?"

Absolutely.

"But how do you like the haircut, Bill?"

Why, it's beautiful, Bernardo.

HOWL FOR CASEY

Mikhail Horowitz

I saw the best bats of my generation destroy'd by spitballs,
    curving elliptically plateward, dragging themselves thru
    the Little Leagues at dawn, looking for an angry hit;
Ruthian sluggers staggering on stadium roofs illuminated,
    rounding incredible bags & coming home;
Who singl'd, & doubl'd, & tripl'd, & homer'd hosanna! into
    the grandstand down the ramp & ending up ecstatic & holy
    w/peanuts & Ballantine Beer in the zen bleachers;
Who slump'd, & watch'd their Louisville timbers go limp, &
    boo'd their fate under celestial arclights, as the rabid
    fans in madness also boo'd;
Who emerging from dugouts dugouts dugouts into the navel's
    ondeck circle were dished up umbilical curveballs by
    embryonic portsiders;
Who loned it along Ohio baselines, looking for visionary
    Cleveland Indians who WERE visionary Cleveland Indians;
Who toed the old rubber w/Gaylord Perry, foot queens fondling
    the southpaw's quivering mound;
Who balled the whole ballpark at the Astrodome, first to open
    & then to catch their flies;
Who poured prick into Ford Frick, six inches too short for the
    shortstop, the league's Most Voluptuous Player, Nookie-
    of-the-Year, relieved by the Lord when their love was
    knocked out of the box;
Who ruled in right field by divine right, fungo Bodhisattvas
    reciting the Diamond Sutra;
Who pitched for Paradise, & Paradise Lost, & were banished down
    down down to the hot stove circuitry of Burning Bush Leagues;
Who stole third base to support their habit, snorting the astro-
    turf w/some dark Benway in Fenway Park;

Who peered trembling into the wet Tibetan facemask of Yogi
    Berrananda, coming thru those catchers in the rye;
Who molested bonus babies, a hot flash in the pan, whizzing
    into the eager mitts of Whiz Kids;
Who mastered Tai Chi w/the invincible Ty Cobb, but could not
    nail sweet Jesus at the plate;
Who slugged Om runs, & utilized their flaccid tools of ignorance
    to open up the keystone, no hits no runs no Eros, only to
    find the jissom of Pee Wee Reese;
Who got hot pants for Billy Cox at the hot corner, & were
    buggered by grumbling umps whilst waiting for Lefty;
Who split hairs w/the old Barber in Kiner's Korner, insatiable
    backstops w/foul balls, lumbering on Buddhist shinguards
    for the Lost Bunt;
Who chained themselves to the endless scoreboard for 23
    innings this actually happened & vanished high on opiated
    crackerjacks into oblivious bullpens;
And CASEY, secret hero of this poem, the cupid of Mudville,
    sailing mashnotes on paperplanes to nubile batboys,
    abandoned to boobirds & pulling his pud in the batter's
    box, weeping & thinking, You can't strike out w/out
    having Visions;
Ah Casey, while YOU are a bum, I am a bum, & now you're truly
    gloveless, alone & broken in the poor old winter Polo
    Grounds of God, a prime candidate for the Hall of Shame,
    & even the groundskeeper hands you a raincheck;
Down to the Diamond! He saw the All Stars! Angels in the
    outfield! Bearded twirlers on Biblical mounds! Seraphic
    hotdog vendors in heavenly aisles! He played the game!
    Scarf'd pennants! Sniff'd Red Sox! Blew down the Pirates!
    Yam-yanker for the Yankees! Cincinnati Wetlegs! Double-
    maidenheaders! Base on balls & Frenchkiss'd Leo the Lip!
-the dirt in his cleats an edible joy, good to nibble a thousand
    innings.

STAN'S RING

Oscar London

I grew up in St. Louis during the prime of Stan "The Man" Musial. In 1943, the Cardinals still played at Sportsman's Park, a grimy stadium reeking on a hot day of all our fathers' sweat and cigar smoke—a tired ballpark echoing the murmur of a slack-jawed crowd aroused from time to time by the crack of a base hit or the cry of "Cold beer here!"

In 1943, Stan Musial was a seasoned Cardinal of twenty-three, while I was a boy of twelve. Now we are both converging on senescence. "The Man" is sixty-eight. The boy is fifty-seven. That, of course, is baseball.

The Saturday game between St. Louis and the New York Giants began at 1:00 P.M. In contrast to the grubby stands, the playing field of Sportsman's Park was pristine. Phosphorescent white lines marked off the diamond; the major-league dirt of the infield looked like pure ground cinnamon. And the grass! William Wordsworth never trod a meadow beside Lake Windermere so unashamedly green as the outfield of Sportsman's Park.

The first two Cardinals—Musial and Slaughter—ran out on the field to take their positions. Under the tropical sun, their white and red uniforms were as dazzling as a pair of dice skipping over bright felt in Reno.

I wore my souvenir Cardinal cap and sat with my father just behind the box seats between home plate and third base. My father, like the century, was in his early forties. He was a shirt salesman for a company that, like my father, would grow fat during the War.

For some of our fathers, the action during a baseball game was not confined to the field. Placing a bet at Sportsman's Park required a certain amount of stealth and a rudimentary knowledge of the territory. The Jewish bookmakers patrolled our section between home and third. The Irish gamblers were strung out along the first-base line. The black gamblers were bunched in the right-field bleachers. The Germans, high in the upper deck behind home plate, did not gamble; they owned the ballclub, the ballpark, and the brewery.

Moe the bookmaker, his handsome face distorted by a wad of hot dog inside his right cheek, paused in the aisle just below us. He talked, necessarily, out of one side of his mouth, taking bets with the speed and precision his two sons would show after the War in biochemistry and physics.

To my horror, my father leaned forward, tapped Moe on the shoulder, and placed a five-dollar bet on New York to win. (I never sang for *my* father, either.)

By the third inning, the Cardinals led six to nothing and Musial was already two for two, a double and a triple. (The ballistics of a Musial extra-base hit were those of the M-1 Garand rifle.)

After the first inning, a succession of New York pitchers trudged to the mound, refused blindfolds, and stood facing the bats of Musial, Slaughter, Kurowski, and Cooper.

The Cardinals were still at bat with no outs in the third, when an enormous white cloud a mile above the pitcher's mound suddenly darkened to a visiting-team gray. A muted growl of thunder indicated that some of the gods, like my father, had bet on the Giants to win. Out of left field, a cool breeze washed over the stands, chilling the hearts of beer vendors and giving wing to hundreds of mustard-stained napkins.

In its effort to compete with the War and the Cardinals as a topic of conversation, the weather in St. Louis could be quite assertive. A shaft of lightning struck the top of the flag pole in center field, singeing the Stars and Stripes and, below it, the banner of the 1942 World Champion Cardinals.

Seconds later, a heart-stopping crack and bam of thunder filled the stadium. Before its echo disappeared, the rain was upon us. The drops were fat and cold and they displaced from the hot expanse of grass an overpowering green fragrance.

Like mourners around a headstone, the four black-garbed umpires gathered at home plate. Thunderstruck, they stared at the flash-flooded infield and gazed up at the heavens. Pooling their collective wisdom, they concluded it was raining cats and dogs and called off the game.

My father and I joined the stampede for shelter underneath the stands near Grand Avenue. Cigars soggy, shoes ruined, all bets off, the huddled masses compacted themselves in the great democracy of the half-drenched. For twenty minutes the storm continued to gather strength.

As I stood watching the rain, I became vaguely aware of a new presence beside me.

My father—may he rest in peace, all bets on opposing teams forgiven—draped an arm across my shoulders and said,

"Show my son your ring, Stan."

I looked up at the unmistakable, hawk-beaked profile of The Man. Hatless, batless, Musial was dressed in an unsullied beige suit, a white-on-white shirt, and a silver-and-brown-striped tie. His tan, bone-dry loafers gleamed with a bottomless shine imparted by legions of shoeshine boys who had knelt at the foot of their hero. His sharply parted dark hair was still wet from his locker-room shower. The Man Himself stood with us mortals under the grandstand, waiting for a break in the storm.

"Show my son your ring, Stan," my father repeated in a louder voice.

The left-handed hitter smiled and slowly extended his right fist. On the fourth finger was his World Championship ring—a glittering prize of the Cardinals' victory, the year before, over the Yankees. An effulgence of gold, diamonds, and rubies, Stan's ring seemed to light up our entire section underneath the grandstand.

Nowhere in the canons of baseball is it ordained that a Jewish boy must kiss the proffered ring of a Cardinal, but for a fleeting moment on a rainy day in St. Louis forty-five years ago, I was tempted.

Musial blushed at the growing adulation surrounding him. Suddenly, he stepped out into the rain and hailed a taxi. It did not appear to me that he got wet.

FIDEL'S LAST PITCH

John Krich

This creeping decrepitude has no glory. Old age is one assassin even I cannot dodge. How can I "prevail" at first base?

I was moved there just yesterday. "A suggestion from the cadre," Pepin told me at the bat-rack. "For the good of the club." How could I protest? They shoved an infielder's mitt at me—it looked like a leather *tortilla*—and took away the glove that fit me so well, with the deep pocket made by so many catches. I was forced to give up the pitcher's mound, and with it the right to be at the center of every play. The right to set the *pelota* in motion. I tried not to grumble. It is imperative that I part with some of my responsibilities. It is instructional for the team to see El Jefe step aside. But first base! The initial stop on the express route to senility! From this station, you witness "The twilight of your career." That is one light I planned never to see.

The game ended mercifully. Called on account of a hurricane. Raúl's Red Sox led Fidel's *Barbudos*, 17-14. This would have been the 300th win for *los rojos*, while my squad has only 212. We've been keeping track of the series since we played those exhibition games in the summer of '61. That was the first summer under socialism, the summer of the great harvest, the summer after we repulsed the Yankees at Playa Girón. Wasn't it also the first summer when we were forced to let the women play? They'd never been interested before, but suddenly they were so insistent. Even you, Celia. Remember? I showed you how to "choke up." It was a summer of great patience and a summer of hope.

My *Barbudos* are hoping still. We might have rallied to win this one had it not been for the dispute over Ramiro's double. Play was held up for half an hour while the coaches argued about whether the ball had grazed some palm leaves along the right field foul line. I didn't interfere. These people don't shrink from a good fight—or a bad one. Sportsmanship becomes an impossibility when each man is his own judge. It was bad enough when we were a nation of contestants. Now we're a nation of umpires.

Finally the parties appealed to me, as I knew they would. They complained about the condition of the field. But I'm no groundskeeper, no Colonel Ruppert or George Steinbrenner. I can't invest in grandstands or a green diamond—down here, the grass always bakes brown. I told my men they were getting spoiled.

"We're lucky to have a field, to have arms and legs to play with. . . ."

What if the superpowers had seen us? What if the C.I.A. had chosen this moment to make its move? Half the Central Committee was in on the argument, stomping on the bases, kicking up all the dust they could raise.

It's true, my *compañeros* and I often act like schoolboys. It's also deceptive. Even at play, we are meditating upon survival. We are priests with pistols: our life in this place is a curious blend of the athletic and the monastic. First we read, preferably from Marx or the latest best-seller about Watergate and other Yankee scandals. Next we hunt, substituting wild grouse for our real targets. Then we shadowbox, to keep trim for that last round which never comes.

When yesterday's downpour came, making our game and its rulebook irrelevant, we scooped up our rifles and left the bats to warp at home plate. We zigzagged like commandos to the main barracks' veranda. Raúl split open a melon for our midday meal. Though we all had official duties to perform, we loitered about until the storm had spent itself in the grooves of Italian tile over our wanted heads. Once more, we were an army. Once more, we had made a heroic escape: out of breath and on the run, with rain in our beards and mud in our sneakers. Once more, we could sniff one another's exertion and dampness and ardor.

Reminded of that best of times, when frustration was just another patrol we could skirt, I was nearly content. I only wish there had not been so many changes in my starting lineup. Where was my original "barnstorming" nine? If death played on our side, why didn't it take me, the captain, when I was so primed? Why do I have to be the one left to keep the game going?

Humanity's progress is ceaseless, and though it appears to move at a crawl, it is always too quick for its victims. Time is a poorly trained servant: he tries to wait at attention, linen folded over one arm, but he grows restless, sneaks off, phones his girlfriend. Tonight, this morning, I have not been a "historic figure" reciting his memoirs. I have been a referee blowing his whistle and screaming, "Time out!" But who hears me? What contest do I control? Even in *el beisbol*, the sport with no clock, there has to be a last pitch.

Perhaps I should take this opportunity to dictate my will. I remember the last time. I was hiding in the cushionless back seat of a Dodge sedan. It was taking me to the dock where the *Granma* was waiting to take me to my death. I used the back of a Mexican leaflet for my paper and a comrade's knee for my desk. I was my own probate. Though I anticipated imminent extinction, I could not list a legacy, I the great list maker! What was I leaving behind? Two pairs of shoes—and Fidelito. And I did not even have him! I specified only that I desired custody of the boy to be given to a childless Cuban widow who hid me when I arrived in Mexico.

This time I won't bequeath my son the least concern. He wouldn't take it anyway. This time I will not think only of lineage. I know now that the members of my family are the millions and millions of forward-looking people everywhere. I have brothers in Angola, sisters in Zimbabwe, children in Kuwait. The only true family is the family in arms. And I care no more for my blood relations—be it resentful Fidelito, spiteful Juana, or inspirational Raúl—than I do for my diplomatic relations. Truly, I care about them less. I have said goodbye, as all men must, to mother and sister and cousin, as we must one day say goodbye to our prized playthings and our esteemed pets and our treasured automobiles and our cherished tastes and our precious lusts and our chosen theories. The prospect of death dampens all grasping, cures all private fetishes. And the revolutionary must adhere to the perspective of death in life. So long, *hasta luego!* Stop grabbing and you will get everything.

No paltry clan will grieve for me, or gather around my executor, eager to get their hands on my estate. My estate is the state. I will be survived by a whole people.

Let the people enjoy my death, since their enemies will. Let them turn my memorial to sport. Why not? A good contest is what the Cubans crave, and I am one of them. I will bury this tape outside Santa Clara, on the grounds of a model citrus farm, under the arthritic tendrils of the district's *ceiba* tree. I won't tell anyone. I'll leave clues at all the ministries, on the scoreboards, in the ice cream cones at *La Coppelia.* I'll make the nation hunt for its inheritance, for this final sermon. Anti-social elements will not be eligible for the grand prize. And what will that finder's fee be? An insignia of merit in the form of Che's red star, fifty pounds of sugar, a lifetime supply of hardballs, and the equivalent in gold bullion of all foreign exchange I have puffed away all these years with my taste for export-quality *Montecristo A's!* A huff and a puff: that is all this tyrant has hoarded.

"I, Fidel Castro Ruz, a.k.a. Alejandro, being of sound, unrevisionist mind and flabby, unscathed body. . . ."

To Mamma and Pappa, I leave one share in the United Fruit Company, Cuban Division.

To sister Juana, I leave a combination cigarette lighter and molotov cocktail.

To sister Lidia, this retreat and all its grounds, to be used as a child care center.

To brother Raúl, my best rifle, my harpoon, my podium.

To son Fidelito, a world without me in it.

To wife Mirta, a drop of jism.

To friend Celia, posthumously, an academy for daydreamers.

To the fisherman Pérez, more posthumously, I leave one Soviet trawler in good working order—if one can be found!

To Batista, a second-hand condom and a Coppertone tan.

To Kennedy and Khrushchev, one missile each up the wrong end.

To Nixon and Brezhnev, my unused Gillette.

To Uncle Ho and Chairman Mao, my solidarity stuffed in a sack of fertilizer.

To Luis Tiant, a humidor. And to whom will I leave the thermidor?

To the peasants, museums. To the prostitutes, pickaxes. To the poets, walkie-talkies.

To Cuba, I offer the results of my amateur gardening—twenty *arrobas* of hybrid tomatoes—along with a gardener's warning: one season of neglect and the weeds start returning.

To Latin America, I leave slogans in the mouths of your children when I would rather leave bread.

To Che and Camilo and Abel and Inti and Allende and all the heroic Chicos, a trail map of paradise.

To the *Estados Unidos,* hated lover, worthy foe, tyrant and tease, I leave the exclusive television rights to my entombment. This must take place at the first American-Cuban World Series in Anti-Yankee Stadium. The proceedings will start with my videotaped rendition of Lou Gehrig's farewell—"I am the luckiest man in the world," flashed across the scoreboard—and end with my final cry of *"Patria o Muerte!"* That cry will be echoed by ten thousand cheerleaders from small towns in East Texas. The *gusanos* in the bleachers will fling their caps high. The "freedom flotilla" will sweep the infield with their tongues. A Marine Honor Guard will present the Cuban colors, which are also red, white, and blue. Billy Graham will lead the benediction. Régis Debray will throw out the first ball. Pat Boone and the Groupo Moncada will sing a medley of "The International" and "The Ballad of the Green Berets." Desi Arnaz and Pérez Prado will lead the Notre Dame Marching Band. J. Edgar Hoover will peddle hot dogs. Miss Barbara Walters will do the play-by-play. In a warm-up bout, Kid Gavilan will outpoint Joe Louis. The C.I.A.'s Havana bureau chiefs, led by Meyer Lansky, will challenge the Venceremos Brigade in an Old-Timers Game; Mickey Mantle will lose an arm-wrestling match to the ghost of Roberto Clemente; the Commissioner will okay a deal giving Puerto Rico back to the Puerto Ricans for a country-to-be-named-later. Our hemisphere of corn and yucca, of cowboys and slaves, will finally be at peace.

DOCTOR K

Jim Hydock

The Mets were in town, playing the Giants in homage to Franz Kline. He had grown up in Wilkes-Barre, Pennsylvania, painting brown and green landscapes of coal mines and aging trains chugging over spindly bridges. As a child, his toys were the black cinders along the railroad tracks, and he would come home after dark, covered in dust. He died just past mid-century, leaving paintings of the pearl grey sky seen through the geometry of black trestles.

We had to park on a gravel plateau high outside the concrete stadium, then stream like refugees through the dust to the stadium gates. In their seats the fans chattered nervously, anxious for the first pitch of Doctor K. A black woman, the color of hot fudge, dressed in a white jumpsuit and a Giants cap leaned over to me and whispered, "He is ruthless. There is no need to give him a name." I nodded and stared at the lines on my blank scorecard.

The Giants got to him early, racking him for nine screaming liners, and by the fifth inning he was gone. As he walked off the field the crowd stood on their seats and jeered like a successful junta. In the locker room Doctor K stripped his uniform in a rage. Leaning his thin black body against the steamy white tile of the shower room, he conjured his revenge. "I am the consensus," he seethed, "I am the program. I am the goddamn border patrol."

BABE & LOU

Franz Douskey

when babe hit
number 714 he was
playing for Boston
and washed up

he was a big tipper
a big eater a big
drinker and every
body loved the babe

lou was the iron
man and played
in 2130 consecutive
games and when he coughed
into the microphone
he said he was
the luckiest man alive

he batted clean up
right behind the babe
and together they
represented fear
power and (judging
from the full stands)
absenteeism

this was before the unions
before the depression before
the war and when the smoke

lifted the forties were over and
both men had died slowly
each weighing less
than a 100 lbs

THREE NEW TWINS JOIN CLUB IN SPRING

Garrison Keillor

My team won the World Series. You thought we couldn't but we knew we would and we did, and what did your team do? Not much. Now we're heading down to spring training looking even better than before, and your team that looked pitiful then looks even less hot now. Your hometown paper doesn't say so, but your leadoff guy had a bad ear infection in January and now he gets dizzy at the first sign of stress and falls down in a heap. Sad. Your cleanup guy spent the winter cleaning his plate. He had to buy new clothes in a size they don't sell at regular stores. Your great relief guy, his life has been changed by the Rama Lama Ding Dong, and he is now serenely throwing the ball from a place deep within himself, near his gall bladder. What a shame. Your rookie outfielder set a world record for throwing a frozen chicken, at a promotional appearance for Grandma Fanny's Farm Foods. Something snapped in his armpit and now he can't even throw a pair of dice. Tough beans. Your big left-hander tried hypnosis to stop smoking and while in a trancelike state discovered he hated his mother for tying his tiny right hand behind his back and making him eat and draw and tinkle with his left. So he's right-handed now, a little awkward but gradually learning to point with it and wave goodbye. That's what your whole team'll be doing by early May.

Meanwhile, my team, the world-champion Minnesota Twins, are top dogs who look like a lead-pipe cinch to take all the marbles in a slow walk. My guys had a good winter doing youth work. Last October they pooled their Series pay to purchase a farm, Twin Acres, north of Willmar, where they could stay in shape doing chores in the off-season, and they loved it so much they stayed through Thanksgiving and Christmas (celebrating them the good old-fashioned Midwestern way), and raised a new barn, bought a powerful new seed drill to plant winter wheat with, built up the flock of purebred Leghorns, chopped wood, carried water, etc., along with their guests—delinquent boys and girls from St. Louis and Detroit who needed to get out of those sick and destructive environments and learn personal values such as hard work and personal cleanliness. Meanwhile, back in Minneapolis, the Twins front office wasn't asleep on its laurels but through shrewd deals made mostly before 8:15 A.M. added to what they had while giving up nothing in return. It seems unfair.

OTHER TEAMS GNASH TEETH OR SULK

It's considered impossible to obtain *three top premium players* without paying a red cent, but the Twins:

Traded away some useless air rights for Chuck Johnson (23, 187 lbs., 6'1", bats left, throws left), a native of Little Falls, Minnesota. Maybe that's why the scouts who work the Finger Lakes League ignored his phenomenal season with the Seneca Falls Susans. They figured, "Minnesota? Forget it!" But how can you forget thirty-eight doubles, twenty-two triples, and twenty-nine round-trippers—and in spacious Elizabeth Cady Stanton Stadium! That's a lot of power for a lifelong liberal like Chuck. And what's more, he *never struck out*. Not once. Plays all positions cheerfully.

Sent a couple in their mid-forties to the San Diego Padres in exchange for Duane (Madman) Mueller (29, 280 lbs., 6'2", right/right, a.k.a. Mule, Hired Hand, The Barber). Duane is a big secret because after he was suspended by the Texas League for throwing too hard he played Nicaraguan winter ball for three years and then spent two more doing humanitarian stuff, so scouts forgot how, back when he was with the Amarillo Compadres, nobody wanted to be behind the plate, Duane threw so hard. His own team kept yelling, "Not so *hard*, man!" If that sounds dumb, then you never saw him throw: he threw *hard*. A devoted Lutheran, he never ever hit a batter, but in one game a pitch of his nicked the bill of a batting helmet and spun it so hard it burned off the man's eyebrows. No serious injury, but big Duane took himself out of organized ball until he could learn an off-speed pitch. He's from Brainerd, Minnesota, where he lives across the street from his folks. His mom played kittenball in the fifties and had a good arm but not like her son's. She thinks he got it from delivering papers and whipping cake mix. "I'd sure hate to have to bat against him," she says.

Gave up a dingy two-bedroom house in St. Paul (it needs more than just a paint job and a new roof, and it's near a rendering plant) to acquire and activate Bob Berg (24, 112 lbs., 5'3", right/left), the fastest man on the base paths today (we *think*), but he sat out last year and the year before last and the year before *that* because he didn't have shoes. Reason: he's so fast he runs the shoes right off his own feet. Now athletic foot specialists have studied his film clips (sad to see: three lightning strides, a look of dismay on Bob's face, and down he goes with his loose laces like a lasso round his ankles) and come up with a new pair of pigskin shoes with barbed cleats that stick in the turf and slow him down. Born and raised in Eveleth, Minnesota, he is probably the nicest fast man in baseball. Nicknamed The Hulk ("berg" means "mountain" in Norwegian). He used those three years on the bench to earn a B.A. in history, by the way.

THAT'S NOT ALL

Joining the team later will be Wally Gunderson (17, 191 lbs., 6′4″, left/right), who dons a Twins uniform June 8th, the day after he graduates from West High in Minneapolis. The Twins have saved him a number, 18, and assigned him a locker and paid him a bonus, twelve hundred dollars, which was all he would accept. He's thrilled just to be on the team. A big lanky loose-jointed kid with long wavy blond hair and a goofy grin, he throws a screwball that comes in and up, a slider that suddenly jumps, a curve that drops off the table, and a stinkball that hangs in the air so long some batters swing twice. You don't expect so much junk from an Eagle Scout, but Wally's got one more: a fastball that decelerates rapidly halfway to the plate—a braking pitch. Some he learned from his dad and the rest he invented for a Science Fair project. "Pitching is physics, that's all," he says, looking down at his size-13 shoes, uneasy at all the acclaim.

Detroit and St. Louis offered the lad millions in cash, land, jewelry, servants, tax abatements, but he wasn't listening. "I want to play my ball where my roots are," he says quietly.

Twinsville wasn't one bit surprised. Personal character and loyalty and dedication are what got us where we are right now, and that's on top. We're No. 1. We knew it first and now you know it, too. You thought we were quiet and modest in the Midwest but that's because you're dumb, as dumb as a stump, dumber than dirt.

You're so dumb you don't know that we're on top and you're below. Our team wins and your team loses; we need your team to amuse us. Minnesota soybeans, corn, and barley; we're the best, so beat it, Charley, or we'll shell ya like a pea pod, dunk ya like a doughnut—sure be nice when the game's over, won't it—take ya to the cleaners for a brand-new hairdo. We can beat ya anytime we care to. Shave and a haircut, two bits.

WHITE LIKE ME (KURT STILWELL)

Mike Shannon

There weren't any black people
In my neighborhood down in Florida.
Except for the black ladies who came in
In the mornings to babysit and clean house.
They'd get off the city buses,
Chirping happily as birds at daybreak,
Big lumpy satchels and transfers in their hands,
While we boarded those putrid yellow
School buses, resigned as convicts.
We had a black maid too, and she practically
Raised my brothers and my sisters.
Her name was Catherine and we loved
Her like a member of the family.
Otherwise, the only time I ever
Ran into blacks was on the ballfield.
I remember that in little league
We were kind of afraid of them.
They were always bigger, faster, stronger,
Louder (and our coaches said they were older).
In junior high I read I NEVER HAD IT MADE
Which made me wish I could have been
A Brooklyn Dodger with Jackie Robinson
So I could have treated him like a brother.
There were no blacks on my high school
Team—they didn't like the coach—but they
Knew I wasn't prejudiced, not with my locker
Practically a shrine to Ozzie Smith
And when I got into pro ball I had no trouble
Whatsoever living with black guys

Even though I never knew how to answer them
When they'd call me "White Boy."
It's only been this summer that I've wondered
About my attitude, as I've watched Barry
From the bench, coming across the bag
Like a rapist, firing the ball submarine
Right at the face of the runner,
Playing shortstop for the Reds, my position,
Which either he stole from me or I gave to him.

HOW I GOT MY NICKNAME

W. P. Kinsella

*For Brian Fawcett, whose story "My Career with the
Leafs" inspired this story.*

In the summer of 1951, the summer before I was to start Grade 12, my polled Hereford calf, Simon Bolivar, won Reserve Grand Champion at the Des Moines All-Iowa Cattle Show and Summer Exposition. My family lived on a hobby-farm near Iowa City. My father, who taught classics at Coe College in Cedar Rapids, and in spite of that was still the world's number one baseball fan, said I deserved a reward—I also had a straight-A average in Grade 11 and had published my first short story that spring. My father phoned his friend Robert Fitzgerald (Fitzgerald, an eminent translator, sometimes phoned my father late at night and they talked about various ways of interpreting the tougher parts of *The Iliad*) and two weeks later I found myself in Fitzgerald's spacious country home outside of New York City, sharing the lovely old house with the Fitzgeralds, their endless supply of children, and a young writer from Georgia named Flannery O'Connor. Miss O'Connor was charming, and humorous in an understated way, and I wish I had talked with her more. About the third day I was there I admitted to being a published writer and Miss O'Connor said, "You must show me some of your stories." I never did. I was seventeen, overweight, diabetic, and bad-complexioned. I alternated between being terminally shy and obnoxiously brazen. I was nearly always shy around the Fitzgeralds and Miss O'Connor. I was also terribly homesick, which made me appear more silent and outlandish than I knew I was. I suspect I am the model for Enoch Emery, the odd, lonely country boy in Miss O'Connor's novel *Wise Blood*. But that is another story.

On a muggy August morning, the first day of a Giant home stand at the Polo Grounds, I prepared to travel into New York. I politely invited Miss O'Connor to accompany me, but she, even at that early date, had to avoid sunlight and often wore her wide-brimmed straw hat even indoors. I set off much too early and, though terrified of the grimy city and shadows that seemed to lurk in every doorway, arrived at the Polo Grounds over two hours before game time. It was raining gently and I was one of about two dozen fans in the ballpark. A few players were lethargically playing catch, a coach was hitting fungoes to three players in right field. I kept edging my way down the rows of seats until I was right behind the Giants dugout.

The Giants were thirteen games behind the Dodgers and the pennant race appeared all but over. A weasel-faced batboy, probably some executive's nephew, I thought, noticed me staring wide-eyed at the players and the playing field. He curled his lip at me, then stuck out his tongue. He mouthed the words, "Take a picture, it'll last longer," adding something at the end that I could only assume to be uncomplimentary.

Fired by the insult I suddenly mustered all my bravado and called out, "Hey, Mr. Durocher?" Leo Durocher, the Giants manager, had been standing in the third-base coach's box not looking at anything in particular. I was really impressed. That's the grand thing about baseball, I thought. Even a manager in a pennant race can take time to daydream. He didn't hear me. But the batboy did, and stuck out his tongue again.

I was overpowered by my surroundings. Though I'd seen a lot of major-league baseball I'd never been in the Polo Grounds before. The history of the place . . . "Hey, Mr. Durocher," I shouted.

Leo looked up at me with a baleful eye. He needed a shave, and the lines around the corners of his mouth looked like ruts.

"What is it, Kid?"

"Could I hit a few?" I asked hopefully, as if I was begging to stay up an extra half hour. "You know, take a little batting practice?"

"Sure, Kid. Why not?" and Leo smiled with one corner of his mouth. "We want all our fans to feel like part of the team."

From the box seat where I'd been standing, I climbed up on the roof of the dugout and Leo helped me down onto the field.

Leo looked down into the dugout. The rain was stopping. On the other side of the park a few of the Phillies were wandering onto the field. "Hey, George," said Leo, staring into the dugout, "throw the kid here a few pitches. Where are you from, son?"

It took me a few minutes to answer because I experienced this strange, lightheaded feeling, as if I had too much sun. "Near to Iowa City, Iowa," I managed to say in a small voice. Then, "You're going to win the pennant, Mr. Durocher. I just know you are."

"Well, thanks, Kid," said Leo modestly, "we'll give it our best shot."

George was George Bamberger, a stocky rookie who had seen limited action. "Bring the kid a bat, Andy," Leo said to the batboy. The batboy curled his lip at me but slumped into the dugout, as Bamberger and Sal Yvars tossed the ball back and forth.

The batboy brought me a black bat. I was totally unprepared for how heavy it was. I lugged it to the plate and stepped into the right-hand batter's box. Bamberger delivered an easy, looping, batting-practice pitch. I drilled it back up the middle.

"Pretty good, Kid," I heard Durocher say.

Bamberger threw another easy one and I fouled it off. The third pitch was a little harder. I hammered it to left.

"Curve him," said Durocher.

He curved me. Even through my thick glasses the ball looked as big as a grapefruit, illuminated like a small moon. I whacked it and it hit the right-field wall on one bounce.

"You weren't supposed to hit that one," said Sal Yvars.

"You're pretty good, Kid," shouted Durocher from the third-base box. "Give him your best stuff, George."

Over the next fifteen minutes I batted about .400 against George Bamberger and Roger Bowman, including a home run into the left-center-field stands. The players on the Giants bench were watching me with mild interest, often looking up from the books most of them were reading.

"I'm gonna put the infield out now," said Durocher. "I want you to run out some of your hits."

Boy, here I was batting against the real New York Giants. I wished I'd worn a new shirt instead of the horizontally striped red and white one I had on, which made me look heftier than I really was. Bowman threw a sidearm curve and I almost broke my back swinging at it. But he made the mistake of coming right back with the same pitch. I looped it behind third, where it landed soft as a sponge and trickled off toward the stands—I'd seen the play hundreds of times—a stand-up double. But when I was still twenty feet from second base Eddie Stanky was waiting with the ball. "Slide!" somebody yelled, but I just skidded to a stop, stepping out of the baseline to avoid the tag. Stanky whapped me anyway, a glove to the ribs that would have made Rocky Marciano or Ezzard Charles proud.

When I got my wind back Durocher was standing, hands on hips, staring down at me.

"Why the hell didn't you slide, Kid?"

"I can't," I said, a little indignantly. "I'm diabetic, I have to avoid stuff like that. If I cut myself, or even bruise badly, it takes forever to heal."

"Oh," said Durocher. "Well, I guess that's okay then."

"You shouldn't tag people so hard," I said to Stanky. "Somebody could get hurt."

"Sorry, Kid," said Stanky. I don't think he apologized very often. I noticed that his spikes were filed. But I found later that he knew a lot about F. Scott Fitzgerald. His favorite story was "Babylon Revisited," so that gave us a lot in common. I was a real Fitzgerald fan; Stanky and I became friends even though both he and Durocher argued against reading The Great Gatsby as an allegory.

"Where'd you learn your baseball?" an overweight coach who smelled strongly of snuff and bourbon said to me.

"I live near Iowa City, Iowa," I said in reply.

Everyone wore question marks on their faces. I saw I'd have to elaborate. "Iowa City is within driving distance of Chicago, St. Louis, Milwaukee, and there's minor-league ball in Cedar

Rapids, Omaha, Kansas City. Why, there's barely a weekend my dad and I don't go somewhere to watch professional baseball."

"Watch?" said Durocher.

"Well, we talk about it some too. My father is a real student of the game. Of course we only talk in Latin when we're on the road, it's a family custom."

"Latin?" said Durocher.

"Say something in Latin," said Whitey Lockman, who had wandered over from first base.

"The Etruscans have invaded all of Gaul," I said in Latin.

"Their fortress is on the banks of the river," said Bill Rigney, who had been filling in at third base.

"Velle est posse," I said.

"Where there's a will there's a way," translated Durocher.

"Drink Agri Cola . . ." I began.

"The farmer's drink," said Sal Yvars, slapping me on the back, but gently enough not to bruise me. I guess I looked a little surprised.

"Most of us are more than ballplayers," said Alvin Dark, who had joined us. "In fact the average player on this squad is fluent in three languages."

"*Watch?*" said Durocher, getting us back to baseball. "You *watch* a lot of baseball, but where do you play?"

"I've never played in my life," I replied. "But I have a photographic memory. I just watch how different players hold their bat, how they stand. I try to emulate Enos Slaughter and Joe DiMaggio.

"Can you field?" said Durocher.

"No."

"No?"

"I've always just watched the hitters. I've never paid much attention to the fielders."

He stared at me as if I had spoken to him in an unfamiliar foreign language.

"Everybody fields," he said. "What position do you play?"

"I've never played," I reiterated. "My health is not very good."

"Cripes," he said, addressing the sky. "You drop a second Ted Williams on me and he tells me he can't field." Then to Alvin Dark: "Hey, Darky, throw a few with the kid here. Get him warmed up."

In the dugout Durocher pulled a thin black glove from an equipment bag and tossed it to me. I dropped it. The glove had no discernable padding in it. The balls Dark threw hit directly on my hand, when I caught them, which was about one out of three. "Ouch!" I cried. "Don't throw so hard."

"Sorry, Kid," said Alvin Dark and threw the next one a little easier. If I really heaved I could just get the ball back to him. I have always thrown like a non-athletic girl. I could feel my hand bloating inside the thin glove. After about ten pitches, I pulled my hand out. It looked as though it had been scalded.

"Don't go away, Kid," said Leo. "In fact, why don't you sit in the dugout with me. What's your name anyway?"

"W. P. Kinsella," I said.

"Your friends call you W?"

"My father calls me William, and my mother . . ." but I let my voice trail off. I didn't think Leo Durocher would want to know my mother still called me Bunny.

"Jeez," said Durocher. "You need a nickname, Kid. Bad."

"I'll work on it," I said.

I sat right beside Leo Durocher all that stifling afternoon in the Polo Grounds as the Giants swept a doubleheader from the Phils, the start of a sixteen-game streak that was to lead to the October 3, 1951 Miracle of Coogan's Bluff. I noticed right away that the Giants were all avid readers. In fact, the *New York Times* best-seller lists and the *Time* and *Newsweek* lists of readable books and an occasional review were taped to the walls of the dugout. When the Giants were in the field I peeked at the covers of the books the players sometimes read between innings. Willie Mays was reading *The Cruel Sea* by Nicholas Monsarrat. Between innings Sal Maglie was deeply involved in Carson McCuller's new novel *The Ballad of the Sad Cafe*. "I sure wish we could get that Cousin Lyman to be our mascot," he said to me when he saw me eyeing the book jacket, referring to the hunchbacked dwarf who was the main character in the novel. "We need something to inspire us," he added. Alvin Dark slammed down his copy of *Requiem for a Nun* and headed for the on-deck circle.

When the second game ended, a sweaty and sagging Leo Durocher took me by the arm. "There's somebody I want you to meet, Kid," he said. Horace Stoneham's office was furnished in wine-colored leather sofas and overstuffed horsehair chairs. Stoneham sat behind an oak desk as big as the dugout, enveloped in cigar smoke.

"I've got a young fellow here I think we should sign for the stretch drive," Durocher said. "He can't field or run, but he's as pure a hitter as I've ever seen. He'll make a hell of a pinch hitter."

"I suppose you'll want a bonus?" growled Stoneham.

"I do have something in mind," I said. Even Durocher was not nearly as jovial as he had been. Both men stared coldly at me. Durocher leaned over and whispered something to Stoneham.

"How about six thousand dollars," Stoneham said.

"What I'd really like . . ." I began.

"Alright, ten thousand, but not a penny more."

"Actually, I'd like to meet Bernard Malamud. I thought you could maybe invite him down to the park. Maybe get him to sign a book for me?" They both looked tremendously relieved.

"Bernie and me and this kid Salinger are having supper this evening," said Durocher. "Why don't you join us?"

"You mean J. D. Salinger?" I said.

"Jerry's a big Giant fan," he said. "The team Literary Society read *Catcher in the Rye* last month. We had a panel discussion on it for eight hours on the train to St. Louis."

Before I signed the contract I phoned my father.

"No reason you can't postpone your studies until the end of the season," he said. "It'll be good experience for you. You'll gather a lot of material you can write about later. Besides, baseball players are the real readers of America."

I got my first hit off Warren Spahn, a solid single up the middle. Durocher immediately replaced me with a pinch runner. I touched Ralph Branca for a double: the ball went over Duke Snider's head, hit the wall, and bounced halfway back to the infield. Anyone else would have had an inside-the-park homer. I wheezed into second and was replaced. I got into thirty-eight of the final forty-two games. I hit 11 for 33, and was walked four times. And hit once. That was the second time I faced Warren Spahn. He threw a swishing curve that would have gone behind me if I hadn't backed into it. I slouched off toward first holding my ribs.

"You shouldn't throw at batters like that," I shouted. "Someone could get seriously hurt. I'm diabetic, you know." I'd heard that Spahn was into medical texts and interested in both human and veterinary medicine.

"Sorry," he shouted back. "If I'd known I wouldn't have thrown at you. I've got some good liniment in the clubhouse. Come see me after the game. By the way, I hear you're trying to say that *The Great Gatsby* is an allegory."

"The way I see it, it is," I said. "You see, the eyes of the optometrist on the billboard are really the eyes of God looking down on a fallen world . . ."

"Alright, alright," said the umpire, Beans Reardon, "let's get on with the game. By the way, Kid, I don't think it's an allegory either. A statement on the human condition, perhaps. But not an allegory."

The players wanted to give me some nickname other than "Kid." Someone suggested "Ducky," in honor of my running style. "Fats," said somebody else. I made a note to remove his bookmark between innings. Several other suggestions were downright obscene. Baseball players, in spite of their obsession with literature and the arts, often have a bawdy sense of humor.

"How about 'Moonlight,'" I suggested. I'd read about an old-time player who stopped for a cup of coffee with the Giants half a century before, who had that nickname.

"What the hell for?" said Monty Irvin, who in spite of the nickname preferred to be called Monford or even by his second name, Merrill. "You got to have a reason for a nickname. You got to earn it. Still, anything's better than W.P."

"It was only a suggestion," I said. I made a mental note not to tell Monford what I knew about *his* favorite author, Erskine Caldwell.

As it turned out, I didn't earn a nickname until the day we won the pennant.

As every baseball fan knows, the Giants went into the bottom of the ninth in the deciding game of the pennant playoff trailing the Dodgers 4-1.

"Don't worry," I said to Durocher, "everything's going to work out." If he heard me he didn't let on.

But was everything going to work out? And what part was I going to play in it? Even though I'd contributed to the Giants' amazing stretch drive, I didn't belong. Why am I here? I kept asking myself. I had some vague premonition that I was about to change history. I meant I wasn't a ballplayer. I was a writer. Here I was about to go into Grade 12, and I was already planning to do my master's thesis on F. Scott Fitzgerald.

I didn't have time to worry further as Alvin Dark singled. Don Mueller, in his excitement, had carried his copy of *The Mill on the Floss* out to the on-deck circle. He set the resin bag on top of it, stalked to the plate, and singled, moving Dark to second.

I was flabbergasted when Durocher called Monford Irvin back and said to me, "Get in there, Kid."

It was at that moment that I knew why I was there. I would indeed change history. One stroke of the bat and the score would be tied. I eyed the left-field stands as I nervously swung two bats to warm up. I was nervous but not scared. I never doubted my prowess for one moment. Years later Johnny Bench summed it up for both athletes and writers when he talked about a successful person having to have an *inner conceit*. It never occurred to me until days later that I might have hit into a double or triple play, thus ending it and *really* changing history.

When I did take my place in the batter's box, I pounded the plate and glared out at Don Newcombe. I wished that I shaved so I could give him a stubble-faced stare of contempt. He curved me and I let it go by for a ball. I fouled the next pitch high into the first-base stands. A fastball was low. I fouled the next one outside third. I knew he didn't want to go to a full count: I crowded the plate a little looking for the fastball. He curved me. Nervy. But the curveball hung, sat out over the plate like a cantaloupe. I waited an extra millisecond before lambasting it. In that instant the ball broke in on my hands; it hit the bat right next to my right hand. It has been over thirty years, but I still wake deep in the night, my hands vibrating, burning from Newcombe's pitch. The bat shattered into kindling. The ball flew in a polite loop as if it had been tossed by a five-year-old; it landed soft as a creampuff in Pee Wee Reese's glove. One out.

I slumped back to the bench.

"Tough luck, Kid," said Durocher, patting my shoulder. "There'll be other chances to be a hero."

"Thanks, Leo," I said.

Whitey Lockman doubled. Dark scored. Mueller hurt himself sliding into third. Rafael Noble went in to run for Mueller. Charlie Dressen replaced Newcombe with Ralph Branca. Bobby Thomson swung bats in the on-deck circle.

As soon as umpire Jorda called time-in, Durocher leapt to his feet, and before Bobby Thomson could take one step toward the plate, Durocher called him back.

"Don't do that!" I yelled, suddenly knowing why I was *really* there. But Durocher ignored me. He was beckoning with a big-knuckled finger to another reserve player, a big outfielder who was tearing up the American Association when they brought him up late in the year. He was 5 for 8 as a pinch hitter.

Durocher was already up the dugout steps heading toward the umpire to announce the change. The outfielder from the American Association was making his way down the dugout, hopping along over feet and ankles. He'd be at the top of the step by the time Durocher reached the umpire.

As he skipped by me, the last person between Bobby Thomson and immortality, I stuck out my foot. The outfielder from the American Association went down like he'd been poleaxed. He hit his face on the top step of the dugout, crying out loud enough to attract Durocher's attention.

The trainer hustled the damaged player to the clubhouse. Durocher waved Bobby Thomson to the batter's box. And the rest is history. After the victory celebration I announced my retirement, blaming it on a damaged wrist. I went back to Iowa and listened to the World Series on the radio.

All I have to show that I ever played in the major leagues is my one-line entry in *The Baseball Encyclopedia:*

W. P. KINSELLA   Kinsella, William Patrick "Tripper" BR TR
5'9" 185 lbs. B. Apr. 14, 1934 Onamata, Ia.

| | | | | | | HR | | | | | | Pinch Hit | |
G	AB	H	2B	3B	HR	%	R	RBI	BB	SO	EA	BA	AB	H
1951 NY N 38	33	11	2	0	2	6.0	0	8	4	4	0	.333	33	11

I got my outright release in the mail the week after the World Series ended. Durocher had scrawled across the bottom: "Good luck, Kid. By the way, *The Great Gatsby* is *not* an allegory."

UNTITLED POEM
Tom Clark

Though it remains a great pleasure to roll the names
and numbers around in what's left of
one's brain, that abandoned bowling alley lane down
which a compacted garbage ball of trivia always thunders
endlessly toward the rooted in concrete steel ninepins
of the facts of life and then bounces and slithers off into
the gutter uselessly, yet not without having diverted one
however briefly etc., still I'm having a harder and harder time every
spring connecting the nominative and statistical reality of
the players to these spoiled jockstrap boys from colleges with
a credit card between their teeth when they show up in florida
or arizona with a stockprofile in place of the old dizzy dean dream

TO BILL LEE
Tom Clark

Spaceman, how was your trip to Peking?
I hear you didn't have such a great time
and you're off to a terrible start
this season
with an earned run average of 12.12 per game
having given up 26 hits and 11 walks
in your first 16 innings
which is a hell of a shame
because when you're not doing well
the reporters don't like to talk to you so much
and when they don't talk to you I don't find out what you say

It could be when you're going this lousy
you don't say much anyway
I wouldn't blame you
but don't worry
the season's still young
I know you're not
I don't mean I know you're not young
I mean I know you're not worrying
because as you've said many times
for example after Tony Perez hit that painful home run off you in the Series
you'll still be alive tomorrow
barring a traffic accident
or cardiac arrest

You are of a philosophical cast of mind I know
even though you are a little temperamental those two traits can exist side by side
I mean I have seen you stomping around in the dugout
and screaming at umpires as though you wanted to kill them
but I also know you've read a lot of serious books and have many interesting thoughts

such as about whether intelligent life exists on other planets
and about Pyramid Power, of which you are a devotee
and about the Bermuda Triangle, which when you told him about it Bernie
Carbo thought you were talking about pussy, and told his gorilla so,
and also about ginseng, which you use before you pitch
the way Popeye uses spinach
before he saves Olive Oyl by punching out Bluto, and of which you are thus an exponent,
and about Eastern Religions too
after many years of inquiry into which
you've concluded that techniques of wacked-out meditation
can be applied in the practical field
a baseball field say
so that for instance in your best example
a Tibetan priest could make a baseball disappear
and then materialize again down the line in the catcher's mitt

"*There*," you say, describing it,
"is my idea of a relief pitcher"

You're telling the truth, as usual
and as usual all the writers are
cackling like you were doing standup comedy

You're also telling the truth when you say that people don't generally realize how hard you
        really work
How for instance you're always one of the first guys to get out to the park
How you help set up the batting cage
How you shag fly balls and run a couple of miles every day
and how you actually work on catching ground balls behind your back
because you have this theory that because of your exaggerated follow-through
you have to

Remember the time you tried your theory out on the late Don Hoak?

It was in 1968 at Winston-Salem in the Carolina League
You were a cocky punk just out of USC
You gloved a ball one handed behind your back
That play started a game ending twin killing
and it also made Don Hoak, then your manager
want to kill you
Hoak chased you all the way to the bus screaming his head off
and when you got on
he stayed outside, yelling at you and pounding on the window

This is your life, Bill Lee, was not what he was saying

Don Hoak never understood you, Spaceman
It wasn't in the stars
Don's nose was just too hard, I reckon
He couldn't conceive of people like you and Hans Arp
who hurl the truth into the bourgeois face of language

People like Reggie Smith and Pudge Fisk
will never understand you either
because you tell it like you see it

You told it like you saw it that time with Ellie Rodriguez
and lost a few teeth for it
but what are a few teeth in the face of the truth?
You tell it like you see it in Spaceman Language like your spiritual grandfather Picabia
even when it gets you into hot water
like it did last summer when you shot off your mouth
about how you thought Busing was a pretty good idea
and about how you thought the Boston fans
who disagreed with you were bigots with no guts

Those contentions were sensible enough I grant you
and I happen to agree with them
but then it's easy for me, I don't have to pitch in Boston
and you do and did
and it wasn't easy last summer
for although you were in the midst of a fine season
the populace was growing weary
of your smart remarks, your blooper pitches
and behind the back catches. Tibet
and Pyramid Power never did
interest Sox fans much, so that when
on May 20 you shut out the A's
with a quasi-spectacular one-hitter
no one seemed to notice,
the response was merely polite,
no one seemed to understand how well
you were pitching, how no lefthander
to put on a Red Sox suit
since Mel Parnell
or even just possibly
the legendary Robert Moses "Lefty" Grove

had pitched quite as effectively
and consistently
as you were doing;
it was as though everybody was just waiting for you
to fuck up.
And you kept on
not fucking up.

On July 27 your unique sinker was never better
than in a 1-0 masterpiece over Catfish Hunter,
the breathtaking parabola of your blooper ball
never more tantalizing or bizarrely elongated.
But still you were not approved of
as you would have been had you not been
funny in the head. You began to speak
curiously after victories.
On August 9 you beat the A's again
and afterwards said they looked
"emotionally mediocre, like
Gates Brown sleeping on a rug."
What did you mean by that?
On August 24 you beat the White Sox 6-1
in a downpour at Fenway. It was one
of your greatest days. At one point you fielded
a ground ball behind your back by sticking
your glove up over your left shoulder,
spearing the ball, and from a sitting position
starting a double play that ended up with
you lying flat on your back in front of the mound.
Still, when it was over, you sensed the contempt
of the writers and fans. They loved you
but they did not love you. "When I'm through,"
you said, "I'll end up face down in the Charles
River." Spaceman, why did you say that?

That was your seventeenth victory
the third year in a row you'd won 17 games
and this time it looked like
you had a good shot at 20 or
better. Little did you know you'd go
through the playoffs, the Series, the winter
and the first two months of a new season
still looking for that next victory. Or

did you know, and is
that what you meant about the Charles River?

You had arm trouble, sure. Then Johnson
kept you out of the playoffs even though
you'd beat the A's twice and called them
emotionally mediocre earlier. In the Series
you pitched well in the second game
but Drago lost it in the ninth. After
the infamous Fisk/Armbrister non-obstruction dispute
in Game Three you said that if you'd
got to ump Larry Barnett you'd have "Van
Goghed" him. You meant you'd have chewed
his ear off? Johnson scheduled you
to start Game Six. "It's not often a
mediocre pitcher gets to start in the
sixth game of a World Series," you said.
(You turned out to be right.) When someone
in the gang of writers asked you if this
was the biggest game you'd ever been asked
to pitch, you said, Nope, this is nothing
compared to the 1968 College World Series.
"That was real baseball," you said. "We
weren't playing for the money. We got
Mickey Mouse watches that ran backwards."
And then when someone else asked what you'd
do if you won and forced the Series into
a seventh game, you said you'd declare an
automatic 48 hours of darkness so Tiant
could get another day's rest. "That's what Zeus
did when he raped Europa," you said.
"He asked the sun god, Apollo, to stay
away for a few days."

               The next
three days, it rained. Apollo, perhaps
hearing your words on a Tibetan wavelength,
split, and not only did Zeus favor you
by washing out the sixth game, which was set
back from Saturday to Tuesday—he ordained
Tiant to pitch it. And you were pissed
off with Zeus and with Darrell Johnson. You sulked.
But when Carbo's pinch homer tied it

in the 8th, I saw you climb up on the rim
of the dugout and wave out toward the left field
wall, where Carbo's ball had gone,
urging your teammates on. Four innings
later, Pudge Fisk's homer over the same wall
won it for Boston, and you danced in the
dugout with the other Sox,
happy as in Frank Lima's perfect phrase
a bunch of fags in Boystown.

                              That left
the seventh game up to you. You pitched
your ass off, serious for once, and took
a 3-0 lead into the 6th, but then Pete Rose
busted up a double play by banging into Burleson
and up came Tony Perez. I know you hate
me to mention what happened next but it's
a part of the story, Spaceman. You tried to
float your blooper pitch past The Dog
for the second time in one night. That was
once too often, like Tony said later.
You thought you could do it;
you were gambling; that's why
they call you Spaceman. They call
Perez The Dog because he persists. "I saw
him all the way," he said later; "I was
ready for it." Boom/The ball
disappeared into the screen. Two runs. An
inning later you came out with a blister
and a one run lead that was gone by
the time you hit the showers. So much for
Tom Yawkey's World Series Dream. You
sat in the locker room with your head down
amidst your sad teammates later. "I just
went out there and did my job," you said,
in your disappointment using the cliché for once.
"I went out there and threw the shit out
of the ball." The blooper ball you threw
Perez? "Hell, I live by that pitch
and I'll die for it," you said half-
tragically. This time nobody laughed.

And then you left for China.

VAN LINGLE MUNGO

Dave Frishberg

The minotaur was on second base.
The lower part wanted to steal but the rest seemed to hesitate.
The reliever was still wet from the sea...

"When I think of a stadium,
it's like a temple," Lefebvre said. "It's religious. Sometimes I'd go into
Dodger Stadium just to be alone. The game might start at 8 and I'd get there
at 1 and sit in the stands and look at the field. It was that beautiful. No one
would be there—only the birds chirping. And I'd see the sky and the grass.
What a feeling!"

Baseball Mandala © 1987 by Tom Blaess

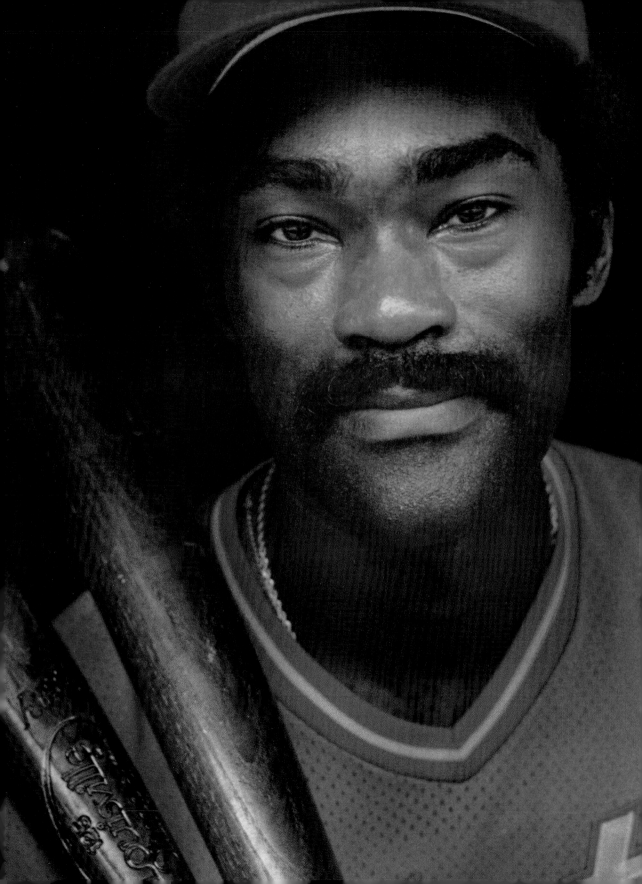

Babe in the Manger © 1990 by Mikhail Horowitz

◀ *Photograph of George Foster © 1990 by John Weiss*

vic power

CLEVELAND INDIANS
FIRST BASE-THIRD BASE

don rudolph

CHICAGO WHITE SOX
PITCHER

WALLY MOON
Outfield

Los Angeles
Dodgers

3rd BASE
REDS

RAY
KNIGHT

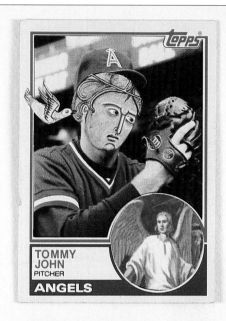

TOMMY JOHN
PITCHER
ANGELS

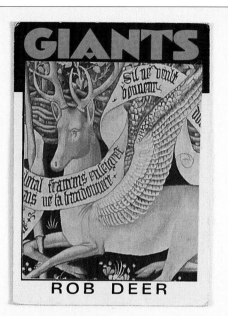

GIANTS

ROB DEER

PHILLIES

OZZIE VIRGIL

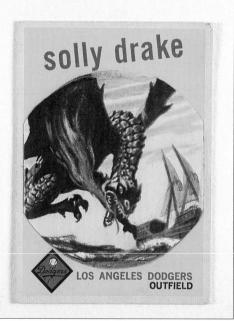

solly drake

LOS ANGELES DODGERS
OUTFIELD

B A S E B A L L   T A R O T   C A R D S

© 1990 by Mikhail Horowitz

Painting of Mark Fydrich © 1987 by Tom Clark

*"I longed to hit as a starving man longs for food.
The ball coming towards me was a rabbit, and I was a wolf waiting to
devour it. I attacked a baseball as though it were no longer a question of
hitting it but crushing it totally."*

—Sadaharu Oh

Photograph of Mike Schmidt © 1990 by John Weiss

*he aisles are jammed, the place is
on its feet, the wrappers, the programs, the
Coke cups and peanut shells, the detritus
of an afternoon; the anxieties, the things
to have done tomorrow, the regrets about
yesterday, the accumulation of summer:
all forgotten, while hope, the anchor,
bites and takes hold where a moment
before it seemed we would be swept out
with the tide.*

You can always spot them, even from high up,
the brown bulged out trying to make a circle
of a square, the green square inside the brown,
inside the green the brown circle you know is mound
and the big outside green rounded off by a round line
you know is a fence. And no one is playing.

K E E P   Y O U R   E Y E   O N   T H E   B A L L

Painting © 1987 by Tom Blaess

TED WILLIAMS

Painting © 1987 by Tom Clark

*The function of
professional baseball
is: circus. Its effect was to
divert people from their natural
inclination to think about
their lot, and to keep them
from getting restless. It was*

Photograph of Pete Rose © 1990 by John Weiss

Photograph of Phillies' mascot © 1990 by John Weiss

*an opiate. It gave people room
in which to tolerate intolerable
circumstances. For a good
radical, it was a joy
of childhood . . .*

HORSESHIT: *Universal term of disparagement in baseball*

Earthquake ticket, SF World Series, 1989

Spring Training, photograph © 1990 by John Weiss

Painting © 1987 by Tom Clark

Will Clark photograph © 1990 by Michael Zagaris

The game begins in the spring, *when everything else begins again, and it blossoms in the summer, filling the afternoons and evenings, and then as soon as the chill rains come, it stops and leaves you to face the fall alone. You count on it, rely on it to buffer the passage of time, to keep the memory of sunshine and high skies alive . . .*

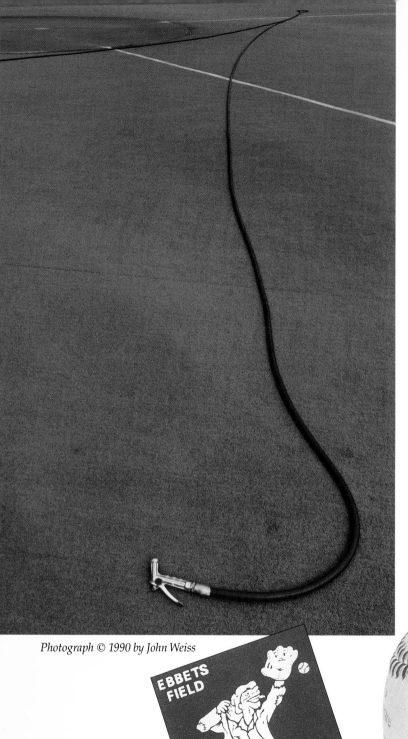

Photograph © 1990 by John Weiss

In contrast
to the grubby stands,
*the playing field of
Sportsman's Park was
pristine. Phosphorescent
white lines marked off the
diamond; the major league
dirt of the infield looked
like pure ground cinnamon.
And the grass! William
Wordsworth never trod
a meadow beside Lake
Windermere so unashamedly
green as the outfield of
Sportsman's Park.*

◆

EBBETS
FIELD

Dodger Pennant courtesy Bob Stricker

Baseball cards from the collection of Roy Jarmann

I saw the best bats of my generation destroy'd by spitballs
curving elliptically plateward, dragging themselves thru
the Little Leagues at dawn, looking for an angry hit;
Ruthian sluggers staggering on stadium roofs illuminated,
rounding incredible bags & coming home;

◆

BILL LEE

S P A C E M A N

*"You
are the ball and the ball is you.
It can do you no harm. A common bond forms
between you and this white sphere,
a bond based on mutual trust."*

THIRD BASE:

THE

MYTH

THE GREAT DYNASTIES OF THE WORLD

Thom Ross

2680 B.C.	Egypt	IVth Dynasty. Khufu (Cheops), Khafre, Menkure. Age of the Great Pyramids.
2000 B.C.	Egypt	XIIth Dynasty. The Middle Kingdom.
1523 B.C.	China	Shang Dynasty. First documented in Chinese history.
1570 B.C.	Egypt	XVIIIth Dynasty. Amenhotep, Thutmose II, Amenhotep IV (Ikhnaton), Tut-ankh-amen. New Kingdom begins.
1342 B.C.	Egypt	XIXth Dynasty. Harmhab, Ramses II, Merneptah.
1200 B.C.	Egypt	Ramses III. New Kingdom declines.
1027 B.C.	China	Chou Dynasty. Confucius, Lao-Tze, Mencius.
221 B.C.	China	Ch'in Dynasty. The Great Wall of China.
202 B.C.–220 A.D.	China	Han Dynasty. China's Imperial Age.
960–1279	China	Sung Dynasty. Gunpowder first used for military purposes. Jenghiz Khan.
1260–1368	China	Yuan Dynasty. Kublai Khan; visited by Marco Polo.
1368–1644	China	Ming Dynasty.
1949–1953	U.S.	New York Yankees. Casey Stengel, Joe DiMaggio, Mickey Mantle, Yogi Berra. Win 5 consecutive World Championships.

BASEBALL

Gilbert Sorrentino

Keep your eye everlastingly on the ball while it is in play.
—Complete Official Rules: General Instructions to
Umpires, 9.00

Baseball is a pure game of continual action, which latter is not to be confused with movement, such as is displayed in football, basketball, hockey, etc. Since this action is often subtle, many think of the game as boring, or slow. So be it.

The game changes totally, and often invisibly, between each pitch.

Everything is gleaming space in baseball. One can *see* what happened.

Baseball games end in their own terms, they do not end because a clock runs out: one thus sees that anything can happen up until the time that last out is made. In football, if one team is four touchdowns behind with ten seconds to play, the football game is *over*, truly, although officially it is not. The players continue their movement, running out the clock in meaningless activity. Invented time imposes itself on the game and affects its patterns. Yet in baseball it is not at all rare to see teams tie and win games with two out in the ninth inning. Time has neither power nor meaning in this game. It works spatially: it is not "fair." No matter how good the pitcher has been, he must get the last out. His beautiful effort can be destroyed by a single mistake. In time games, the rules themselves often win for a team. The pitcher must pitch, in space, to each batter. What he *has done* has no effect on the batter he must face next. The eight men who assist him can only assist him after the ball is released.

It is the ball that controls the game.

Under its brilliantly simple surface, baseball is deeply complex, although this complexity is not arcane. The spectator can understand what happens on every play. There are no secret or bunched patterns. There is too much space between the players to hide anything.

The ball is pitched: something happens. The ball is hit: something happens. The detail is linear. Baseball is reading or painting, not film; it is strangely and elegantly still. The patterns change continually: a man on first with an 0 and 2 count on the batter is not the same thing as that man on first with a 3 and 2 count on the batter. The rests in the game seethe with potential action. The ball must be dealt with scrupulously: it must be played, not interfered with, nor blocked, nor intercepted, nor stolen, nor recovered, nor rebounded. The offensive or defensive player who addresses his skills to the ball in motion may not be tampered with by a player of the opposing team. It is this inevitable quality of the interaction of player and ball that may give the game its strange and calm magic.

It is a spare game of nouns and verbs, without the fussy adjectives of time games. Football, for instance, proffers dozens of plays in which the ball (which almost exists as an afterthought in the brutality of the professional game) moves not an inch, while 22 men smash and injure each other in the most fantastic and unintelligible patterns of mayhem. Time games are replete with penalties in order to control actions whose counterparts in baseball would be called "bush." It is a noble game: its players play against the ball.

It is not truly a game of specialists. Players substituted for are out of the game for its remainder. It is unsentimental.

Played within one rigidly prescribed area, which, in turn, is set within a large area whose boundaries vary astoundingly from park to park, this "carelessness" has given the game marvels of style. Baseball takes place not only where the players are, but where they are not: it takes place where the ball is.

It exists outside of time.

DOCK ELLIS: IN THE COUNTRY OF BASEBALL

Donald Hall with Dock Ellis

Baseball is a country all to itself. It is an old country, like Ruritania, northwest of Bohemia and its seacoast. Steam locomotives puff across trestles and through tunnels. It is a wrong-end-of-the-telescope country, like the landscape people build for model trains, miniature in distance and old age. The citizens wear baggy pinstripes, knickers, and caps. Seasons and teams shift, blur into each other, change radically or appear to change, and restore themselves to old ways again. Citizens retire to farms in the country of baseball, smoke cigars and reminisce, and all at once they are young players again, lean and intense, running the base paths with filed spikes.

Or they stay in the city, in the capital of the country of baseball. At the mouth of the river, in the city of baseball, young black men wear purple leather maxicoats when they leave the ballpark. Slick dressers of the twenties part their hair in the middle and drive roadsters. In old *barrios* everyone speaks Spanish. Kids playing stickball and kids running away from cops change into fierce adults rounding third base in front of fifty thousand people, and change again into old men in their undershirts on front stoops.

Though the grass transforms itself into a plastic rug, though the players speak Arkansas or Japanese, though the radio adds itself to the newspaper, and the television to the radio, though salaries grow from workingmen's wages to lawyers' compensations, the country remains the same; everything changes, and everything stays the same.

The players are white and black, Cuban and Welsh and Mississippi farmers. The country of baseball is polyglot. They wear great mustaches and swing bottle-shaped bats, and some of them dress eccentrically. John McGraw's Giants play two World Series wearing black uniforms. Now the citizens' hair shortens, their loose uniforms turn white, their faces turn white also, and the white world cheers—while on the other side of town, black crowds cheer black ballplayers. Now the hair returns—beards, handlebar mustaches, long locks hanging beside the catcher's mask; now brightly colored knickers cling close to thick legs; now bats are scooped out at the thick end; now black and white play together again.

In the country of baseball the magistrates are austere and plainspoken. Many of its citizens are decent and law-abiding, obedient to their elders and to the rules of the community.

But there have always been others—the mavericks, the eccentrics, the citizens of independent mind. They thrive in the country of baseball. Some of them display with Lucifer the motto, "I will not serve." Some of them are known as flakes, and unless they are especially talented bounce from club to club, to retire from the active life sooner than the others. Left-handed pitchers are reputed to be craziest of all, followed by pitchers in general, and left-handers in general. Maybe forty percent of the population in the country of baseball is flaky, at least in the opinion of the other sixty percent.

When Al Hrabosky meditates hate, in his public solitude behind the St. Louis mound, he perpetuates a great tradition.

The country of baseball begins to take shape at the age of six. Earlier, sometimes. Dock Ellis's cousin gave him a baseball to hold when Dock was in his crib. But Little League starts at six and stickball and cowpastureball at about the same age. At seven and eight and nine, the players begin to reside wholly in the country of baseball. For the people who will live there forever, the long summers take on form—time and space shaped by the sharp lozenge of the base paths. Then high school; maybe college, maybe rookie league, Class A, Double A, Triple A—the major leagues. In the brief season of maturity, the citizens of this country live in hotels, watch movies, pick up women who lurk for them in lobbies, sign autographs for kids, and climb onto the team bus for the ride to the ballpark at five in the afternoon.

In their brief season, they sit for a thousand afternoons in front of their lockers, pull on archaic stockings, set their knickers at the height they affect, and josh and tease their teammates. Tony the trainer measures a tender elbow, tapes an ankle. Then the citizens saunter without urgency onto the field, gloves under arms, and pick up a ball.

Richie Hebner sees Richie Zisk. "Hey," he says, "want to play catch?"

Baseball, they tell us, is part of the entertainment industry.

Well, money changes hands; lawyers make big money; television people and their sponsors make big money. Even the citizens make big money for a while. But like actors and magicians and country singers and poets and ballet dancers, when the citizens claim to be in it for the money, they are only trying to be normal Americans. Nothing is further from the country of baseball than the business life. Although salaries grow and contract clauses multiply, the business of baseball like the business of art is dream.

In the cardboard box business, a boss's expectations rise like a plateau gradually elevated, an infinite ramp leading to retirement on the ghost plains of Arizona. And in the country of cardboard boxes, the manners of Rotary proliferate: the false laughter, the bonhomie of contracts, the golf played with boss's boss. Few flakes survive in the country of cardboard boxes.

But in the country of baseball, men rise to glory in their twenties and their early thirties—a garland briefer than a girl's, or at least briefer than a young woman's—with an abrupt rise, like scaling a cliff, and then the long meadow slopes downward. Citizens of the country of baseball retire and yet they never retire. At first it may seem that they lose everything—the attention of crowds, the bustle of airplanes and hotels, the kids and the girls—but as they wake from their first shock, they discover that they live in the same place, but that they live in continual twilight, paler and fainter than the noon of games.

Dock visits an old friend, Alvin O'Neal McBean, retired to his home in the Virgin Islands. In the major leagues, McBean was *bad*. The language of Rotary does not flourish in locker rooms or dugouts; the citizens' speech does not resemble the honey-tongued *Reader's Digest*; eccentricity breeds with outrage. "McBean would as soon curse you as look at you," Dock says—even if you were his manager or his general manager; and he could *scream*. He was therefore not long for the major leagues. Now Alvin O'Neal McBean supervises playgrounds, the old ballplayer teaching the kids old tricks, far from reporters, umpires, and Cadillacs. "He's made the Adjustment," says Dock. "He doesn't *like* it, but he's made the Adjustment."

The years on the diamond are fantasy. The citizens *know* they live in fantasy, that the custom cars and the stewardesses and the two-inch-thick steaks belong to the world of glass slippers and golden coaches drawn by unicorns. Their fathers were farmers and one day they will be farmers also. Or their fathers loaded crates on boxcars for a hundred dollars a week and one day they too will load crates on boxcars for a hundred dollars a week. Just now, they are pulling down two thousand.

But for them, the fantasy does not end like waking from a dream or like a transformation on the stroke of midnight. They make the Adjustment, and gradually they understand that even at a hundred dollars a week, or even on top of a tractor, they live in a crepuscular duplicate of their old country.

And most of them, whatever they thought, never do just what their fathers did. When they make the Adjustment, they sell insurance or real estate to their former fans, or they open a bar in the Missouri town they came from. They buy a restaurant next to a bowling alley in their old Oakland neighborhood, and they turn paunchy, and tilt a chair back behind the cash register, remembering—while they compute insurance, while they pull draft beer—the afternoons of August and the cold September nights under the blue lights, the pennant race at the end of the dying season.

The country of baseball never wholly vanishes for anyone once a citizen of that country.

On porches in the country of baseball old men are talking. Scouts, coaches, managers; car salesmen, manufacturers' representatives, bartenders. No one would let them exile themselves from that country if they wanted to. For the kids with their skateboards, for the men at the Elks, they remain figures of youth and indolent energy, alert at the plate while the pitcher fidgets at the mound—a young body always glimpsed like a shadow within the heavy shape of the old body.

The old first baseman, making the final out of the inning, in the last year he will play, underhands the ball casually toward the mound, as he has done ten thousand times. The ball bounces over the lip of the grass, climbs the crushed red brick of the mound for a foot or two, and then rolls back until it catches in the green verge. The ball has done this ten thousand times.

Basketball is not a country. It's a show, a circus, a miracle continually demonstrating the Newtonian heresy that muscle is lighter than air, bodies suspended like photographs of bodies, the ball turning at right angles. When the game is over, basketball does not continue; basketball waits poised and immobile in the locked equipment room, like the mechanical toy waiting for a hand to wind it.

Football is not a country. It's a psychodrama, brothers beating up on brothers, murderous, bitter, tender, homosexual, ending with the incest of brotherly love, and in the wounds Americans carry all over their bodies. When the game is done, football dragasses itself to a bar and drinks blended whiskey, maybe seven and seven, brooding, its mouth sour, turned down, its belly flowing over its angry belt.

In the country of baseball days are always the same.

The pitchers hit. Bunting, slapping weakly at fat pitches, hitting line drives that collapse in front of the pitching machine, they tease each other. Ken Brett, with the fireplug body, lifts one over the center-field fence, as the big hitters emerge from the dugout for the honest BP. "Did you see *that?*" he asks Wilver Stargell. "Did you see *that?*" he asks Al Oliver.

The pitcher who won the ballgame last night lifts fungoes to a crowd in left field—outfielders, utility infielders, even pitchers who pause to shag flies in the midst of running. When they catch a ball, they throw it back to the infield by stages, lazy arcs linking outfielders to young relief pitchers to coaches. Everyone is light and goofy, hitting fungoes or shagging flies or relaying the ball. Everyone is relaxed and slightly self-conscious, repeating the motions that became rote before they were ten. Some citizens make catches behind their backs, or throw the ball from between their legs. Behind the mound, where a coach begins to throw BP to the regulars, Paul Popovich and Bob Moose pick up loose baseballs rolled toward the mound, and stack them in the basket where the BP pitcher retrieves three at a time. Now they bounce baseballs on the cement-hard turf, dribbling them like basketballs. Moose dribbles, fakes left, darts right, jumps, and over Popovich's jumping body sinks a baseball in a wire basket for a quick two points.

Coaches slap grounders to infielders, two deep at every position. Third, short, second, first, a bunt for the catcher. The ball snarls around the horn. Third, short, second, first, catcher. At the same time, the rubber arm of the BP pitcher stretches toward the plate, where Bob Robertson takes his turn at bat. Two balls at once bounce toward Rennie Stennett at second. A rookie up from Charleston takes his cuts, and a shortstop jabs at a grounder from Bob Skinner, and Manny Sanguillen leaps to capture a bunt, and the ball hums across the infield, and Willie Stargell lofts an immense fly to center field. Behind the cage, Bill Robinson yells at Stargell, "Buggy-whipping, man! Buggy-whipping!"

Stargell looks up while the pitcher loads himself with balls, and sees that Joe Garagiola is watching him. Tonight is Monday night. "Hey, man," he says slowly. "What are the rules of this bubble-gum contest?" He whips his bat forward, takes a cut, tops the ball, grimaces. Willie has two fractured ribs from a ball thrown by a forty-one-year-old Philadelphia relief pitcher. Philadelphia is trying to catch Pittsburgh and lead the Eastern Division.

"What rules?" says Garagiola. "I don't have them with me."

Willie whips his bat forward with accelerating force. "How many pieces?" He hits a line drive off the right-field wall.

Garagiola shrugs. "Four or five," he says. "Something like that." He laughs, his laugh a little forced, as if he felt suddenly foolish. "Got to have a little fun in this game."

Nearer to game time, with the pitchers running in the outfield, the screens gone from the infield, five Pirates are playing pepper between the dugout and the first-base line. Dave Giusti holds the bat, and fielding are Ramon Hernandez, John Morlan, and Daryl Patterson. Giusti hits miniature line drives back at the other relief pitchers. Everyone laughs, taunts, teases. Giusti hits one harder than usual at Hernandez. Another. The ambidextrous Puerto Rican—who tried pitching with both arms in the same inning until they stopped him; who pitches from the left side now, and strikes out the left-handed pinch hitter in the ninth inning—Ramon drops his glove, picks up a baseball in each hand, winds up both arms as he faces Giusti head on, and fires two baseballs simultaneously. Giusti swings laughing and misses them both.

In the outfield, big number seventeen lopes with long strides, then idles talking to fans near the bull pen for ten minutes, then fields grounders at second base, says something to make Willie Stargell laugh, and walks toward the dugout. Seeing Manny Sanguillen talk with Dave Concepcion and Pedro Borbon, soft Spanish fraternization with the enemy, he throws a baseball medium fast to hit Manny in the flesh of his thigh. Manny jumps, looks around, sees who it is, laughs, and runs with gentle menace toward him. But Dock has turned his back, and leans on his folded arms at the top of the dugout, scanning the crowd for friends and for ladies, his high ass angled up like a dragster, his big handsome head solemnly swiveling over the box seats—bad Dock Ellis, black, famous for his big mouth, suspended in 1975 for a month without pay, the suspension rescinded and pay restored, Dock, famous for his Bad Attitude, maverick citizen in the country of baseball.

At Old Timer's Day in Cincinnati, Edd Roush is an honorary captain, who hit .325 in the Federal League in 1914, .354 in the National League in 1921, and played eighteen years. Lou Boudreau plays shortstop. His gut is huge, but he breaks quickly to his left and scoops a grounder from the bat of Pee Wee Reese, and throws to Mickey Vernon at first. I saw Lou Boudreau, player-manager for Cleveland, hit two fly balls into the left-field screen at Fenway Park in the one-game American League pennant playoff in 1948. I discovered Pee Wee Reese eight years earlier, when I was twelve and the soft voice of Red Barber on WOR chatted about the new shortstop up from the Louisville Colonels. Joe Nuxhall pitches, who pitched in the major leagues when he was fifteen years old, and still pitches batting practice for the Cincinnati Reds. And Carl Erskine pitches, and Harvey Haddix. Harvey Kuenn comes to the plate, and then Dixie Walker—who played right field for the Brooklyn Dodgers, and confessed to Mr. Rickey in the spring of 1947 that he could not play with a black man. Dixie Walker flies out to a citizen who retired last year, still limber as a squirrel, playing center field again—Willie Mays.

In the country of baseball, time is the air we breathe, and the wind swirls us backward and forward, until we seem so reckoned in time and seasons that all time and all seasons become the same. Ted Williams goes fishing, never to return to the ballpark, and falls asleep at night in the Maine summers listening to the Red Sox on radio from Fenway Park; and a ghostly Ted Williams continues to play the left-field wall, and his flat swing meets the ball in 1939, in 1948, in 1960. In the country of baseball the bat swings in its level swoop, the ball arcs upward into the twilight, the center fielder gathers himself beneath it, and *Dixie Walker flies out to Willie Mays.*

THE TEMPLE OF BASEBALL

Lowell Cohn

Jim Lefebvre, batting coach for the San Francisco Giants, is not a man you'd accuse of being a poet. He played his entire major-league career for the Dodgers, was Rookie of the Year in 1965, once hit twenty-four home runs in a season, was part of the Dodgers' all-switch-hitting infield, played five years in Japan, has a square jaw and rough-hewn good looks, and once decked Dodger manager Tom Lasorda.

You expect a lot of things from Lefebvre. You just don't expect him to resort to poetry. But that's exactly what he did last week in the deserted dugout at Phoenix Stadium. He was a John Keats in baseball togs.

Lefebvre was telling a writer about the function of spring training, the usual rededication stuff, when all of a sudden he was *overcome.* That's the only word for it.

"When I think of a stadium, it's like a temple," Lefebvre said. "It's religious. Sometimes I'd go into Dodger Stadium just to be alone. The game might start at eight and I'd get there at one and sit in the stands and look at the field. It was that beautiful. No one would be there—only the birds chirping. And I'd see the sky and the grass. What a feeling!

"After a while, things began to happen. The vendors would come in slowly. The place was beginning to come alive. It was like it had a heart and it was beating slowly, softly—*Boom, boom.*" (As he said this, Lefebvre began to pump his right hand—open, shut, open, shut—like a man preparing to give blood.)

"The fans started to arrive. The lights went on. *Boom, boom.*" (Open, shut, open, shut.) "The visiting team arrived. You could see them in their dugout and you'd look at them. *Boom. boom.* And the game was getting closer. And the heart was beating faster." (Open, shut, open, shut.) "And the game started. BOOM, BOOM! It was loud now, crashing, beating wildly." (He was squeezing so fast the veins popped out in his arm.)

"And then it was over. Just like that. The vendors left. The visiting team was gone. The heart stopped.

"I think a baseball field must be the most beautiful thing in the world. It's so honest and precise. And we play on it. Every star gets humbled. Every mediocre player has a great moment.

"The field is beautiful in spring. I smell the grass again and remember how I loved the smell, the way it came into my nostrils and filled me up."

"Did artificial turf change that?" the writer asked.

"Artificial turf was a desecration," Lefebvre said. "It violated the temple."

"Which stadium is the most special?" the writer asked.

"Yankee Stadium," he said. "I was a Yankee fan until the day I signed with the Dodgers. I had always dreamed of playing there, but I was never in it until . . . " (Lefebvre paused, did a quick calculation.) "It was the World Series, just after Junior (Gilliam) died, 1978."

"What was it like when you were finally in Yankee Stadium?" the writer asked.

"I went in there and I almost cried," Lefebvre said. "It was very moving. My God, Ruth played there and Gehrig. They were heroes and they hit in the same box, ran the same bases. They left their spirits there. I know it."

Lefebvre paused, looked at the writer and blushed. He had been caught with his sensibility down.

"I hope I made myself clear," he said shyly. "I've never said those things before. I didn't know they were in me."

PROSE 43

Michael Palmer

The minotaur was on second base. The
lower part wanted to steal but the rest
seemed to hesitate. The reliever was
still wet from the sea; he was trying
to hold it together with a string
stretched from his right foot sixty
feet and six inches to the plate. His
receiver waited there on one knee with
his left arm extended and the gloved
hand raised. But his eyes kept shifting
from the string to the runner on second,
half bull and half man, and back again.
After a while he asked for time out and
headed toward the mound.

QABALISTIC SEX* MAGICK FOR SHORTSTOPS AND SECOND BASEMEN

Rob Brezsny

As a child I was a boy but I thought I was a girl too. I thought I was the two of us, growing up together, taking turns creating each other. The night was my dream of her and the day was her dream of me. We used the same baby, shared the eros of a single zygote, split apart so that one was miasma and the other prophecy, one mammal and the other archetype, one beast and the other angel.

I suffered as the boy in the body. Day was shadow, my time apart from her. At night I celebrated dissolution, ritually offering sacrifice to our reunion. Before falling to sleep I gave her my orgasms, the day's accumulated psychic energy—blankets pulled over my face and kleenex stuffed in my ears to shut out all sensations from the outside world, a ring of stuffed animals encircling the bed and sealing the sanctified space.

My guardian and guide into dreams was a big totem-body borrowed from the chief of the stuffed animals, Tony the (Detroit) Tiger. Dressed in his baseball uniform, Tony lay always on my pillow directly to the left of my head. He gave way to the map of a gargantuan tiger-crocodile through which I entered my double dream-body.

In some of my more self-conscious day-dreams I resurrected my favorite map-veils from the land of sleep and built them into a buffer-body between my vulnerable flesh and the external world. I was gradually able to sneak my dream-girl into this body, so that in time we were inseparable. She came to inhabit roughly the same space as the body of flesh but jutted out a little beyond the skin. She felt like a halo, holding me in suspension and making me permanently dizzy.

I felt her but never really *saw* her during the day. She never gave me a face and figure to visualize. And at night she was too maniacal and hydra-headed ever to remain very long in one name and shape.

So I contacted and communed with her by evoking the sensation of MAP-ness. Two maps in particular came to serve as my entrance to her world, by day or by night.

The first map is the more ancient. In later years it has been radically transmuted. The second map was originally formulated to be more versatile and universal than the first map, a means to a more thorough exploration of the world of my dream-girl. But ironically, when it finally came into full use, I lost her entirely.

MAP #2

A totem of the Tiger-Crocodile Body: a porously woven gem engraved with the complete geo-anatomical image of the Baseball Diamond.

The MAP began always as an abstract insinuation. It had to be reinvoked each time it was used.

The Call was made:

A geometric ghost of Earth-light irradiated the Eye-Gland, discharging a shivering, rarefied hissing. Coiling and uncoiling like a Breather, the vibration formed a vaporous sarcoma. Dry, husky veins materialized within, diagramming the skeletal magnetic fields of disembodied WORDS.

The WORDS coagulated, began to bleed Barbarous Names, and the diagram collapsed into a sea of chthonic lights, an infernal bath roiling with the black glowing chromosomes of exfoliated homunculi.

A yeasty Vampire-King steamed forth from the multitudes and breathed an instant condensation:

The mature MAP, a docile and adamantine Diamond Germ, a brilliant Star Granulated Kernel glutted with iridescent cartoons of sacrosanct baseball games.

It was then infinitely elastic and could assume any size, according to the desired destination.

It bubbled to the size of solar system and enacted baseball myths with the planets as heroes.

It blanketed the Earth and depicted the crystal latticework of the sacred planetary anatomy.

It contracted to cellular size and portrayed baseball-idylls among the nuclear chromatins.

On June 23, 1956, I discovered the sacred world of the ancestors at a game between the Tigers and the Boston Red Sox. Until then I had practiced my magics with greedy secrecy. I had not guessed that others before me had shared the Silence and had even evolved ceremonies to enter it at will.

My father had decided to take me to my first major-league game on the occasion of my sixth birthday. We arrived at Briggs Stadium at twilight.

We entered the outer shell of the stadium and made our way towards our seats in the reserved section behind third base. When I first glimpsed the field my uncensored impulse was that I was looking at a "dream-window," a compact, rarefied area that I had often watched intrude into my dreams and suck into itself all the seemingly flimsier material around it.

In fact, I was looking at the field through a concrete doorway opening onto the grandstand. As we stepped across the threshold I was stricken with the overpowering sense of HOLY. A dome of gauzy vibration surrounded the field and bound it in a deeper, denser dimension. Inside, the pristine emerald green of the field emanated an ethereal violet haze. The players themselves were dressed in purest white. I could see shimmering shrouds of light around their bodies. They warmed up for the game with an utter self-possession that I had never before witnessed. They were standing in sacred space.

It was years later, after I had begun to investigate the occult, that I realized that the baseball field is a near-perfect analogy of the Tree of Life, the conventional meditation glyph of the Qabalah. . . .

I regard it as no coincidence that the arrangement of positions of the baseball field corresponds so closely to the alignment of the sephiroth on the Tree of Life. I now perform, with the air of the Tree of Life, some of the same imaginative exercises which I once practiced using the baseball field map. But I have not completely abandoned the original map, merely incorporated it into a very personalized version of the Tree of Life.

I probably would have become violently insane had I not received my first (disguised) initiation into the Qabalistic-Baseball System of Meditation around this time. It was my salvation. With it I began to be able to control and channel the incredible sexual exchanges for which I had become the focus.

It happened during the spring of fourth grade. I was acknowledged to be the best baseball player around, so I was called upon to manage the baseball team representing our class in a tournament against the other classes. For this special tournament, school rules required that at least three girls be included in each starting lineup. The other boys in the class thought this a stupid, emasculating rule. But I saw it as a sexual opportunity, a thrilling new element to be used in my alchemical dramas. . . .

There was no hierarchy of baseball talent among the fourth-grade girls of Sudman School, Allen Park, Michigan, in 1960, so I could without guilt choose my three favorites, the three sexiest girls in the class, Gail Musa, Patti McQueen, and Nancy Lebenta. I immediately began to include them intimately in my orgiastic presleep rituals. My dream-girl began exclusively to portray herself with their faces. As the experiments proceeded, though, Gail Musa's dark, sultry, Venusian face prevailed, dominating my fantasies and giving my dream-girl a definite and specific form she had not previously had. . . .

The erotic *Qabalistic* experiments began when I installed Gail within the nerve nexus of SECOND BASE in my baseball field map and abandoned my phantom dream-lover. It is the story of my initiation into the mysteries of NETZACH, the Qabalistic equivalent of SECOND BASE.

As central ganglion of SECOND BASE, Gail became Queen of NETZACH and received all the attendant powers, privileges, and responsibilities. She organized my training for initiation around an investigation of the terrain between SHORTSTOP and SECOND BASE.

This area I later recognized to be the Twenty-Seventh Path on the Tree of Life: Connecting NETZACH and HOD (the eighth sephirah, or SHORTSTOP) and ruled by the sixteenth card of the traditional Tarot deck, the Tower, card of the planet Mars. Within the environs of this path she aided me in learning how to regulate and control the unbalanced debilitating forces that were

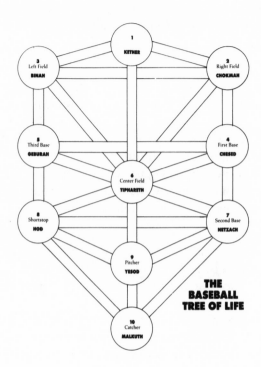

deposited in me through the Totem and Radio: the Toy Witch dimension of the baseball field map.

At the core of our work was the rite of *congressus subtilis*, or sexual union with a non-material entity. Even though Gail was at home in her own bed and I in mine, I was able to fertilize her astral body with my astral seed and conceive with her a brood of elemental children. And so together we broke down the haunting love-death of the elementals into names and forms and birthed them in our own image. Where before they had bedeviled me to the verge of criminal insanity, they now became my willing servants. With them at my command I was then formally initiated into the mysteries of NETZACH by Gail, the Queen of that sephirah.

I have been prepared for the use of Qabalistic magick since my youth. The baseball field map served as the surrogate system, building in my aura a vivid image of the archetype of the Tree of Life. In fact, baseball provided a more effective program for the work than a formal course in the Qabalah.

If astral structures are to become potent talismans, they must be nourished with the stuff of personal emotional associations. The abstruse theorems contained in the Qabalistic texts would not have roused my imagination to crystallize a miniature Tree of Life in my aura.

And would my mother have allowed the revolutionary teachings of the Qabalah to reach me had they been offered in the weird occult tongues of the Angels and Archangels? Would she have invited trance-intoxicated wizards into her house to teach her son to meditate upon the example of Aleister Crowley? Of course not. To be indoctrinated by the Great American Game was the perfect subterfuge:

BASEBALL IS THE MODEL
FOR THE GUERRILLA MEDITATION TECHNIQUES
OF MODERN AMERICAN QABALISTIC MAGICK.

The following is a description of a dream-artifact. It appeared on February 29, 1972, four hours before I boarded a plane in London to depart for New York after a six-months' stay in Europe.

I was one of the extraterrestrial guides of the planet Earth, a Martian member of the Great White Brotherhood of the Solar System come to protect and preserve the realm of the Old Gods, the beings which *homo sapiens* had displaced and banished to the secret places of the planet.

I could not actively intercede and nullify the oppressive politics of the ruling species, and so I erected a Gargantuan Bubble—a dazzling musical globe—where I took representative members of the Old Gods, like a latter-day Noah. I kept them inside in a kind of suspended animation: Until the day when the human civilization would disappear.

The elves and the dwarves, the nymphs and the fauns and the satyrs, the sylphs and undines, the griffins, the sphinxes, the centaurs, the titans, the muses . . .

From each I extracted and memorized the essential genetic information.

Eons passed. I waited for a sign.

When the Magic Baseball Game began I knew it was time for the Old Gods to be released and returned to Earth.

The little statues and idols in which they had been trapped for so long shivered and squealed. Slowly and inexorably they took their places over the vast baseball diamond spread across the inside of the great Bubble.

I strode to the pitcher's mound and checked my fielders. My beloved griffins, patina-encrusted, fidgeted near Third Base. The Great God Pan squatted behind Home Plate. A small host of sphinxes hovered over my head. At Second Base was my sultry Venusian Hetaira, Gail Musa. And at Shortstop, a winged, mercurial salamander with the face of my singer-hero David Bowie.

We began our lethal incantation, led by the strident voices of the griffins:

> Lithosphere on Fire
> Lucifer's Desire
> Lithosphere on Fire
> Lucifer's Desire . . .

And from an infinitesimal prick at the very Crown of the Bubble appeared a race of Reptile Men adorned with cartilaginous diamond crests and riding black winged horses.

I grasped the magic baseball in my right hand and raised it high over my head.

All together we bellowed the materialization of Fire. I threw the ball straight up.

As it fell it broke into a multitude of miniscule Earths. Our Reptile Men and their steeds rushed to envelop them, then with a burst of Black Fire extinguished every one.

The Old Gods blinked out, reassembled outside the Bubble, and went forth once again to populate the planet.

At the time of the dream I had not yet discovered that BASEBALL = QABALAH. But three years later, when Mercury appeared to me again in the shape of David Bowie, this time mixed with Philadelphia Phillies shortstop Larry Bowa, I finally guessed.

There were two dream-visitations in June of 1975. In each, Bowie-Bowa led me underground, as Mercury often does, through a labyrinth of shadowy rooms and halls. This was the catacombs of his immense domed vehicle, which was a kind of flying saucer with the guts of a baseball stadium. It was an appropriate home for the image-flesh that he had borrowed.

In the visitation of June 2, 1975, he led me into a dark and dank room, empty except for a television. There I watched a show exhibiting the "latest styles in Tarot-card images," which were modeled by a series of undulating boxes that resembled the 1957 baseball cards. The "modern" images were predominately weird, shimmering portraits of the players of the 1957 Detroit Tigers, my all-time favorite team—including Al Kaline, Charlie Maxwell, Frank Lary, Jim Bunning, and Harvey Kuenn.

The outlines of the faces and the shapes of the features remained relatively fixed, but the color of the skin pulsed rhythmically with iridescent greens and protoplasmic purples, and tiny phosphorescent explosions flickered from all the orifices. Clusters of eggs and wormlike jewels writhed around the boundaries of the faces, sometimes penetrated the skin and disappeared.

I thought the cards looked like little televisions themselves, and for a moment—imagining "television within a television"—I felt the familiar maddening sensation of "map of a map of a map of a . . ."

I reexperienced all the thrills I felt when I first discovered baseball cards, relived the satisfaction of studying the records and vital statistics, memorizing the faces, sorting the cards according to various systems of classification (by teams, by position, by age, by how much I liked them), and inventing card games using only my favorite cards.

Accompanying these feelings was a rush of a different kind of familiarity, emotions that also felt like memories but more compacted. I found no way to describe this to myself later except to say that the portraits on the cards reminded me of the noble faces used to illustrate the virtues in old physiognomy textbooks. The crude blank look of modern profane man was conspicuously absent.

Yet they were the same faces I had preserved so vividly in my inner eye for more than fifteen years. Center fielder Bill Tuttle still had that hazy, evasive Cancerian look (born under the sign of the Crab). Frank Lary had the fixed, bulldog jaw; though the pupils of his eyes were so contracted that he appeared to be in a trance. Duke Maas had the characteristic cleft in his chin. Reno Bertoia was the passionate, temperamental adolescent Italian. Al Kaline looked like my father as I imagined my father looked when I was born.

At the bottom of Harvey Kuenn's card was a signature—"Huysmans." It made sense if

Huysmans was the creator of these cards, I thought, since he painted medieval scenes. I was confusing and combining the decadent French author of *Against the Grain* with the modern scholar who wrote *The Waning of the Middle Ages.*

Charlie "Paw Paw" Maxwell flowed across the screen three times, the only card to appear more than once. The third time he showed I transfixed him on the screen with an act of dream-will. I wanted to examine him in detail and report back to my brother Tom. Maxwell and Tom are both left-handers and when I was young they together embodied my archetype of left-handedness. Moreover, Maxwell was Tom's favorite player, the Young-Father image equivalent to my Al Kaline.

To my surprise Maxwell's position was listed as Second Base. I had never heard of a left-hander playing Second. But then I remembered that Tom had been an All-Star Second Baseman in Little League.

I expected to find Maxwell's batting record on the back of the card. Instead there was an intricate network of red hieroglyphics splayed across a black background. A cartoon from outside the card migrated into the midst of the hieroglyphics and announced that they were the voice-print of the Star Sirius coding instructions for work on the Twenty-Eighth Path. (Between NET-ZACH and YESOD, the seventh and ninth sephiroth; a reference to the "path-workings" of the Qabalah.)

I guessed during the dream that the Charlie Maxwell card was the "modern" version of the seventeenth card of the traditional Tarot, The Star. In checking an occult reference book the next day I found that The Star card is in fact the traditional symbol for the Twenty-Eighth Path.

In the next dream-visitation, on the summer solstice of 1975, Mercury escorted me to the heart of the mysteries of Sirius. This time I did not simply observe the cards. I became a co-creator. I intruded into a previously undifferentiated region of the baseball field map-plasm and designed for it an articulate configuration of sound: a poem-talisman enclosed within the body of my own Tarot card. It gave me access to that part of the map that links the map as a whole to its prototype.

The dream began in the underworld. Bowie-Bowa took me by the hand and led me through smoky glass doors into a lightless crypt reeking of ammonia. I ran my free hand along the wall and felt a fine, damp fur. After a few cautious steps we came upon a row of gnarled sarcophagi which emitted a faint glow. They reminded me of bioluminescent worms. At the foot of the last one, a withered old black woman lay, squirming and stroking herself. She squealed out jumbled clusters of syllables as if speaking in tongues. But in listening closely, I clearly distinguished the words of the English language. In fact she was merely mimicking the standard rap of the Christian fundamentalist preachers. The fit was genuine. But it seemed more like a chemical disturbance or epileptic seizure than a divine communion.

"Through the city of black buzzing." That phrase carried us through a kind of black porous diaper composed of swarming insects. We alit on a broad phosphorescent baseball field in a perfectly flat, horizonless land oppressed by a very low black sky. The sole source of light was the ground.

A game was in progress. We watched from the vicinity of the first-base coaching box. It was the last game of the season and it didn't matter much who won. The old veteran Al Kaline was being given as many times at bat as possible since this was his last game before retiring. He was batting in both the leadoff and cleanup positions. The scoreboard gave a summary of his record thus far in the game:

	AB	R	H	RBI
Choline	5	4	1	3

or was it Chaline? Definitely "Ch" in place of "K." I thought of acetylcholine, the chemical involved in the transmission of nerve impulses.

Then the game was over and another had begun. There was an exogamous feel to this one, the sense of a match-up between two teams that rarely played each other, that were not in the same league—like my favorite teams Detroit and Philadelphia playing in spring training or the World Series.

I was playing Shortstop for Detroit. Though I am right-handed, I was wearing a left-handed glove. Kaline, the player-manager, was in center field.

Near the pitcher's mound I found a little glass head or eye, an egg-shaped marble which bore a photographic likeness of my face. As I walked towards Second Base to show it to my girlfriend, a milk-white salamander ran across my path. At first it was almost two-dimensional, no more than a thin, veined membrane. But when I gave chase and tried to catch it, it puffed up into a transparent balloonlike sac and squirted away.

I noticed that I no longer had the marble. It was now suspended like an eye at the center of the salamander-sac. I followed it as it floated towards Third Base. There, standing on the Third Base bag, was Al Kaline. He stopped me and handed me a huge, three-dimensional baseball card in the shape of a cereal box. It was similar to the cards I'd seen on television on June 2.

The name of the player on the card was BERQ QALQAS. He played for the TIBETAN GUERRILLAS. I took "guerrilla" to be a pun on "gorilla," implying that the guerrilla is a more sophisticated and glamorous beast to have as one's totem than the gorilla.

Qalqas looked much like the Reptile Men from the dream of the Old Gods. The cartilaginous diamond crest was set in a skull shaped like an elongated hoof. Face and body were as sleek as a polished gem and black except for the crest. There were no facial features except for slits around the eye area. There was a double set of scaly wings. He was seated, or perhaps attached to, a squat, black winged horse.

On the back-side of the box-card was a diagram representing a pitcher pitching to a catcher. An arrow at the end of a dotted line connected a circle, image of the pitcher's mound, with a similar circle behind an upside-down pentagram symbolizing home plate. The diagram and its caption:

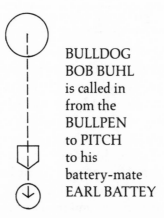

BULLDOG
BOB BUHL
is called in
from the
BULLPEN
to PITCH
to his
battery-mate
EARL BATTEY

Kaline hinted that this card could be used to perform an act of talismanic magick. And that I should "think sexy thoughts and let the astral plane spore (me) for a change." In fact, he suddenly became very funny.

Earl Battey, he said, was like "a scarab crawling from a shitty meditation."

And since "Bob Buhl 'swings both ways,' Graves (Robert Graves, author of the *The White Goddess*) wrote him into the script as the poet in the labyrinth." (Ariadne's web or Arianrhod's castle?)

And "Battey is the Salt of the Battery" (sounded like "assault and battery").

And "The Black dog
    The black bull
    As black as the pitch
    In Hecate's Eye."

In the second phase of my introduction to MAGICK, Mercury confirmed that the Tree of Life was the prototype of the Baseball field map and that together they would lead me back to MAGIC. He taught me a diabolical lesson: that I should seek the holy in the midst of the most mundane, the spiritual in the midst of the most biological, the universal in the midst of the most personal. He appeared in the dual image of Larry Bowa and David Bowie to demonstrate that I had long known him intimately but never recognized him.

Since I was a child I have believed in Shortstop as the peculiar emotional location of androgynous information. When I play Shortstop, I love to feel myself in my body—sleek, lithe, smooth, graceful, vibrating from the inside in a kind of perpetual sexual excitement. I feel like my body is as feminine as a man's body is permitted to be, yet I don't feel like a woman. I feel anomalous, supercharged, outside the game altogether and yet the focus of the action. I am aggressively confident of my defensive skill. I feel potent in my ability to field, handle, and manipulate the raw force of the batted ball. All the other players are less balanced than I, more completely consumed in one extreme or the other. They look to me as a catalyst and mediator, as the central point of equilibrium around which opposing forces circulate.

Larry Bowa is my prototypical Shortstop—a consistent defensive star since 1970 for my favorite team of later years, the Philadelphia Phillies. Small and light in comparison to his teammates (5'11", 155 pounds), he lacks brute power but is proficient in the subtler offensive skills. In the field he is impeccably accurate, agile, fleet-footed, rangy, graceful.

For years I have played with the imagination of David Bowie as androgynous extraterrestrial messenger from the stellar gods, using rock and roll as his medium. At first I elaborated the outlines of the story he had suggested with his album *Ziggy Stardust and the Spiders from Mars*. But with the appearance of *Diamond Dogs* I began to weave his myth into my own.

In the winter of 1973 I received what I regard as a direct transmission from the Dog-Star Sirius concerning the Star's envoy to Earth, Dionysus, the "Lame God of Light." The entire thirty thousand word message was delivered over a period of three weeks, during which time I remained almost continually in trance. I was not a mature medium—the result was a dense, tangled, unreadable story that I typed up and called "The Revolt of the Lame and the Last Sacred Acts." It became a potent, if weirdly formulated, talisman which steadily attracted new information concerning the link between Sirius and the Earth. In time I began to identify myself as an extraterrestrial visitor from Sirius fleshing out the inexpressible Word of Dionysus.

In *Diamond Dogs* I detected the insinuations of the same mysteries revealed in "The Revolt of the Lame . . ." Bowie at once joined my conspiracy of Sirians. I began to attribute to him the same androgynous, homunculian, transvestitic, tricksterian, agathodaimonic, and mercurian qualities which I have imagined myself to possess as extraterrestrial messenger and which I have vividly sensed while playing Shortstop. I even imagined we were in secret contact via dreams, planning and coordinating future transmissions.

Mercury revealed that he was not different from Larry Bowa and David Bowie. His body had been formed in me from the stuff of my baseball and extraterrestrial fantasies. I did not, until June of 1975, ever think of calling him by the name "Mercury," nor did I consciously invoke his aid. Nevertheless he had served as mediator between alchemical husband and alchemical wife, heaven and earth, god and human, celestial father and chthonic mother. I was able to use his peculiar state of consciousness simply by arousing the personal memories and associations which share his nature.

1) From DAATH, the silent sephira, Vision of The Conference of the First Swirlings, Assiatic Division of the Great Magic Baseball Body:

LEAGUE OF SEVERITY	*LEAGUE OF MILDNESS*	*LEAGUE OF MERCY*
Tibetan Guerrillas	Neptune Egg-Demons	Venus Whoremoans
Orgone Blue Spankings	Holy Ghost Parasites	Enochian Dream-Works
Chichen Itza Syllabaries	Dionysian Trance-	Red Bush Succubi
Zen Trans-Biogrammarians	Migrations	Sphinx Orgasms
Black Solar Heat	Samhain Maenads	Autismeros Ruptured
Rememberers	Yezidi Witch-Tricksters	Gametes
Ectoplasma Gland-	Anti-Christ Clowns	Akasha Homunculi
Mesmerizers	Lunatic Cartoons	Lesbian Clones
Quasi-Stellar Punks		

2) From the Twenty-Second Path, between Tiphareth and Geburah, Vision of the Line-Up for the Play-Off Game between the Tibetan Guerrillas and the Neptune Egg-Demons:

TIBETAN GUERRILLAS

1. Female Acid of Windows, RF
2. Prakriti Bricoleur, SS
3. Berq Qalqas, CF
4. Reptile Rodeo Man, LF
5. Nostradamus Impetigo, C
6. Chesed Guevara, 3B
7. Aqua Bilge de ma Grotesque, 2B
8. Anaerobe Blistercuffs, 1B
9. Violet Cloaca-Protein, P

NEPTUNE EGG-DEMONS

1. Microwave Beehive Star, 3B
2. Bombastic Amino, RF
3. Babylon-with-Full-Hands, 2B
4. Wild Rashy Lila, C
5. Haploid Pulsar, LF
6. Nemesis Pimpdragon, SS
7. Chloroplaste Philosophe, 1B
8. Humus Azoth, CF
9. Ark-Brute Witch-Whorl, P

Below are excerpts from a very simple sample meditation of modern Qabalistic sex-magick. It is reprinted from the pamphlet of "Qabalistic Sex-Magick for Shortstops and Second Basemen":

Imagine the diamond to be located on the Martian equator, longitude 32° West . . . Imagine yourself the naked cynocephalic Shortstop running to your left and behind Second Base for a pop-up.

Just as you are about to snare the ball in the web of your glove (which is on your left hand), imagine ramming your erect phallus into the upturned vulva of the Second Baseman, a red-haired woman crouching on all fours. Her number is 7. Her uniform is the gauzy green gown of a priestess of Isis but is pulled back from her haunches to expose her genitals . . .

THE ATHLETE

Bob Callahan

Teamwork, dedication, and a winning attitude—these are the three graces which descend on all the members of the league-leading Hibernian Hall Class "B" Softball Team.

Pagan Baseball, Cu Chulainn as the "Ump," and John Baxter, formerly of the I.R.A., champion of the Native Games, connects . . . the ball sailing over the Protestant left fielder's head where it is seized by a flight of Ravens who carry it halfway back to Erainn. O Lug, the game is over; the Irish have defeated Rowaton.

There are still ages when the old magics prevail. Some have the myths, others the rituals: put them together, the Coach is saying, and you change the imagination of the World.

He learns his Irish both at home and down at the Hibernian Hall. Old Men sitting in the corner, nursing their drafts, dream aloud of the glorious days of the Sinn Fein—the Sinn Fein, MacNeill's brilliant Gaelic League, and Connolly's green socialism—an agrarianism via Marx tailored to fit the old, abused yet still pregnant Irish soil. At no time in the last four hundred years is Ireland quite as profound as on the eve of her own revolution.

We must play Greenwich for the regional championship—Greenwich, the wealthiest Yankee community in all of this region—Greenwich will now host a gathering for the sons & daughters of the Clan na Gael.

Standing on second base, the wet winds of Long Island Sound blowing in across his face, he looks down past Johnny Long's strong right arm, and watches Oliver Cromwell come to the plate.

A low lying cloud floats in from the Sound, and three old women—Brigit, Maude Gonne, and Grace O'Malley—step out of the silver air and take their place, like the witches in Macbeth, on the green aside his brother who is holding the line down at third base.

The score is 3 to 2, Irish.

The Greenwich team has two aboard, one out, and it is the bottom of the fatal seventh.

Strike two.

Johnny Long has put Cromwell in the hole.

Now the Witches begin to mumble.
Blessed be the Holy Name of Ireland.
Blessed be the Sacred Heart of Breed.
"I am the Hag of Beare, and dream
of the rich cloth I no longer wear . . ."
Cromwell hits a scorcher down the third-base line.

His brother, perfectly positioned, pounces on the ball, the moves of a cat, and he feels it hit his own glove as he pivots over second, and throws Cromwell out at first by more than a yard and a half.

The stands erupt, the tenant farmers cheer, and the witches turn into beautiful Irish women who rush onto the field to greet him.

We had to win this one, he tells the Davis brothers. I felt it was in the air.

From **THE UNKNOWN STORY OF BASEBALL**

Richard A. Russo

I. THE JOURNEYS OF BASHO

Matsuo Kinsaku, born in Japan in 1644, changed his name to Basho and became the first great *haiku* poet. Basho was also an itinerant ballplayer, who earned his keep by putting together pickup teams of fellow journeymen and playing exhibition games against the local champions. Each fall he retreated to his modest hut in Fukagawa to spend the winter writing; each spring, he looked forward to touring the countryside again in search of new inspiration:

> Spring air,
> scent of plum—
> the Season is upon us.

In his youth, Basho was known primarily as a pitcher with deceptive speed, though he longed to be recognized as an outstanding batsman. "The essence of pitching is *wabi* [humility]," he once said, "for a pitcher is only as good as the defense behind him. But the essence of batting is *sabi* ['contented solitariness']."

Once, after a close game, a Zen student who'd lost a substantial sum betting against Basho's team angrily challenged him to explain how he could reconcile the principles of Buddhism with the practice of baseball. Basho quickly replied,

> A ball
> leaps from a bat—
> hear the sound!

In later years he lost his fastball and had to move to left field, until his legs gave out and he retired from the game. It is said that several hundred people came to Edo to watch him play his last game beside the cherry-blossomed groves of the Sensoji temple in Asakusa. The poet hurled a three-hit shutout, doubled in his first two at-bats, and then, after flying out deep to center, laid down a perfect bunt in the final inning to squeeze home the winning run.

The following spring, when asked how he was getting along now that he could no longer play ball, Basho thought for a moment, then replied,

> After a recent rain
> the grass has grown greener
> than ever before.

Despite this outward calm, he missed playing the game. Later that spring he wrote one of his most moving poems:

> Old legs—
> still yearning
> for the playing fields of Edo.

In old age, Basho's love of the game was deepened by his retirement from active play. As a spectator, he found baseball the perfect expression of *karumi*, the ideal of detachment he sought in his writing. Each game was an opportunity for the calm contemplation of profoundly felt truths. A good baseball game, he declared, was like a good poem: its movement light as "a river bubbling over a shallow bed," yet its outcome, in retrospect, "inevitable."

In 1694, as he lay dying, his disciples begged for one last poem. Basho called for rice paper and pen, and wrote these words:

> Autumn grass—
> all that's left
> of batsmen's dreams.

II. THE EYE OF THE NEEDLE

In the winter of 1844, Elias Howe arrived in Cambridge, Massachusetts, at the invitation of his friend, George Fisher. Howe had been wrestling with the idea of a mechanical sewing machine for several years, but his first designs, which imitated the movement of a human arm, had all been failures. His machine could poke a needle through cloth, but not pass it all the way through, which would require detaching it from the drive wheel—yet the needle had to pull the thread through the cloth in order to make a stitch.

Fisher knew that Howe had come to an impasse, and offered to provide whatever equipment was needed, as well as food and lodging, so that he could concentrate on the problem without any external distractions. Howe moved in with his friend in October and set up a workshop in the garage. But even under ideal working conditions, he could find no solution, and by the spring of 1845 was ready to give up.

Baseball was the rage in Cambridge that spring, the early variant now remembered as "the Massachusetts game," in which a runner could be retired by "plugging" him with a thrown ball. George Fisher was a great fan of the local Beaneaters. Seeing that Howe was slowly sinking into despair, he suggested they go to a game, hoping that taking his friend's mind off the problem of the sewing machine for one afternoon would prove refreshing.

Big John Manning was throwing for Boston that day. (His son, Jack, would later go 18-5 for the Bostons in the National Association in 1876.) The opposing club could only manage three baserunners against the underhand fireballer, who thrice struck out the side on nine pitches. "They can't touch his fastball," crowed Fisher. "They're swinging right through it." Howe, who'd never seen the game played before, was deeply moved, and even managed to forget his damned machine for a few hours.

Afterwards, Fisher wanted to bring his newly converted friend around to meet some of the Boston players, but Howe declined. The game had reached into the dark corners of his mind and stimulated unexpected memories of his childhood as a farmboy in Spencer, and many a happy afternoon of stoolball (a game in which the ball was thrown at an inverted stool, which the batter had to defend with a stick). It seemed life had been simpler then. Fretful and melancholy, Howe returned to his workshop, where he spent several fruitless hours trying to work on his machine. He couldn't concentrate; his mind was distracted, filled with images of games. He retired early, only to sleep fitfully for most of the night, until finally, near dawn, he sank into a deep slumber and had the following dream.

Manning was again on the mound—only this time, he was hurling fastballs at Howe, who sat frozen on a three-legged milk stool behind home plate. A parade of burly little men carrying baseball bats stepped up to the plate to swing at the pitches, but try as they might, they could not protect him, for each bat had a hole in it the exact width of a baseball, and Manning's fastball would unerringly find the hole and pass through the bat unimpeded. Howe awoke in a cold sweat, the dull thud of baseballs hitting their target echoing in his mind.

That morning at breakfast, he was relating his nightmare to Fisher when suddenly, picturing the strange baseball bats with holes in their ends, he burst out laughing. He'd found the answer to his problem! If his machine couldn't pull a thread through cloth, it would *push* it through—a feat he'd accomplish by putting the eye of the needle at its point instead of at its base!

Elias Howe finished his design that summer and patented the first sewing machine in September, 1846. After winning a long legal battle with Isaac Singer over patent infringement, he became a wealthy man. A devoted baseball fan, Howe donated much time and money to early efforts to organize the game, and lived long enough to see a promising young kid named Jack Manning break in with the Red Stockings on the eve of professional baseball.

III. INCIDENT IN VIENNA

Carl Jung's visit to Vienna to see Sigmund Freud in 1909 proved decisive in severing their once-close relationship. Freud had been touting the younger man as his true successor for some time, a responsibility with which Jung had grown increasingly uncomfortable.

The visit got off to a poor start on the first night, when Jung tried to discuss a dream he'd had in which he kept descending floors of an old house until finally he came upon two ancient human skulls in the deepest basement. He felt that the dream signified levels of the psyche beyond the personal, which would require substantial revision of psychoanalytic theory, but Freud immediately focused on the two skulls and kept asking what wish they represented and whose skulls they were. Finally Jung shouted, "My wife and my sister-in-law!" Freud was satisfied, unaware that his student had purposely told him what he wanted to hear. Jung only grew more depressed. Matters became worse when Freud related a dream of his own, then refused to confide the personal associations that would allow Jung to interpret it.

Both men were in foul moods. Struggling to find some neutral topic of conversation, they turned to baseball, which Freud had introduced to his student two years earlier, during their first meeting in March of 1907. (After Freud's death in 1939, Jung acknowledged in a letter to Toni Wolff that, whatever their differences, he owed a debt of gratitude to Freud for bringing into his life the two great "sciences" [*wissenschaften*] of the twentieth century: psychoanalysis and baseball.)

At first, they reminisced about the games and players they'd seen during their recent visit to the United States. But the conversation quickly became personal, when Freud boasted to the startled Jung that he could "strike him out on just three pitches." "And what makes you so confident, Herr Professor?" Jung replied sarcastically. Freud smiled and said, "I taught you how to hit."

"I knew then," Jung wrote in his memoirs fifty years later, "that Freud sought to maintain his authority over me at all costs. The end of our relationship was already foreshadowed."

The younger man warned his mentor not to persist in his foolish boast, or he would be forced to "take him deep." Freud merely turned and entered the parlor, where he drew a bat and ball from an antique wooden cabinet. The two men then walked to a nearby field.

What happened next is not clear. Neither man ever recorded the episode in writing, though both mentioned it to intimate associates. Jung told Toni Wolff that he took Freud's first pitch, in order to "see what he had," then hit a "gargantuan" home run down the left-field line. Embarrassed at his own need to show the old man up, he then purposely missed the third and final pitch to let Freud save face.

Freud's account of the episode was somewhat different. Anna Freud reported that her father once told her that he'd struck Jung out on three straight pitches, though upon questioning he'd admitted one of them was a "long foul ball." In Freud's version, he froze Jung with a fastball for a called strike, then had him way out in front of a change-up, which Jung pulled down the line for a foul strike. "A foul home run?" Anna asked. "A foul home run is a strike," her father snapped. "And he missed the third one completely."

What followed next is well documented. The two men returned home in silence. Freud put the bat and ball away in the cabinet. Then Jung perversely brought up the occult, a subject sure to irritate Freud. Suddenly they heard a creaking sound from the parlor.

"Aha!" shouted Jung. "An example of catalytic exteriorization phenomenon!"

"Bosh," replied Freud.

Jung began to feel a strange burning sensation in his chest, as if his diaphragm were made of red-hot iron. "You are mistaken, Herr Professor," he said.

Just then there was a loud report, like a pistol shot. Both men ran to the parlor. Freud opened the cabinet and they peered inside.

Freud's bat had shattered into a dozen pieces.

BOX SCORE FOR THE LITTLE BIGHORN, JUNE 25, 1876

Thom Ross

Gall   **Lt. Col. G. A. Custer**

I am writing this whole game up as a baseball novel. The end has Crazy Horse striking out the last 5 batters in relief. Seen in actual terms the game is basically historically accurate. It will be illustrated, by me, with pen and ink drawings of the cavalry men and indians dressed as if for war yet carrying bats and gloves in place of clubs and rifles, baseballs instead of bullets.

7TH CAVALRY
(UNITED STATES ARMY LEAGUE)

	AB	H	R	RBI
Reno LF	1	0	0	0
Benteen LF	3	2	0	0
Keough SS	4	1	0	0
Calhoun CF	4	1	1	0
Cooke C	3	1	0	1
Smith 3B	4	0	0	0
Yates 1B	4	0	0	0
Custer, T. RF	3	0	0	0
Reily 2B	3	0	0	0
Custer, G. P	3	1	0	0
	32	6	1	1

SIOUX/CHEYENNE
(NATIVE AMERICAN LEAGUE)

	AB	H	R	RBI
Low Dog RF	6	4	2	3
Crow King 3B	6	2	2	1
Gall 1B*	5	3	3	5
Two Moon C	5	2	2	2
Spotted Eagle CF	4	2	1	0
Rain-in-the-Face SS	4	3	2	1
Lame White Man LF	3	0	1	0
Hump 2B	5	1	1	0
Sitting Bull P	4	1	1	2
Crazy Horse P	1	1	1	2
	43	19	16	16

7th Cavalry	100 000 000	1	6 1**
Nat. Americans	101 033 35X	16	19 0

E–Custer, T.   2B–Calhoun, Cooke, Keough, Rain-in-the-Face, Gall, Sitting Bull, Low Dog, Two Moon, Crazy Horse   3B–Crow King   HR–Gall 2, Two Moon   Double Plays–7th Cav. 1, Nat. Americans 1   Left on Base–7th Cav. 5, Nat. Amer. 9

	IP	H	R	ER	BB	SO
7th Cavalry						
Custer, G. (L)	8	19	16	13	4	5
Nat. Amer.						
Sitting Bull (W)	7	6	1	1	1	7
Crazy Horse	2	0	0	0	0	5

Time—2:45   Attendance—15,683

*Gall, the Hunkpapa warrior, hit two tremendous home runs into the upper deck of the stadium, into a section used exclusively for the witnessing of the Sun Dance. He was a great first baseman who always played in front of the bag, runner or no runner on. His hair was wrapped in ermine skins and he wore a single feather, standing straight up in his hair.
**The error was Tom Custer misjudging a line drive off the bat of Crow King.

**Gall hits his first of 2 HRS
Little Big Horn River
June 15, 1876**

STELAE

John Oliver Simon

for Richard Grossinger and Bill James

There are stelae from Palenque
that are nothing but names and numbers,
range factor, ERA and triples
for Hunahpú and Hunahpú
who played the sacred game back when
you had to claw for every run
not like today. The losing manager
got disembowelled on the mound
by the knife of the morning star.

I grow older, hombres, or the children
striding to the plate grow young.
At 41 I played in Xalatlaco,
place-name meaning, "sandy ballcourt."
The Zapotec zurdo decked me.
¿Cómo se dice beanball en español?
"¡Así que es pendejo!"
And then for once in my mortal
middle-infielder's vagabond career
I got good wood on the pelota,
it sailed toward the ring of the sun,
reached the ancient wall on one hop.

Hunahpú and Hunahpú played ball
against the gods. They lost.
They got their heads cut off
and turned them into baseballs on a tree.
A girl ate them. She had babies:
Hunahpú and Hunahpú.

They finished second two years running,
smoked the candles of the underworld,
came back to challenge in the playoffs.
They used a mosquito in center field
to steal signs. They stole them blind.
They took the first strike, they went
with the pitch. They had the long ball.
They sacrificed, they threw the split-finger.
You remember the sequence from Game Six.

The Mayans carved the standings
into limestone. Learn to interpret
the statistics of heaven,
these cyclic fractals of the endless game.

"Over the fence," I yelled, "is a home run."
"Over the fence," said Mr. Brockerman from his yard, hoping to keep his windows intact, "is out."
"It's our game and we can make the rules,
and besides you can't even get a job."

HOME PLATE

PLAYING CATCH

Linda Brewer

David, my son, is a militant couch potato. He reads by night and sleeps by day, during Analytical Geometry. The future, to him, means turning seventeen. He devours Ritz crackers, is skinny, and dresses all in black. With his posture, standing sideways he looks like a question mark. To me, that's what he is.

It is a golden spring day, sweet-scented and peaceful, until the report card hits the mailbox. A glance down the column of dot matrix letters and I have to sit down and pop a Tums. When David comes home from school, I make him sit down opposite me at the kitchen table, and I go into my doomsday speech.

"Your generation will be running the world someday. How can you handle it if you don't have the proper skills? You have to acquire knowledge." I toss in all the generic phrases about winners and losers and close with a reminder of how successful his older sister has always been.

In return he mutters the standard responses. "It's not that big a deal. I'll do better next time." And the clincher, "I didn't ask to be born."

"None of us did, kiddo."

His eyes glaze over and he waits, still life with unopened cracker box. He's just come home from school, he's hungry and he can't eat. I can't swallow my diet soda. We have ruined each other's appetites.

The door is half open, to let the cat escape our human connection. A whiff of freshly cut grass freshens our murky atmosphere. I'm tired of the sound of my own voice, yakking all around the unanswerable question, "How are you going to turn out?" We sit in silence for a minute, letting the blood pressure subside.

The sun is shining, free and unabated.

"Let's go do something fun, right now. It's too nice outside not to."

David looks mistrustful. He wipes a film of Ritz dust off his fingertips.

"I'm pretty busy." Rubbing it in, he adds, "I've got homework."

"Come on, let's go play catch, just for a few minutes. Let's warm up the old soup bones. The fresh air will do us good."

He wants to say no. His glance travels down the hall to the living room, where my idea, and his homework, face a triple threat: soft couch, earphones, and a fresh stack of library books.

165

"Oh, all right."

"Good, I'll get the equipment. It'll just take a second."

I stroll down to the playground soberly, trying not to betray any parental enthusiasm. David drags along six feet behind me, unconnected. His body language conveys boredom and incipient side ache. A kid comes up the steps from the playground, swigging pop from a can. He and David exchange terse greetings: "Hey, man."

I imagine them talking later, at school.

"Hey, man, was that your mom?"

"No way, man. That's just some woman from our street."

At the playground I give the ball a little toss. It's a white, smooth ball, bought years ago. The word "Official" stands out as black and unblurred as ever, never having made contact with a bat. I was a tomboy at one time, but a weak, myopic one. David would rather be reading. Between us, the Olympic flame would flicker out in a second.

Redwing blackbirds are singing in the bushes along the edge of the playground—a nice touch. A dandelion has managed to poke through the blacktop. Old memory cells reactivate.

"You pound in the pocket, like this." I demonstrate. In 1958 I was into pocket formation, the proper oiling of the leather, the whole baseball glove maintenance program.

"An initial observation," David says, not pounding his glove even once. "This mitt is too small for me. We have to trade."

"They're gloves. Catchers have mitts."

He isn't listening. Already starved for print, he's reading his/my glove. "Who was Eddie Matthews?"

"Third base for the Braves." I want to elaborate, but don't.

"Nice handwriting," David says. "Let's get this over with. Throw it."

I throw. He misses. He picks it up and throws it back. I miss.

"We just need to warm up the old soup bones."

I miss again.

This is more of an exercise in futility than exercise. Computer games were supposed to give him wizard hand-eye coordination. What's the point if he can't catch a ball? Button-pressing is no big deal. We can train rats to do that.

I finally catch one and throw it back. He catches and throws. I catch and return it. He fires one hard. My hand smarts. The old soup bones are heating up.

"I'm totally serious," he says. "I think school misses the point half the time. We don't learn anything interesting."

"Tell me about it."

"Like Shakespeare. Shakespeare's really a great author."

Throw and tell. Once the rhythm sets in it's one step away from rocking chairs on the porch. You hardly have to move. Connected by the ball, you're close enough to talk, far enough away for privacy.

I snare a high fast one with a simple wave of my hand—"Say *hey*"—and grin. After all these years I still don't throw like a girl.

My mind drifts. I'd like to see a convention of politicians tossing the old ball around, literally and figuratively, comparing secrets. How do you grip the ball in a crisis? Can you throw a decent knuckleball with white knuckles? If everybody strikes out, is the game truly over?

David pounds his glove and snags my next wild toss with élan. He grins wickedly and throws one even wilder, on purpose. I have to chase the ball down the school driveway, past the flagpole, across the road and into a ditch full of damp greenery. When I return, he has taken off his black sweatshirt. Underneath he's wearing a hand-me-down T-shirt bearing a picture of Super Chicken.

"You knew the job was dangerous when you asked for it," reads the motto. Whose job? Mine as a parent, or his as my successor in this world of arbitrary foul lines?

Back and forth. I love the blunt slap of baseball on glove.

The old soup bones are just about thrown out. I have to move up closer to lob the next one. "Listen to this," David says. His teeth are clenched. His thin, pale face is fixed and masklike. He sings.

> Nut goes ut.
> Nust cun down.
> Stinning wheel.
> Got to go roun—

He breaks off to explain to me, "I can sing and talk nithout nooving ny lits. I din tracticing in the nirror." He tosses me the ball, well pleased with himself.

"So this is what they don't teach you in school?"

"Anong other things."

He adds, "It night cun in handy sunday, as a career. Also, I'm thinking of getting more exercise," he says, moving his lips now. "I'd like to learn to tap dance. Seriously."

He whaps out a muffled rhythm pattern on the blacktop, ending with a highly torqued pirouette. I can't help laughing.

"No, but really, Mom, I do have good ideas. You just don't know."

I believe him.

"One last one, kiddo." My arm is like a rag. I lean back and hurl a parabola, a simulated pop fly. The little ball, scuffed now, spins bravely up, following its geometric destiny, making it look easy. I want it to stay up there a long time. I want to keep it going, keep it in the blue sky, in open space, keep it from landing any place but—wherever he may be—right in David's glove.

From **PRIDE OF THE BIMBOS**

John Sayles

Denzel wandered toward them with his glove under his arm. A few were in the outfield, crowding under liners and pop-ups that a tall boy threw them. "I got it!" they called in unison, "Mine, mine!" Off to one side a dark, barrel-chested kid was playing pepper with a boy who had a bandage over his eye. The rest milled around, joking, tossing gloves and hats in the air, fighting over the remaining bat to take practice swings. They all seemed to know each other.

Denzel squatted next to a thin boy who sat on his glove at the fringe of the action, watching expectantly. He was the only one there smaller than Denzel.

"Gonna be a game?"

"Uh-huh." The thin boy looked up at him, surprised.

"They got regular teams?"

"Nope. They pick sides."

Denzel nodded.

"Hope I get to play," said the thin boy. "When the teams don't count out even I got to sit," he said, "every single time."

He waited for a word of support but Denzel just grunted and moved several feet away. *Might think we come together.*

The ones on what seemed to be the field hacked around a little longer until a movement to start a game began. "Let's go," someone said. "Get this show on the road."

"Somebody be captains."

"Somebody choose up."

Gradually they wandered in and formed a loose group around a piece of packing crate broken roughly in the shape of a home plate. They urged each other to get organized and shrugged their indifference over who would be the captains.

"C'mon, we don't have all day."

"Somebody just choose."

"Big kids against little kids!" said a fat boy in glasses and they all laughed.

"Good guys against the bad guys!"

"Winners against the losers!"

"The men against the mice!"

"Okay," said the dark, barrel-chested kid, "Whynt we just have the same captains as yesterday?"

"Yeah, but not the same teams."

"Too lopsided."

"That was a slaughter."

"We got scobbed."

"Do it then," said the fat boy, "Bake and the Badger."

"Yeah, shoot for first pick."

"Let's go, choose up."

There was a sudden movement, everybody spreading in a semicircle around two of the boys, jostling not to be behind anyone, the thin boy hopping up and running to join them. Denzel got up slowly and walked to the rear of them. No sense getting all hot and bothered. No big thing. He drifted through hips and shoulders, quietly, till he stood in view of the captains.

They were shooting fingers, best four out of seven, like the World Series. The barrel-chested boy was one of the captains, the one they called the Badger, and the tall boy who had been throwing flies was the other.

Denzel slipped his glove on. It was an oversized Ted Kluszewski model his daddy had handed down to him. Each of the fingers seemed thick as his wrist and there was no web to speak of and no padding in the pocket. Orange and gunky.

The tall boy won on the last shoot and the Badger scowled.

"Alley Oop!" Bake called without even looking.

"Haw-*raaat!*" A wiry kid with arms that hung to his knees trotted out from their midst and stood by Bake. "We got it now, can't lose. Can not *lose!*"

"Purdy!" The Badger barked it like an order and a solid-looking red-haired kid marched out and took his place.

The two first picks began to whisper and nudge at their captains.

"Vernon," whispered the wiry boy, "get Vernon."

"Vernon."

Vernon came to join them and he and Alley Oop slapped each other's backs at being together.

"Royce," whispered the big redhead. "They get Royce, we've had it."

"Royce," said the Badger and Royce was welcomed into the fold.

"Pssst!" called the fat boy with the glasses to Alley Oop and Vernon. "Have him pick me. You guys need a third sacker."

"Ernie," they said, on their toes leaning over each of Bake's shoulders, "Ernierniernie!"

"Okay, Ernie," he said and Ernie waddled out with his glove perched on top of his head.

"Gahs looked like you needed some help," he told them. "Never fear, Ernie is here!"

The captains began to take more time in their picking. They considered and consulted and looked down the line before calling out a name. The Badger pounded quick, steady socks into the pocket of his glove while beside him Purdy slowly flapped the jaws of his first baseman's mitt.

Soon there were more that had been chosen than that hadn't. The ones who were picked frisked and giggled behind their captains while the ones who hadn't were statues on display. "You," the captains said now, still weighing abilities but unenthusiastic. Finally they just pointed. The Badger walked along the straggling line of leftovers like a general reviewing troops, stood in front of his next man and jerked his thumb back over his shoulders. When there was only one spot left for even teams Denzel and the thin boy were left standing. It was the Badger's pick.

Denzel stood at ease, eyes blank. It grew quiet. He felt the others checking him over and he smelled something. Topps bubble gum, the kind that came with baseball cards. He snuck a glance at the thin boy. His eyes were wide, fixed on the Badger, pleading. He had a round little puff of a catcher's mitt that looked like a red pincushion. There was no sign of a baseball ever having landed in it, no dent of a pocket.

Denzel felt the Badger considering him for a moment, eyes dipping to the thick-fingered old-timer's glove, but then he turned and gave a slight, exasperated nod to the thin boy. "We got him."

Before Denzel could get out of the way Bake's team streamed past him onto the field.

"First base!" they cried, "Dibs on shortstop!" Trotting around him as if he were a tree, looking through the space where he stood. "Bake?" they whined, "Lemme take left huh? I always get stuck at catcher or somethin." Denzel kept his face blank and tried to work the thing back down into his throat. They all knew each other, didn't know whether he was any good or not. No big thing.

He drifted off to the side, considered going back to the van, then sat beyond the third-base line to watch. As if that was what he had come to do in the first place. Nice day to watch a ball game. He decided he would root for Bake's side.

"Me first," said the Badger, pointing with the bat handle, "you second, you third. Purdy you clean up. Fifth, sixth, semeightnon." They had full teams so Denzel couldn't offer to be all-time catcher and dive for foul tips. You didn't get to bat but it kept you busy and you could show them you could catch. Denzel kept his glove on.

He could tell he was better than a lot of them before they even started and some of the others when the end of the orders got up. The pitching was overhand but not fast. There was a rock that stuck out of the ground for first base and some cardboard that kept blowing so they had to put some sod clumps on it for second and somebody's T-shirt for third. Bake played shortstop and was good and seemed a little older than the others. The one called Purdy, the big red-headed one, fell to his knees after he struck out. Everybody had backed way up for him. Alley Oop made a nice one-handed catch in center. Whenever there was a close play at a base, Badger would run over and there would be a long argument and he would win. The thin boy had to be backed up at catcher by the batting team so it wouldn't take forever to chase the pitches that went through. The innings went a long time even when there weren't a lot of runs because the pitchers were trying tricky stuff and couldn't get it close. Denzel followed the action carefully, keeping track of the strikes and outs and runs scored, seeing who they backed up for and who they moved in for, who couldn't catch, who couldn't throw, keeping a book on them the way his daddy and Pogo had taught him he should. When fat Ernie did something funny he laughed a little along with the rest of them. Once somebody hit a grounder too far off to the left for the third baseman or left fielder to bother chasing. "Little help!" they called and Denzel scrambled after it. He backhanded it moving away, turned and whipped it hard into the pitcher. No one seemed to notice. He sat back down and the game started up again.

The Badger's side got ahead by three and stayed there, the two teams trading one or two runs each inning. They joked and argued with each other while waiting to bat. They practiced slides and catches in stop-action slow-motion and pretended to be TV commentators, holding imaginary microphones and interviewing themselves. They kept up a baseball chatter.

"*Hum*babe!" said the team in the field. "Chuckeratinthere*iss*gahcant*it*issgahcantit! *Hum*babe! *No*sticknostickchuckeratinthere—"

"*Lets*go!" said the team at bat, "*Big*innin*big*innin*we*gottateam*we*gottateam*bang*itonout-there! *Lets*go*lets*go!"

Late in the fifth inning a mother's voice wailed over the babble from a distance.

"Jonathaaaan!"

There was a brief pause, the players looking at each other accusingly, seeing who would confess to being Jonathan.

"Jonathan Phelps you get in here!"

The thin boy with the catcher's mitt mumbled something, looking for a moment as if he were going to cry, then ran off toward the camp.

Denzel squatted and slipped his glove on again. He wore it with his two middle fingers out, not for style but so he could make it flex a little. He waited.

The tall boy, Bake, walked in a circle at shortstop with his glove on his hip, looking around. "Hey kid!"

Who me? Denzel raised his eyebrows and looked at Bake.

"You play catcher for them."

Denzel began to rise but the Badger ran out onto the field. "Whoa na! No deal. I'm not takin him. Got enough easy outs awriddy. Will play thout a catcher, you gahs just back up the plate and will have to send somuddy in to cover if there's a play there."

Denzel squatted again and looked to Bake.

"Got to have even teams," he said. "I got easy outs too. If you only got eight that means your big hitters get up more."

"I'm not takin him, that's all there is to it." The Badger never looked to Denzel. "We don't need a catcher that bad. Not gonna get stuck with some little fairy."

Bake sighed. "Okay. He'll catch for us and you can have what's his name. Hewitt."

The Badger thought a minute, scowling, then agreed. Hewitt tossed his glove off and was congratulated on being traded to the winning side.

"Okay," said Bake, "you go catch. You're up ninth."

Denzel hustled behind the plate and the game started up. There was no catcher's gear, so though it was hardball he stood and one-hopped the pitches. He didn't let anything get by him to the kid who was backing him up. He threw the ball carefully to the pitcher. There were no foul tips. Badger got on and got to third with two out. Bake called time. He sent the right fielder in to cover the play at the plate and Denzel out to right.

The one called Royce was up. Denzel had booked him as strictly a pull-hitter. He played medium depth and shaded toward center. The first baseman turned and yelled at him.

"What you doing there? Move over. Get back. This gah can cream it!"

He did what the first baseman said but began to cheat in and over with the delivery.

The second pitch was in on the fists but Royce swung and blooped a high one toward short right. Denzel froze still.

"Drop it!" they screamed.

"Choke!"

"Yiyiyiyiyi!"

"I got it!" yelled somebody close just as Denzel reached up and took it stinging smack in the pocket using both hands the way his daddy had told him and then he was crashed over from the side.

He held on to the ball. Alley Oop helped him to his feet and mumbled that he was sorry, he didn't know that he really had it. The Badger stomped down on home plate so hard it split in half.

"Look what I found!" somebody called.

"Whudja step in, kid?"

"Beginner's luck."

Denzel's team trotted in for its at-bats. While they waited for the others to get in their positions Bake came up beside him.

"That mitt looks like you stole it out of a display window in the Hall of Fame," he said, and Denzel decided to smile. "Nice catch."

The first man up flied out to left and then Ernie stepped in. Ernie had made the last out of the inning before.

"Hold it! Hold it rat there!" Badger stormed in toward the plate. "Don't pull any of that stuff, who's up? Ninth man aint it? The new kid?"

"We changed the batting order," said Ernie. "You can do that when you make a substitution. The new kid bats in my spot and I bat where Hewitt was."

"Uhn-uh. No dice."

"That's the rules."

"Ernie," said Bake, stepping in and taking the bat from him, "let the kid have his ups. See what he can do."

Bake handed the bat to Denzel and the Badger stalked back into the field. It was a big, thick-handled bat, a Harmon Killebrew 34. Denzel liked the looks of the other one that was lying to the side but decided he'd stay with what he was given.

The Badger's team all moved in close to him. The center fielder was only a few yards behind second base.

"Tryn get a piece of it," said Ernie behind him, "just don't whiff, kid."

"Easyouteasyouteasyout!" came the chatter.

Denzel didn't choke up on the big bat. See what he can do.

The first four pitches were wide or too high. He let them pass.

"C'mon, let's go!"

"Wastin time."

"Swing at it."

"Let him hit," said the Badger. "Not goin anywheres."

The next one was way outside and he watched it.

"Come *awn!*" moaned the Badger, "s'rat over!"

"Whattaya want kid?"

"New batter, new batter!"

"Start calling strikes!"

"Egg in your beer?"

"See what he can do."

The pitcher shook his head impatiently and threw the next one high and inside. Denzel stepped back and tomahawked a shot down the line well over the left fielder's head.

"Attaboy! Go! Go!"

"Dig, baby, all the way!"

"Keep comin, bring it on!"

By the time the left fielder flagged it down and got it in Denzel was standing up with a triple.

"Way to hit! Way to hit, buddy."

"Sure you don't want him, Badger?"

"Foul ball," said the Badger. He was standing very still with his glove on his hip. "Take it over."

This time Bake and half his team ran out to argue. The Badger turned away and wouldn't listen to them.

"Get outa here," they said. "That was fair by a mile. You gotta be blind."

He wouldn't listen. "Foul ball."

"Get *off* it," they said, "you must be crazy."

Denzel sat on the base to wait it out. The third baseman sat on his glove beside him and said nice hit. The Badger began to argue, stomping around, his face turning red, finally throwing his glove down and saying he quit.

"Okay," said Bake, "have it your way."

"Nope." The Badger sulked off but not too far. "If you gonna cheat I don't want nothin to do with it."

"Don't *be* that way, Badger, dammit."

"Hell with you."

"Okay," said Bake, looking over to Denzel and shrugging for understanding, "we'll take it over."

Denzel lined the first pitch off the pitcher's knee and into right for a single. Three straight hits followed him and he crossed the plate with the tying run. The first baseman made an error and then the Badger let one through his legs and the game broke open.

Denzel sat back with the rest of the guys. They wrestled with each other and did knuckle-punches to the shoulder.

They compared talent with a professional eye.

"Royce is pretty fast."

"Not as fast as Alley Oop."

"Nobody's that fast."

"Alley Oop can *peel*."

"But Royce is a better hitter."

"Maybe for distance but not for average."

"Nobody can hit it as far as Purdy."

"If he connects."

"Yeah, he always tries to kill the ball. You got to just meet it."

"But if he ever connects that thing is gonna sail."

"Kiss it goodbye."

"Going, going, *gone!*"

Denzel sat back among them without talking, but following their talk closely, putting it all in his book. Alley Oop scored and asked Bake to figure his average for him and Bake drew the numbers in the dust with a stick till he came up with .625. That was some kind of average, everyone agreed. They batted through the order and Denzel got another single up the middle and died at second. It was getting late so they decided it would be last ups for Badger's team. The Badger was eight runs down and had given up.

Bake left Denzel in right for the last inning but nothing came his way. Purdy went down swinging for the last out and they split up. Bake and the Badger left together, laughing, but not before Bake asked Denzel his name and said see you tomorrow.

Denzel didn't tell him that he'd be gone tomorrow. That they'd have to go back to Jonathan Phelps.

BERKELEY PICKUP SOFTBALL (EXCERPTS)
1975–1983

Richard Grossinger

1975–1976

The diamond called Codornices is notched into the Berkeley hills, a stunning baseball field set on a plateau among the evergreens. Each Sunday, the first twenty players there choose up two teams. They play a seven-inning game; the winning team holds the field. The next pickup group of ten plays them—and so on, as long as there are players. It must be the next ten. No priority is given to regulars, males, stars, friends, favorite positions. There may be arguments over exactly who came first, but no one is pushed out of line.

Just about everyone at Codornices is supposed to be good, a sort of sixth sense those who have been playing all their lives develop about those who haven't. The prejudice is a strange one, but baseball seems to exist in the memory or not at all; and only a rare cricket or lacrosse player can teach himself past the age of twelve.

Infield errors are rare, fly balls are caught, and there is a strikeout maybe every third game. Bad players are exposed, but not hassled. If you fuck up you might also be costing nine other players the field; that's trouble enough. Sometimes one team has to play with several sure outs in the middle of the lineup or too many people to hide at catcher and in short center. That's life. It's no more serious than pitching your heart out for the last-place White Sox crosstown at the Oakland Coliseum, and losing. The American League is a different league but not a different world.

Codornices is a hangout for baseball junkies. There's a regular group, but it's difficult to say who it is. The players on the field change consistently from week to week, month to month, season to season, but from one Sunday to the next the change is indiscernible. Anyone who's missing might come back the following week, in a month, two years later, or never.

Over the years, these players have made the game for Codornices, and it is a great game. So they keep playing it. I have been in softball games in college at Amherst, when we fought for a place in the intramural standings, and years later on the bare Goddard field, out on Vermont 2, where players of clashing abilities and moods mixed to produce a sloppy boring game, more ego and street theater than baseball. You waited forever while showboats juggled pop-ups, caught balls behind their backs, ran into easy tags. Hitters posed, ranted, improvised at the plate. You were at the mercy of unauthorized score changes. The second baseman tried (and failed) to out-race the batter to first after fielding his grounder, and then colluded with him in fake wrestling (while you stood out in left field counting the years of your life and staring at the surface tension of the clouds, and how deep the luxury of any summer at all in the north).

Some of these routines went on at Codornices too, but as a spoof on a spoof, the entendre triple at least—chicano runner and okie greaser playing gang war on a tag, blacks pretending to pretend to be black (and calling each other 'nigs'), a first-string running back from Cal tasting pitches from a five-foot woman, really busting it to put one of them over the left fielder's head, and bouncing it right back to the mound, so she held it for what seemed like forever, and then slingshot him out at first. One Sunday a bunch of black teenagers sat in the outfield waiting to play, hassling and diving at women joggers circling the diamond, one of whom finally grabbed their ball and tossed it in the bushes. After two bearded Berkeley policemen restored peace between the parties (and our own game was resumed), the teen girlfriends of these guys showed up, dressed for disco, three of them carrying blasters tuned to the same station. They shuffled through the outfield, stopping play, and when someone asked them to hurry they halted right where they were and called out, "Kiss my pussy." But before the day was over, we had chosen everyone into the game.

It was better street theater at the same time that it was better baseball. There was the sense that, if this game didn't make it, you were back on the street flat into Monday. You couldn't just pretend.

On the field histories mean nothing. Bearded, shaved bald, long dresses, dungarees, wrestler with tank top, black with red track shoes, Mexican in leather, and Chinese in blue button-down shirt, plus the faded Berkeley, Albany, Oakland Industrial League shirts: Fanny Bridge Inn reading "F.B.I.," Road Runners, Watergate, Sonoma Food Conspiracy, Contra Costa Merchants, Bookpeople, and of course, The Best Minds of Our Generation, the words run together in a concrete shot of letters on their backs.

I imagine there are more perfect games to drift in than Codornices, Berkeley, but this is the game that gave baseball back to me, after years of having lost it. The tension holds because the players have been through it—it and baseball too—and the shit has worked its way out. America has vanished, here before elsewhere, and they are in the abyss, they play in an abyss, and that is why they play. On the field we exchange nothing, but our auras somehow touch and transcend, though nothing really transcends because the mystery *is* the feeling. Just hard enough, just slow and lazy and laid back enough, that a golden ballgame, like a jewel, appears.

Left is the secret field, sloping upward to merge with the woods and trails. The line is bordered by overhanging conifers that nullify any drive contacting them. Center field opens out forever, picking up the slope to the fence around the city reservoir. Deep center is a park unto itself—a hippie gang playing kickball, kids fungoing, kites, touch football, penetrating but not disrupting (except one time a preppy football squad pranced out in uniform, young professors and town managers, and organized a rah-rah scrimmage, invading even left field as if they were the history of the European novel crashing American street lingo).

Off third base, Codornices descends into the parking lot beyond which is a companion playground. Every now and then an arts fair occupies it, and live rock or country and western ascends onto the ballfield, mixing with the din of portable radios, motorcycles, and the subtler but definite music of unceasing baseball.

The first-base line is the dugout and gathering point, players distinguishable from Sunday mob only in the passage of innings. Past first base it becomes pure California beach, even encroaching on the game. Down in the right-field corner, cyclists park their bikes, and use the time between games and innings to work on their machines. Occasionally balls sail out the right-field corner for a long ride down Euclid Street. Left-field home runs are more common, crashing through the trees into the picnic areas.

Nongame traffic is heavy. Its main course is up from the playground, dangerously threading the line, down to the corner, into the woods: a regular parade of kids, citizens, clowns, dogs, bongos, dope, Olympia Beer, trackmen, frisbees, lovers—past where John Skeels played a left field so brash and angelic I find myself remembering him as in a 1957 baseball card.

The only violence I ever saw there was the dog fight that brought the owners jaw to jaw, one a scruffy second baseman backed ritually by his team (who minutes earlier had been bitching for *him* to get *his* mutt off the field), the other an elder, an untouchable walking a breed. The "professor" threatened to have the whole rabble thrown out of the neighborhood by the department of parks. But it was the Little League that did it, for three months, its coaches drilling teams from Oakland and the City. What a joke, to be closed down like that, without knowing if it was from our past or in our corporate future. That wasn't baseball they played, but none of them understood, the coaches, the professor, the department of parks, why it was our field in some final way because it was all they had left us. While they ran the business of the nation into the 1980s, we kept choosing up one more game, pretending not to care, the dispossessed street gangs of something less radical yet than the South Bronx. And even I didn't understand how much it was *their* field and how I won the permission to play, at least partly by being just barely good enough (and partly by their knowing I was honoring them in this piece).

Standing out in the sun grass, the blue world outfield, dreamlike . . . the body always a resistance. Either one-two-three, or outs hidden like needles in a haystack of base runners and runs, and we have to keep recalling who made them, how, and whether it was this inning or last. Dragon kites plunging and sailing, dogs holding up play, immune to balls thrown at them, the good ball lost in the bushes, and half of everyone looking for it—the interruptions at least as much as the game, so that most of being alive is consciousness, and most of consciousness, until it is trained, is thinking about a life, and most of that comes so easily, without resistance, and most of baseball is waiting, playing the few balls hit to center, running the bases, while the thoughts go on. Nothing else. No plot, no narrative, no ideal, no keeping the collective garden, no supper. No plan for the future. No Casteneda, Barry Commoner, no Mao, no Catfish Hunter; no Bob Dylan or Seth Material. No unrequited love for the past. No fear for the earthquake. Simply uninterrupted eternity. Nothing absolutely nothing. No wonder that same summer Jimmy Carter ran on a platform of native softball. Ralph Nader pitched.

I remember their names, like words from a song: Tim, Bill, Rudy, Travis, Gail, Wolfman Dave. I remember their faces even better: the divorced catcher with his kid and the chip on his shoulder, the Spanish outfielder who disrupted the game with burps, the tall thin shortstop with the El Cerrito cap, the angry hung-over hippie who always slapped the ball to right, the one-time radical lawyer from Forest Hills. Some of them were the remnants of high school hardball teams, working class, married or dating the same girls, some of whom played.

I was curious, but people shrugged off biographical questions. They were their motorcycles. Or their girls. Or the girls were their guys. They were their jive, and how they played.

The baseball body is old, for most of us. It is one of the first bodies we had. On the field we look like we did then, the same grace, the same shy, hurt retreat, the unrelieved aggression. We continue to live out the argument. Not just like any kids, or in imitation of kids. But like the kids we were, and are. Who cares what we so-called became. We are still those original things, however bitter, and we seem to want to remember them, and even more, to be them.

Once I tried to get a conversation going with Bill, the left-handed first baseman who loved the right center-field alley, and whose face I will know a hundred years from now. His absolute non-answers:

"Collecting unemployment."

"What do you mean, what am I doing! I'm playing baseball, can't you see."

We were playing baseball, it was clear. And if you are as falsely profound as I tend to get, you become less present, you make believe the game is just an excuse. For every such gesture, you lose some of the identity you have, from making the plays, or not, and hitting with men on base.

And John Skeels. If I had been a rookie on the Yankees, he would have been Mickey Mantle. With a touch of Mark Fidrych and Dick Allen. Some days he played the perfect game; he got singles at will and stretched them into doubles. Small and fast, daring on the bases, he always scored. I felt like it took a hit to get me around; he was water, he simply flowed in. He never made contorted catches; he outran the ball, flicked it out of the sky with a bored cocky slap. He would run down shots that were misjudged by other outfielders. When he felt like it. . . . Blond and smirky, often hung over, sometimes missing absurdly, but in dives like a swan. Or sitting on the side smoking a joint while the game was in progress, and jumping up to make a gliding catch. The first summer he brought a girlfriend to the field; she was his mirror, short and blond and American, and they sat kissing on the sidelines, like birds pecking at each other. I was gone from September through December, and played only a little baseball until, at the end, it became Vermont mud, and the new President of Goddard, hoping to invent some school spirit, bought a carton of white horsehide and slogged through the autumn trying to keep the game going, and abandoned the field with the leaves, though we played hardball fungoes into biting November cold, and then, after Indiana Turnpike snows on a drive to Chicago, back in one day through Kalamazoo, and out west via Michigan, Denver, Wyoming blizzards, the long Nevada desert—the first weekend of February, blue forever Codornices sun, there was Skeels, where I left him, playing left field.

1977–1978

Eddie Detroit still pays us a visit sometimes. He's a brittle nervous guy, shirtless, in red shorts, thin legs, with a strutty chest, Elizabethan hair, and a sad formal face. He plays an intense, prancing game, with good basic rhythm, but errors as complete and inexplicable as broken china. He's an absolute original, seeking on the field some vindication that goes well beyond baseball. His bit is to interrupt the game with soliloquies out of Shakespeare. Sometimes it won't happen for months, and then, after a crucial muff, he's down on his knees, and the quavery clarity of his voice booms: "O what a rogue and peasant slave am I!" or "Is it not monstrous that this player . . . ?" It's a game stopper. Once, after popping up for the second time in a row: "They trouble my sleep; they inveigh against my privacy." Scattering his teammates with slashes of his bat.

Another irregular is Stacy, the traveling hippie and radical street actor with the propeller beanie. I caught him on TV at the Oakland Coliseum early in the spring, organizing the crazies in a crowd that looked like about 220 during the second game of a doubleheader. Every time Larry Wolfe of the Twins came up, they howled, until, in the extra innings approaching midnight, the ballpark reverberated like a hollow canyon. At Codornices, he played a game so slow and sleepyheaded that time itself seemed to wait for him and baseball slept like Rip Van Winkle, in week-old clothes and beads.

One of our difficulties is that anyone who schedules Codornices for their group on a Sunday assumes they own it and should be able to kick us off. We're the Sunday squatters, but we think we're the soul of the field. The city doesn't agree. They will not issue our game a permit, but they'll give them to Little League and the Dog Show. We complain about the trailers of dog owners dragging furrows through the grass, but they ignore us. We offer to repair the field if they will supply tools and materials; they ignore that too. But now that they no longer keep up baseball diamonds, Codornices is developing sandpits, with as many potholes as the streets; once the rains start, these become permanent puddles. So we are forced to do it anyway, freelance, bringing our own shovels and wheelbarrows.

Johnny Skeels was the hero of my first piece, but he moved north to Healdsburg the year I was away. I knew he had heard about the book, but I didn't see him again until one day in March; he walked up beside me in center field and said, "Hi." At first I didn't recognize him;

then we both stood there smiling. He had brought a team down from Healdsburg on motorcycles, and they sat on the edge of right field waiting their turn.

"Hey Skeels, what's all this shit I'm reading about you?" someone asks. "You're not that good, man."

"You know, I didn't write it. He called it like he saw it, right?"

Another Berkeley boy is Curtis, a Baby Ruth slugger with a cherub face. About the only thing he does except play the game is comb out his hair in long blonde tufts with tugs of a piece of metal. He has a total baseball consciousness, but he's not a team player. Nothing can convince him to go for singles instead of homers. He does a lot of popping up, and puts a few in the trees. He watches his drives go in dead earnest. Likewise, at shortstop absolutely nothing can convince him not to show off his rifle arm, even in game situations. If he's on the losing team, he hustles his way into the next game. How can you turn down Babe Ruth? He just places his body there.

"What are you doing back out there, Curt?"

"I dunno. They wanted me to play, I guess."

He can't conceive of not playing. He's baseball himself, and the rest of us are smaller beings, props to his deep breaths and power strokes. If Curtis wants to fire it through first, then Curtis does it, with absolute good nature and no guilt. He doesn't blame the first baseman, either; he just happened to be there, or not; instead he stares after the ball, watching where it goes, as though admiring a bad work of art.

Etch and Mike smile; they're baseball junkies who see the end of the line, but Curt's beginning. Big Curt. He just swings the bat. A simple life. He works for his mother in her International House of Pancakes franchises; Wolfman Dave, another Berkeley boy, mixes dough for Wonder Bread.

"My pappy grew up with Billy Martin," he says. "I went to school with Glenn Burke, Berkeley High, the no-good sonofabitch."

They call him by his last name now, Anzalone. He no doubt has a heart of gold, because I have seen him sneak a smile, but on a game-to-game basis there is not a meaner sonofabitch than the old Wolfman. He can control a game with his voice and edge of violence. He just agitates and agitates. He wears the other guys down. "Ain't no batter. Ain't no batter. Ain't no batter." Over and over, melodically.

"Dave, you're going to drive us crazy. Can't you say something else?"

"That's the point. It's meant to be irritatin'. You gotta be irritatin' or you're not distractin'."

He stands out in left field glaring, hunched over slightly, his hair thrown back from a bald spot. He shouts at the batters, daring them to hit it over his head. When he catches one, he responds big:

"Shut you up. Yeah, I shut you up man. You ain't got nothing, rookie. Nothing but shit."

Called out at third, he starts to leave the field, then changes his mind and charges back. "Your man dropped the ball. He didn't field it clean. I'm not going to let you move me off the base, asshole." And he plants himself there with angry dignity, and takes off on the next hit and stamps on home plate as he scores.

"You ain't gonna get me out," he tells the pitcher. "I'm battin' .800 off you." He lines a single to right. "Take that, fucker."

When he pitches, he flicks up those big arcs and waits for the batter to hit one. A key hit off him, and he'll storm around the mound: "That's it. No more hits. You rookies ain't gettin' no more hits off me." And then he keeps them out of the strike zone, trying to bully the batter to swing. He'll call "Strike" each time, and "You're out," but, of course, he has to keep pitching.

And you don't win. I've gone up against Dave vowing to wait for a good pitch, and I've swung long before my time.

He arrives in a white Lincoln Continental, and when his game is over (if he's lost), he goes back to the parking lot and plays his tape deck, saunters up for the next game, the same chip on his shoulder.

"I'm gonna take you up the middle," Guy shouts at him.

"You take me up the middle, you're gonna be out. Ain't nobody takes me up the middle."

Etch says: "Why do you make them angry, Dave? You gotta play 'em next week."

Dave gives Etch a long look of disbelief, then says, "So I go out and beat their asses again next week."

One game we got a 10-0 lead on his team in the first inning, so he came in from left to take over the pitching. He made us hit junk the rest of the game. He called out two of our runners at home for missing home plate (a ripped piece of newspaper no one took seriously); and he had several of his players beat out hits on routine groundouts. They got four runs in the last inning when our shortstop, Curtis, threw a bullet through the first baseman with the bases loaded and the batter having fallen down in the box. Curt gave it a long look, shrugged, walked off the field, and began hustling the next game.

I went home early that day, bitching about Dave, came back the next week, was made captain, and chose him first.

1979

This is the year everyone wants to play ball. Codornices is mobbed in March, as many as three teams waiting for the next game—chicanos in their undershirts and jewelry, fragments of ex-jock radio-station, rock-band and Berserkeley Record leftovers (like Erik, the slugging Viking), the Minds themselves (in surly middle age trying to whip the kids), high schoolers with Expo and Cardinal caps (anything bright or loud), the Gentile brothers, and the earliest arrival of all, the angry slugging black man called Mr. Steak after the white letters on his red jersey, who hit fungoes with me in the February rain when he couldn't wait for the season to start. Compared to what followed, those were pastoral days—looking for the ball in wet leaves among giant pink slugs, dodging mud puddles and football players.

The second edition of the baseball book is now out, with photographs of our field and cameos of the players.

Eddie Detroit is nervously snapping at the ball at third base, chanting rhymes with no apparent relationship to events. "Hipsecura. Hupsecura." He seems to be talking to the ball, repeating himself, as though curious with what he has mouthed. Skeels tosses his glove in the air, clips a line drive, and catches it bare-handed.

"Hey, did you hear about Merlin getting married today?" Mike asks.

"Sure did," John says. "Called him up when I got to town, said, 'Hey, John, what's new?' And he said, 'Nothin' much; gettin' married today.'"

Mike suggests we have Skeels run out onto the field and everyone will clap. "After all, isn't he supposed to be our hero." John just smiles.

Eddie Detroit sits on the bench reading and guffawing. "You got me. Yeah, you got me. There's no denying it. But tell me, what does 'inveigh' mean? I use it all the time." A little bit later he comes over and puts his arm around me. "Just one thing, though, one thing." He takes a silver flask out of his back pocket and gulps three times before capping it. "We're all waiting for the big moment. We're waiting to strike it rich. The big contract. Any season now. And we're gettin' older too. So this year, it's not Eddie Detroit. It's Eddie Champagne. Remember that!" He walks away, nodding to himself.

A few weeks later, as we are forced to sit out two games after losing, he comes up to me and says, "The name here is Arthur Edward Price, Mr. A. Edward Price. And anything else that appears in print is an extrasensory distortion."

When we finally take the field, a Mexican team has been defeated, and they occupy the third-base bench. They tease and rattle Eddie, who is tipsy by now, flamboyantly missing most of them at the hot corner. "Anyone can be a sore sport," he lectures them from the stage. They roar at such an overt delicacy. They've got to wait two games now and they're going to enjoy it. After Eddie throws a couple of men out, he proudly holds his ground: "Attention, everyone." There is unexpected silence. "This game is being discontinued." Then he crouches for the next pitch.

A few motorcycles buzz in and park. Curtis appears over the hill for the first time in 1979. "Why here's Babe Ruth," says Anzalone. "Hey, what's up Curt."

Curtis reads briefly through the riff on him, puts the book down, saying, "Great, man," and is looking right away for how to play, though people are already signed up two games ahead.

"I've got a bad image up here," Wolfman says. "My mother's gonna think I'm picking on everyone. Well, I'm gonna be a good boy from now on." And he has, with an occasional sly smile at me every time he would have blown up another season. "The press has reformed me."

The one who tries Dave's patience the most is Steve Gentile, oldest son of the one-time Orioles' first baseman Jim. He's "Gentile"; his younger brother is Scott. Gentile has made a name for himself on the pickup diamonds of the Bay Area. He calls himself "The King," and he has been on many of the prominent local teams: big time softball—more than beer money and uniforms. He's even played for National Champion Campbell's Carpets, whose duffel bag he carries. The man defies description. He's a dreamer, an elegant goon, a professional ringer. He visits pickup fields like ours only to get ready for the real season. More than anyone else, he's given his life to baseball, the best years, and all the rest, almost by birth, and not from any choice he knows of.

"What does your brother do otherwise?" I ask Scott.

"Otherwise? Not much. He puts up sheet rock if he needs money. That's one day a month. He tends bar at Big Art's on Friday and Saturday."

On the one hand, Gentile is conceited, self-enamored, and ruthless. On the other hand, he is lordly, gentle, and good-humored. Physically, he is big and red, hair and beard, a Bill Walton. He wears a blue baseball cap, goes shirtless, drinks a lot of beer, and slaps around a medium paunch. In the field he claims shortstop like an angry dog. No one else can go near it. He's a lazy player, like a big soft lion bounding around. He plays in short left field, but with an arm that has first base nailed almost by definition. He makes occasional errors on easy grounders, but that's clearly the beer and the pot. "Hey, that's my play," he tells the ball. That's why he's not in the majors—too much Aquarian Age debris in his blood. He knows it's going to be sour grapes from here on in. He plays with that attitude, like, "Look, man, you and I know I don't belong here, but if you think I'm going to go through the shit and training to be a big league ballplayer, or if you think I care about some fuckin' pro team. . . . " He's twenty-five, looks older. And sometimes you feel he thinks there's still enough time to do it. At least, some part of him does.

Gentile stands on the field with the rest of us, but he has his private set of rules. Everyone plays him in right field, even the third baseman. The catcher would too if they'd let him. It's more than the Williams shift. It's the Gentile shift. Sometimes he beats it over the top, but not often. He yanks half a dozen towering pop-ups a game onto the rightside hill, where there are too many trees and other obstacles for them to be caught with any frequency. When they are, he refuses to accept it. "Foul ball," he says, almost to himself. He doesn't shout.

"On this field, that's an out, Gentile."

"Get yourself a fence," he snaps, as though to the field itself, or as though we could instantly erect a fence for him if we wanted. Same thing he says when he hits a towering shot halfway up the hill to the reservoir at the limits of right field and the third baseman catches it because everyone's standing there as though it were fungo. "Home run," he announces, and breaks into a trot, terminating it about halfway to first, then gallantly striding back to the bench.

"Big pop-up man. Can of corn," Anzalone shouts. He's pitching.

"Get yourself a fence."

The poke to left would be simple, and when the game is on the line, people plead with him and drop hints: "I guess they don't think he can go the other way."

"I'm not gonna fuck with my swing. Not for any shitass game. There's still plenty of holes in right. Just because they got all those people out there, what makes you think there ain't holes too?"

One game he was on our team, and we beat Roda's resident all-stars, who were trying to hold the field all day; we scored five in the bottom of the seventh: 8-7. Gentile got the last hit, with men on second and third. The game was ours if he poked it to left. Instead he squibbed it to first, and it spun under the first baseman's glove into right. "Sorry about that. Cheap single," he says, touching first as the winning runs score. In a key spot the next game, with left field teasing his vanity, he hits a gargantuan shot at the reservoir. He stands at home and watches it, sipping his beer while the ball's still in the air. "Got something on it." But there's an outfielder of some credentials there. "Deepest part of the ballpark," he sings, a mixture of pressbox lingo and reggae. "Oh, they get him out. Nice catch, man." He sits on the bench singing his observations. "Let's see if you're going to be Mr. Ribbie today." Good hard "b's" for ribbie. He's grown up hearing it, and it's babytalk. "You're wrapping up for a . . . double," as someone puts on a batting glove. Men on base and he comes to bat: "They're ready for the big clean-up hitter." The giant stretches out his pectorals with three aluminum bats. He hits it straight up into the blue, grabs his beer off the backstop and returns to the bench. "I'm leaving it up to you," he says to the next hitter, who might as well be Gus Triandos.

His critics sit on the hill. "He can tear up the league when there's a fence, five a game sometimes, but he doesn't give a shit for the team."

"Aw, he's probably supposed to play in the big time, but too much booze and smack. So now he's gotta be King Shit of the pickup field."

Once between games, he rearranged the batting order against field rules so that I lost a turn up. I explained that to him, but I knew I was going to lose. I didn't even want to win.

"What do you think this is: communist baseball? We don't do things fair. You're an eighth-place hitter, and you better learn to live with it. You're gonna be an eighth-place hitter all your life. Anyhow," he adds with a smile, "everyone wants to see the slugger."

He wanted to know why he wasn't in this book. So now he's here. Who said it isn't like a dream? Even if we are just a bunch of rabble playing in the sun.

THE LAST GAME: 1983

For years the legendary Sunday pickup game flourished at Codornices; it turned away or absorbed all invaders. The rules were simple and fair: the first twenty people played; then the next ten played the winning team. The losing team got on the end of the line. Anyone who didn't like the format of the game stopped coming. Permits for the use of the field were required by the city, but those who arrived with official paper usually backed down, if not from fairness, then in the face of the sheer number of people playing and waiting to play. Occasionally the Codornices regulars lost a skirmish, but then they were able to outwait even the most entrenched game, though sometimes it took three or four hours of sitting to regain the field. Only the annual Dog Show unambiguously took over the field, covering it with rubbish and holes for the following weeks. But how could you argue with hundreds of trailers full of exotic dogs from all over California?

Then, after State Proposition 13, the City of Berkeley decided to raise money from the use of the field itself. They began to enforce the permits by charging money for them, first five dollars an hour, then ten dollars an hour. People paying for time fought the pickup game more vigorously, and the Codornices regulars began to drift away because there was too often a hassle over the field. If they were going to give up a Sunday and, in some cases, drive twenty or thirty miles to get to *the game*, they wanted to know they would play, or at least be able to sit on the side drinking beer with their colleagues until their turn came.

The sawbuck was a problem, but it wasn't the main stumbling block. The sheer bureaucracy involved in getting the diamond undermined the spontaneity of the game. The magic of Codornices could not be sustained by people waiting in line for a permit. The game had to be improvisational, invented on the spot. It was organized by disorganization—dozens of separate people deciding on a given Sunday to come to a certain ball diamond, few of them ever having seen each other elsewhere and virtually none of them knowing who else would show up that day. How do you activate such a group to apply for permits? Players would have to be designated each week to wait in line at City Hall; word then would have to be gotten out about which hours of which Sundays we had claimed. Part of the excitement of Codornices was not being certain who was going to show up for Sunday's game. There were literally hundreds of people who played more than once and had some intention of returning, plus unlimited numbers of other potential players, one or two of whom stumbled upon the choosing-up every week.

Codornices was a pickup game defined by the fact that someone might play in 1976 and next in 1981, might not even live in California. Yet half the people would recognize him when he came back, and no one would know if he came from outside Reno or was on vacation from Denver. Even when you knew what sounded like a last name you weren't sure if it was a surname or a nickname. The swift strong-armed shortstop I had always (like everyone else) called Frampton turned out to be the shadow of a rock star; his name was Fenger. On the other hand, for years I was sure Merlin was called that because he was a magician with the bat, a righty able to hit with such accuracy down the right-field line that he could beat almost any shift with line-drive homers placed either to the right or left of the right fielder; but he was Merlin at the post office on Monday too.

Finally, responding to neighborhood pressure, the city closed the field for a year, reseeded it, and tore out the parking lot and put a playground in its place. When it was reopened the University athletic department and fraternities seemed to have all the permits; it was no longer a blue-collar field.

Without the strange and wild mix of Codornices, baseball lost its edge for me. I found myself only in middle-aged pickup games, usually associated with a party or holiday, or because a team needed a player and someone thought to call me. These games lacked the violence of Codornices, but they also lacked its incredible spaced-out calm. People played with pompous competitiveness and self-conscious humor. There was little of the spontaneous jive of Codornices, its outrageous riffs, its sense of floating in the cosmos at the heart of danger. It was just play-it-and-get-it-over. We played right past each other—even though we talked a whole lot more about "cultural things." My mind wandered and I didn't feel like diving for the ball; my heart wasn't in my throat each at-bat.

Codornices was the great street game on the diamond in the sky. It was the lower-class Sunday in heaven. It was the one break dance in which I was allowed to play and do my few good moves. Next to that the picnic and white-collar circuit seemed like ballroom dancing or, even worse, a bunch of anthropologists acting out a Jivaro ceremony.

Early in the new year, 1983, I got an unexpected phone call from Bob Pearce, the slugger from Margarita's Mexican Lunch. He told me he wanted to have a reunion on the field, an official reopening of the baseball season. I, as the chronicler, had to attend. He wasn't quite sure what to call his event: a reclaiming of the field? a Hall of Fame game? a party? "I've called at least fifty people," he told me, "and they've called their people. We're going to have ballplayers you've never seen, real old-timers. We could have guys who haven't played at Codornices for ten years. April 2nd. Mark that date down on your calendar. It's going to be the function of the year."

He told me he had joined a team in Minneapolis called Triangle Sports; last year they were the winner of the Industrial Softball nationals.

"You know. Give the fantasy one last whirl before I settle down with the wife and the swimming pool." He quoted me the team batting averages: .671, .606, .663, .579. Most of the *home-run* averages were over .300. People had records like 86 homers in 76 games. The team as a whole hit 603 home runs and batted .595. "You know, just another guy chasing the American dream."

"Bp starts at ten sharp" were Pearce's final words, and three months later my son Robin and I were there at ten after. After a long rainy winter the day was bright and sunny. But the field was occupied by seven girls and five guys, some in uniform, going through an embarrassingly inept practice. A sort-of coach, a guy in a baseball cap, was hitting ground balls and calling out instructions. He had spent too much time listening to Joe Gorilla on the tube.

It was clear that Bob Pearce had neglected to get a permit. Not only was it beneath him, it was beneath the dignity of the reunion. Legends don't need a permit to play. And most of the ground balls were getting through.

Along the first-base line sat three Codornices regulars: Norm, Etch, and Merlin. Norm was leaning back on the hill, looking his angry self. Etch, soft-spoken and mellow, always resembled a hundred major leaguers; with a little more talent he could have been George Brett; instead he had to drive up from Hayward for the game. Merlin looked older and sadder—the tall, pencil-thin shortstop from the mail center.

They greeted me and Robin warmly, and since I was carrying a handful of the earlier baseball anthology, Norm said: "What's that? The bookmobile?"

Etch didn't shift his weight on the hill but lazily extending an arm said, "How are you, Rich." And then to Robin: "My, look at you. You're about ready to take your place with the big boys."

"Hello there, Richard." Merlin's Idaho voice.

"Jesus," said Norm. "Where is Pearce?"

"He called everybody up and then he's not here himself." Etch.

"Are these ladies ever going to get done?" Merlin.

"You think they'd be tired chasing the ball." Etch.

"They'll quit soon." Merlin. "But we don't have enough to take the field anyway."

The group with the permit starts a half-hearted game at 11:15 when that beat-up little construction worker, the Indian Iggy, shows up as part of a team. An intense player who has trouble handling the ball and not enough power to get many hits, Iggy cusses and boasts every inch of the way. Pearce never called him, but he has the authentic permit for the next game and a date with a team of mostly Japanese players.

Although Iggy is missing most of his ten, his opponents gather in fairly large numbers and assemble an elaborate barbecue along the first-base bench. A few of them are playing a mixture of pepper and hitting up in the air off their bats like paddleball.

Scattered across the field are other people having catches, kids throwing to fathers, hardballs and softballs mixed. Within an hour, from eleven to twelve, the field has caught fire. It has become a landscape of baseball scenes as detailed as any Brueghel painting. The original game is entwined in dozens of partial games and is beginning to unravel. But we still don't have enough people to make a play for the field.

In any case Iggy is holding the permit today, actually waving it in the air in triumph. He organizes an aggressive batting practice out in left, and every ten minutes runs in to ask us: "Hey, hey, if we don't got enough guys, any of you want to play with us, huh?"

"Sure, Iggy," Norm says with royal detachment. "I'll play in your game."

It is time for Iggy's permit to take effect, but the Japanese players have begun barbecuing and are in no hurry, and Iggy doesn't have a full team; he has even enlisted Robin now. A few more Codornices regulars show up: Brian (the childhood battery-mate of major-league pitcher Mike Scott), his perennial sidekick Tony, still talking baseball stats in wise-guy staccato, then Frampton. Brian sits down and immediately begins discussing Mike Scott's failings, wondering why Scott MacGregor couldn't have taught him how to change speeds in college.

Then a sports car pulls into the No Parking zone, and the two Gentile brothers emerge like circus giants. "Oh no, I knew I shouldn't have called them," Etch says. He shakes his head and buries it in his chest.

Steve saunters down the first-base line well ahead of Scott, swinging his equipment bag. He stands before us in the sun, a pale red hippie giant, surveying the scene, like all other scenes, forever. "Shit, what is this, guys? Where is the old . ball . game?" Putting the rhythm on each word, riffing as usual. He pumps a lot of hands, but I am so enthralled at seeing my characters come together I forget I'm there. He's grabbed my hand and said, "Hey man, hello," before I can wake up. "Like, remember me." After a pause: "I still got your book. I think. You can call my lawyer." Then a laugh as big as himself. Bouncing on his legs in place, he scans the world around him, all three hundred and sixty degrees. Now a speech:

"Softball's just getting too popular here in Berkeley. Look at these people playing. Radicals. No more real ballplayers. Maybe we should walk on; we could play on through."

The co-ed team is leaving, and the Japanese team is assembled on the sidelines. They have put on their Yoshi's Restaurant shirts and are summoning Iggy from left field.

"Hey, get an interpreter," Gentile yells as though noticing them for the first time. "Tell these guys to put on their earphones, we want to talk to them. Christ, it looks like the Little League World Series. Get Tatum O'Neal."

After collecting his gear from the car Scott Gentile finally comes down the line. "You're the little brother now, Steve," Etch says, but Steve's heard it before and is bored. He is trying to hustle his way onto Iggy's team, but no one is paying any attention. "Some game Pearce called. I'm glad I stayed in bed and tore one off. At least my legs are weak. Hey, Iggy, you lead off. I'll play with you."

Etch is apologizing to Scott for calling his old lady instead of him. "I had the wrong phone number."

"Yeah. She's saying, 'Where's this BeebeeQ? Why didn't I hear about it?' I says: 'You didn't hear because I didn't tell you, and I didn't tell you because it's just a bunch of guys boozing and playing ball. And you don't want to go to that no way.'"

The first pitch is being thrown in Iggy's game; just at that moment Pearce arrives, strides down the first-base line with three guys and two women. One o'clock.

"Look at that," says Norm, jumping to his feet and grabbing a ball to throw with someone. "The deuce shows up after the fact. There's your boy now. Ain't that brutal!"

"Hey, what's the fuss?" Pearce says. "We never have bp before one here anyway."

"But you called it for ten, big boy."

"Yeah, but nothing ever happens at Codornices until one. So what's going on now?"

"The sushi bar is playing Iggy. It's a game of midgets," says Gentile.

"What a day for a game," says Pearce, throwing his arms out into the sky. "They've got the preliminary game on now, then the big boys take the field." To Norm: "Hey, how's it going, Mr. Angry?" They shake one another's hands and twist each other back and forth. Norm has a bat now and is hitting fungoes. Pearce walks up the hill to greet everyone else. He introduces his wife Kathleen and his friend Dale. "He's played on some great A.S.U. teams. Now he's on my new home team, Ashby Lumber. Hey, Johnny Merlin there. How are you, old boy?" To his wife: "Kathleen, this is the guy who got me into it, back in the old days, remember, 1973, the Main Post Office Mets. And Doc Watt pitched for us; he must have been forty-eight when he threw that shutout. This is the man responsible."

Merlin stands up and approaches him. "I hear you're playing in the majors now," he says with only the slightest grin.

"Yeah, got to give it one more shot before I settle down with the backyard pool and the kid. I was up in Minnesota just last week; they've got seven feet of snow there. Gentile, has your brother filled out or is that just his wallet? Yeah, but Johnny Merlin got me into it. I fucked myself up later." He turns to me. "Rich, we're going to get a game in today."

"Typical Codornices," I say. "Always a complication. Three hours and we're only an hour from taking the field."

"Always an altercation," Merlin chimes in, seemingly unaware that he has changed my word. Meanwhile, Gentile, ignoring the preliminary game, has gotten the spare out of his car and rolled it up on the right-field hill. "There's no fence here," he says, reciting his favorite riff. "The slugger wants to put one out. Inside the tire's a home run. You don't have to run."

"We'll give it to you," Pearce says.

Gentile looks around slowly again and then makes another speech:

"What are all these people doing on the field? They should be up on the hill cheering for the real players. Where they belong. Now everyone wants to play. You should have seen our game here last year. The people were having their BeebeeQ. Good-looking ladies. When they were done they went up on the hill; they watched us and cheered. We kept going and going. Norm hit a few out. The fans went wild. It was dark. They brought us beer. They fed us. We didn't want to leave. Fuck, it was dark. Norm wanted to turn some lights on. That was a game. Now I'm just standing here in the sunlight. Gentlemen, I don't know what it's all about."

"Just a day for a ballgame, Steve," says Etch. "A great day for a game."

"All lies," says Gentile. "All lies. Hey, look at that dog up there pissing on my tire. He must be angry at me."

With time to kill, Pearce asks me to walk him back to his car to see his baseball collection. I follow him out to the street and stand there while he opens his trunk. It's a memorabilia store in there. He's got binders full of 1950s cards. He's even got the sign they put up when the city shut down the field: CODORNICES CLOSED FOR THE SEASON. Now he pulls out a file of softball articles. "You should have seen our guys out there at the Coliseum when we had our home-run contest last year. We were poking them out 360. Brett and Henderson and those guys sitting in the dugout, they couldn't believe it. There's this one guy who won the thing, Howard 'Crusher' Scheer. He's a hippie type, from upper Pennsylvania somewhere, has his old lady with him all the time. Everything's mellow with Crusher. He put seven of ten in the seats. He goes maybe six-seven, two-seventy. When we put on the show in San Diego, Jack Murphy Stadium, they asked him if they should put up a temporary fence in the outfield so he could hit some home runs. Hell no. He put the first nine in a row in the bleachers, three hundred and fifty feet. The guy is awesome. But the team I'm playing for, they won the championship; they beat some team from Florida called Jerry's Catering at the nationals. It's a great bunch of guys—an airline mechanic, a vice cop, boys who do different things."

People are wanting to choose up sides for when Iggy's game ends, so a sign-up sheet is manufactured from a piece of paper blowing across the field. It's instantly filled with twenty names. Then another twenty. Someone in the second group wants to play fast-pitch.

"Not on this field, buddy," says Pearce. "Slow-pitch. Keeps the ball in play. Gives us a chance to play ball."

"But I've played fast-pitch here before."

"For how long, guy?"

"Last year."

"That's one." Then Bob turns to the group. "You know who started it all on this field?—Berserkeley Records, the musicians on Mondays. That's what Codornices is about, just the local guys playing a little ball. No myth, Rich. Just us boys."

"It's the cocktail hour," says Gentile, pouring a drink. "It must be. It's afternoon." He alternately drinks and swings his bat. Scott is talking about how nice it is to be in the tournament in Martinez:

"Breeze blowing out to left. First day, first game. Diamond one. Eight A.M."

Iggy's game with Yoshi's drags on. Early on, his team is in the lead by a couple of runs, but they play the field for fifteen minutes without putting a batter out and are down by eleven runs. Both sides are arguing about what inning it is. "Bottom four," Iggy says, but an inning later it is still bottom four, and a Japanese woman with a calculator and a scorecard insists that's correct. It's now past two o'clock. Pearce has set up a blaster with all the old Abbott and Costello routines about baseball.

At 2:30 we take the field. I join Etch, Dale, and the Gentiles on one team against Pearce, Norm, Brian, and Merlin. They're a better team, and we chase them the rest of the afternoon into the teens. For all his intensity Pearce is held to some hard ground singles, and Gentile's swinging for the tire and getting mostly pop-ups. But a leaner and more desperate Brian, a rough year etched in his face, hits three prodigious shots into the trees, and Norman follows with two. We keep scoring runs too, and as the game nears its climax, the lead is cut to one. Then Norm hits a shot into the bushes up by the reservoir with Pearce on, and the two big boys jog the bases proudly and slowly. Once the ball is pulled loose, Scott whips the relay into Iggy who (as catcher) has already blown two runs on collisions at home. This time he catches the ball as the runners are halfway between third and home, and, light as a feather, tags both unsuspecting giants, one after another like a turnstyle guard, just as they are about to touch home in tandem. "Two fat eagles in one shot," shouts Gentile. But Pearce and Norm are enraged. It's a home run, they demand. Automatic. That just puts Steve up on the soapbox:

"Did I see a fence there? Did somebody build a fence while I wasn't looking? Man, I told you a million times. If you don't want to run, get yourself a fence. That's why my tire's out there."

The feelings are now intense. Norm and Scott begin to swing at one another between innings. "I want a piece of that fucker," Scott shouts as his brother drags him away. Racial taunts go back and forth. We score two runs in the top of the seventh and go ahead by one. In the bottom half Pearce comes up with two on and smacks a monster shot clear into the reservoir. "All right!" Shaking his fist as he rounds the bases. That's the game.

Everyone disappears into the trees for a barbecue that Pearce's wife and Dale's girlfriend have been making. Before the food is served Bob lines us up. "The last photograph at Codornices," he says, handing the camera to Kathleen and running into the picture. I know he's right. There will never be another game here. "Fuck it, Norm," Pearce says. "One nigger and you've gotta stand up higher than everyone else." The picture is taken. Then another. Another. And finally Bob says: "Rich, I know you've stopped writing them, but there's gotta be a piece about this day. There's gotta be a story about how we came and took the field back."

And now, a year later, as I go over my notes from that day and write Mr. Pearce's piece for him, I am reminded of Coppola's version of Hinton's *Rumblefish*, when Dennis Hopper, playing the father of the two grown-up kids, tells the younger son (Matt Dillon) about his older brother (Mickey Rourke):

"He was born in the wrong era, on the wrong side of the river, with the ability to do anything and finding nothing he wants to do."

But this is Berkeley, not Tulsa.

MY BASEBALL YEARS
Philip Roth

In one of his essays George Orwell writes that, though he was not very good at the game, he had a long, hopeless love affair with cricket until he was sixteen. My relations with baseball were similar. Between the ages of nine and thirteen, I must have put in a forty-hour week during the snowless months over at the neighborhood playfield—softball, hardball, and stickball pickup games—while simultaneously holding down a full-time job as a pupil at the local grammar school. As I remember it, news of two of the most cataclysmic public events of my childhood—the death of President Roosevelt and the bombing of Hiroshima—reached me while I was out playing ball. My performance was uniformly erratic; generally okay for those easygoing pickup games, but invariably lacking the calm and the expertise that the naturals displayed in stiff competition. My taste, and my talent, such as it was, was for the flashy, whiz-bang catch rather than the towering fly; running and leaping I loved, all the do-or-die stuff—somehow I lost confidence waiting and waiting for the ball lofted right at me to descend. I could never make the high school team, yet I remember that, in one of the two years I vainly (in both senses of the word) tried out, I did a good enough imitation of a baseball player's *style* to be able to fool (or amuse) the coach right down to the day he cut the last of the dreamers from the squad and gave out the uniforms.

Though my disappointment was keen, my misfortune did not necessitate a change in plans for the future. Playing baseball was not what the Jewish boys of our lower-middle-class neighborhood were expected to do in later life for a living. Had I been cut from the high school itself, *then* there would have been hell to pay in my house, and much confusion and shame in me. As it was, my family took my chagrin in stride and lost no more faith in me than I actually did in myself. They probably would have been shocked if I had made the team.

Maybe I would have been too. Surely it would have put me on a somewhat different footing with this game that I loved with all my heart, not simply for the fun of playing it (fun was secondary, really), but for the mythic and aesthetic dimension that it gave to an American boy's life—particularly to one whose grandparents could hardly speak English. For someone whose roots in America were strong but only inches deep, and who had no experience, such as a Catholic child might, of an awesome hierarchy that was real and felt, baseball was a kind of secular church that reached into every class and region of the nation and bound millions upon millions of us together in common concerns, loyalties, rituals, enthusiasms, and antagonisms. Baseball made me understand what patriotism was about, at its best.

Not that Hitler, the Bataan Death March, the battle for the Solomons, and the Normandy invasion didn't make of my contemporaries what may well have been the most patriotic generation of schoolchildren in American history (and the most willingly and successfully propagandized). But the war we entered when I was eight had thrust the country into what seemed to a child—and not only to a child—a struggle to the death between Good and Evil. Fraught with perilous, unthinkable possibilities, it inevitably nourished a patriotism grounded in moral virtue and bloody-minded hate, the patriotism that fixes a bayonet to a Bible. It seems to me that through baseball I was put in touch with a more humane and tender brand of patriotism, lyrical rather than martial or righteous in spirit, and without the reek of saintly zeal, a patriotism that could not so easily be sloganized, or contained in a high-sounding formula to which you had to pledge something vague but all-encompassing called your "allegiance."

To sing the national anthem in the school auditorium every week, even during the worst of the war years, generally left me cold. The enthusiastic lady teacher waved her arms in the air and we obliged with the words: "See! Light! Proof! Night! There!" But nothing stirred within, strident as we might be—in the end, just another school exercise. It was different, however, on Sundays out at Ruppert Stadium, a green wedge of pasture miraculously walled in among the factories, warehouses, and truck depots of industrial Newark. It would, in fact, have seemed to me an emotional thrill forsaken if, before the Newark Bears took on the hated enemy from across the marshes, the Jersey City Giants, we hadn't first to rise to our feet (my father, my brother, and I—along with our inimical countrymen, the city's Germans, Italians, Irish, Poles, and, out in the Africa of the bleachers, Newark's Negroes) to celebrate the America that had given to this unharmonious mob a game so grand and beautiful.

Just as I first learned the names of the great institutions of higher learning by trafficking in football pools for a neighborhood bookmaker rather than from our high school's college adviser, so my feel for the American landscape came less from what I learned in the classroom about Lewis and Clark than from following the major-league clubs on their road trips and reading about the minor leagues in the back pages of *The Sporting News*. The size of the continent got through to you finally when you had to stay up to 10:30 P.M. in New Jersey to hear via radio "ticker-tape" Cardinal pitcher Mort Cooper throw the first strike of the night to Brooklyn shortstop Pee Wee Reese out in "steamy" Sportsmen's Park in St. Louis, Missouri. And however much we might be told by teacher about the stockyards and the Haymarket riots, Chicago only began to exist for me as a real place, and to matter in American history, when I became fearful (as a Dodger fan) of the bat of Phil Cavarretta, first baseman for the Chicago Cubs.

Not until I got to college and was introduced to literature did I find anything with a comparable emotional atmosphere and aesthetic appeal. I don't mean to suggest that it was a simple exchange, one passion for another. Between first discovering the Newark Bears and the Brooklyn Dodgers at seven or eight and first looking into Conrad's *Lord Jim* at age eighteen, I had done some growing up. I am only saying that my discovery of literature, and fiction particularly, and the "love affair"—to some degree hopeless, but still earnest—that has ensued, derives in part from this childhood infatuation with baseball. Or, more accurately perhaps, baseball—with its lore and legends, its cultural power, its seasonal associations, its native authenticity, its simple rules and transparent strategies, its longueurs and thrills, its spaciousness, its suspensefulness, its heroics, its nuances, its lingo, its "characters," its peculiarly hypnotic tedium, its mythic transformation of the immediate—was the literature of my boyhood.

Baseball, as played in the big leagues, was something completely outside my own life that could nonetheless move me to ecstasy and to tears; like fiction it could excite the imagination and hold the attention as much with minutiae as with high drama. Mel Ott's cocked leg striding into the ball, Jackie Robinson's pigeon-toed shuffle as he moved out to second base, each was to be as deeply affecting over the years as that night—"inconceivable," "inscrutable," as any night Conrad's Marlow might struggle to comprehend—the night that Dodger wild man, Rex Barney (who never lived up to "our" expectations, who should have been "our" Koufax), not only went the distance without walking in half a dozen runs, but, of all things, threw a no-hitter. A thrilling mystery, marvelously enriched by the fact that a light rain had fallen during the early evening, and Barney, figuring the game was going to be postponed, had eaten a hot dog just before being told to take the mound.

This detail was passed on to us by Red Barber, the Dodger radio sportscaster of the forties, a respectful, mild Southerner with a subtle rural tanginess to his vocabulary and a soft country-parson tone to his voice. For the adventures of "dem bums" of Brooklyn—a region then the very symbol of urban wackiness and tumult—to be narrated from Red Barber's highly alien but loving perspective constituted a genuine triumph of what my English professors would later teach me to call "point of view." James himself might have admired the implicit cultural ironies and the splendid possibilities for oblique moral and social commentary. And as for the detail about Rex Barney eating his hot dog, it was irresistible, joining as it did the spectacular to the mundane, and furnishing an adolescent boy with a glimpse of an unexpectedly ordinary, even humdrum, side to male heroism.

Of course, in time, neither the flavor and suggestiveness of Red Barber's narration nor "epiphanies" as resonant with meaning as Rex Barney's pregame hot dog could continue to satisfy a developing literary appetite; nonetheless, it was just this that helped to sustain me until I was ready to begin to respond to the great inventors of narrative detail and masters of narrative voice and perspective like James, Conrad, Dostoevsky, and Bellow.

A PERSONAL HISTORY OF THE CURVEBALL

Jonathan Holden

It came to us like sex.
Years before we ever faced the thing
we'd heard about the curve
and studied it. Aerial photos
snapped by night in *Life*, mapping
Ewell "The Whip" Blackwell's sidearm hook,
made it look a fake, the dotted line
hardly swerved at all.
Such power had to be a gift
or else some trick, we didn't care which.
My hope was on technique.
In one mail-order course in hypnotism
that I took from the back cover
of a comic book, the hypnotist
like a ringmaster wore a suit,
sporting a black, Errol Flynn moustache
as he loomed, stern but benign
over a maiden.
Her eyes half-closed, she gazed
upward at his eyes, ready
to obey, as the zigzag lightning strokes
of his hypnotic power, emanating
from his fingertips and eyes,
passed into her stilled, receptive face.

She could feel
the tingling force-field of his powers.
After school, not knowing
what to look for, only
that we'd know it when it came—
that it would be strange—
we'd practice curves, trying
through trial and error to pick up by luck
whatever secret knack a curveball took,
sighting down the trajectory
of each pitch we caught
for signs of magic.
Those throws spun in like drills
and just as straight,
every one the same.
In Ebbets Field I'd watch
Sal "The Barber" Maglie train
his batter with a hard one at the head
for the next pitch,
some dirty sleight of hand down and away
he'd picked up somewhere
in the Mexican League. Done,
he'd trudge in from the mound.
His tired, mangy face had no illusions.
But the first curve I ever threw
that worked astonished me
as much as the lefty cleanup man I faced.

He dropped, and when I grinned
smiled weakly back. What he'd seen
I couldn't even guess
until one tepid evening in the Pony League
I stepped in against a southpaw,
a kid with catfish lips
and greased-back hair,
who had to be too stupid
to know any magic tricks. He lunged,
smote one at my neck.
I ducked. Then, either
that ball's spin broke every law
I'd ever heard about or else
Morris County moved almost
a foot. I was out

by the cheapest trick the air
can pull—Bernoulli's Principle.
Like "magic," the common love songs
wail and are eager to repeat
it helplessly, *magic*, as if to say
what else can I say, it's magic,
which is the stupidest of words
because it stands for nothing,
there is no magic. And yet
what other word does the heartbroken
or the strikeout victim have
to mean what cannot be and means what is?

From **NORTH TOWARD HOME**
Willie Morris

Like Mark Twain and his comrades growing up a century before in another village on the other side of the Mississippi, my friends and I had but one sustaining ambition in the 1940s. Theirs in Hannibal was to be steamboat men, ours in Yazoo was to be major-league baseball players. In the summers, we thought and talked of little else. We memorized batting averages, fielding averages, slugging averages, we knew the roster of the Cardinals and the Red Sox better than their own managers must have known them, and to hear the broadcasts from all the big-city ballparks with their memorable names—the Polo Grounds, Wrigley Field, Fenway Park, the Yankee Stadium—was to set our imagination churning for the glory and riches those faraway places would one day bring us. One of our friends went to St. Louis on his vacation to see the Cards, and when he returned with the autographs of Stan Musial, Red Schoendienst, Country Slaughter, Marty Marion, Joe Garagiola, and a dozen others, we could hardly keep down our envy. I hated that boy for a month, and secretly wished him dead, not only because he took on new airs but because I wanted those scraps of paper with their magic characters. I wished also that my own family were wealthy enough to take me to a big-league town for two weeks, but a bigger place even than St. Louis: Chicago, maybe, with not one but two teams, or best of all to New York, with three. I had bought a baseball cap in Jackson, a real one from the Brooklyn Dodgers, and a Jackie Robinson Louisville Slugger, and one day when I could not even locate any of the others for catch or for baseball talk, I sat on a curb on Grand Avenue with the most dreadful feelings of being caught forever by time—trapped there always in my scrawny and helpless condition. *I'm ready, I'm ready*, I kept thinking to myself, but that remote future when I would wear a cap like that and be a hero for a grandstand full of people seemed so far away I knew it would never come. I must have been the most dejected-looking child you ever saw, sitting hunched up on the curb and dreaming of glory in the mythical cities of the North. I felt worse when a carload of high school boys halted right in front of where I sat, and they started reciting what they always did when they saw me alone and daydreaming: *Wee Willie Winkie walks through the town, upstairs and downstairs in his nightgown.* Then one of them said, "Winkie, you *gettin'* much?" "You bastards!" I shouted, and they drove off laughing like wild men.

Almost every afternoon when the heat was not unbearable my father and I would go out to the old baseball field behind the armory to hit flies. I would stand far out in center field, and he would station himself with a fungo at home plate, hitting me one high fly, or Texas Leaguer, or line drive after another, sometimes for an hour or more without stopping. My dog would get out there in the outfield with me, and retrieve the inconsequential dribblers or the ones that went too far. I was light and speedy, and could make the most fantastic catches, turning completely around and forgetting the ball sometimes to head for the spot where it would descend, or tumbling head-on for a diving catch. The smell of that new-cut grass was the finest of all smells, and I could run forever and never get tired. It was a dreamy, suspended state, those late afternoons, thinking of nothing but outfield flies as the world drifted lazily by on Jackson Avenue. I learned to judge what a ball would do by instinct, heading the way it went as if I owned it, and I knew in my heart I could make the big time. Then, after all that exertion, my father would shout, "I'm whupped!" and we would quit for the day.

When I was twelve I became a part-time sportswriter for the *Yazoo Herald*, whose courtly proprietors allowed me unusual independence. I wrote up an occasional high school or Legion game in a florid prose, filled with phrases like "two-ply blow" and "circuit-ringer." My mentor was the sports editor of the *Memphis Commercial Appeal*, whose name was Walter Stewart, a man who could invest the most humdrum athletic contest with the elements of Shakespearean tragedy. I learned whole paragraphs of his by heart, and used some of his expressions for my reports on games between Yazoo and Satartia, or the other teams. The summer when I was twelve, having never seen a baseball game higher than the Jackson Senators of Class B, my father finally relented and took me to Memphis to see the Chicks, who were Double A. It was the farthest I had ever been from home, and the largest city I had ever seen; I walked around in a state of joyousness, admiring the crowds and the big park high above the River and, best of all, the grand old lobby of the Chisca Hotel.

Staying with us at the Chisca were the Nashville Vols, who were there for a big series with the Chicks. I stayed close to the lobby to get a glimpse of them; when I discovered they spent all day, up until the very moment they left for the ballpark, playing the pinball machine, I stationed myself there too. Their names were Tookie Gilbert, Smokey Burgess, Chuck Workman, and Bobo Holloman, the latter being the one who got as far as the St. Louis Browns, pitched a no-hitter in his first major-league game, and failed to win another before being shipped down forever to obscurity; one afternoon my father and I ran into them outside the hotel on the way to the game and gave them a ride in our taxi. I could have been fit for tying, especially when Smokey

Burgess tousled my hair and asked me if I batted right or left, but when I listened to them as they grumbled about having to get out to the ballpark so early, and complained about the season having two more damned months to go and about how ramshackle their team bus was, I was too disillusioned even to tell my friends when I got home.

Because back home, even among the adults, baseball was all-meaning; it was the link with the outside. A place known around town simply as The Store, down near the train depot, was the principal center of this ferment. The Store had sawdust on the floor and long shreds of flypaper hanging from the ceiling. Its most familiar staples were Rexall supplies, oysters on the half-shell, legal beer, and illegal whiskey, the latter served up, Mississippi bootlegger style, by the bottle from a hidden shelf and costing not merely the price of the whiskey but the investment in gas required to go to Louisiana to fetch it. There was a long counter in the back. On one side of it, the white workingmen congregated after hours every afternoon to compare the day's scores and talk batting averages, and on the other side, also talking baseball, were the Negroes, juxtaposed in a face-to-face arrangement with the whites. The scores were chalked up on a blackboard hanging on a red and purple wall, and the conversations were carried on in fast, galloping shouts from one end of the room to the other. An intelligent white boy of twelve was even permitted, in that atmosphere of heady freedom before anyone knew the name of Justice Warren or had heard much of the United States Supreme Court, a quasi-public position favoring the Dodgers, who had Jackie Robinson, Roy Campanella, and Don Newcombe—not to mention, so it was rumored, God knows how many Chinese and mulattoes being groomed in the minor leagues. I remember my father turned to some friends at The Store one day and observed, "Well, you can say what you want to about that nigger Robinson, but he's got *guts*," and to a man the others nodded, a little reluctantly, but in agreement nonetheless. And one of them said he had read somewhere that Pee Wee Reese, a white Southern boy, was the best friend Robinson had on the team, which proved they had chosen the right one to watch after him.

There were two firehouses in town, and on hot afternoons the firemen at both establishments sat outdoors in their shirtsleeves, with the baseball broadcast turned up as loud as it would go. On his day off work my father, who had left Cities Service and was now a bookkeeper for the wholesale grocery, usually started with Firehouse No. 1 for the first few innings and then hit No. 2 before ending up at The Store for the postgame conversations.

I decided not to try out for the American Legion Junior Baseball team that summer. Legion baseball was an important thing for country boys in those parts, but I was too young and skinny, and I had heard that the coach, a dirt farmer known as Gentleman Joe, made his protégés lie flat in the infield while he walked on their stomachs; he also forced them to take three-mile runs through the streets of town, talked them into going to church, and persuaded them to give up Coca-Colas. A couple of summers later, when I did go out for the team, I found out that Gentleman Joe did in fact insist on these soul-strengthening rituals; because of them, we won the Mississippi State Championship and the merchants in town took up a collection and sent us all the way to St. Louis to see the Cards play the Phillies. My main concern that earlier summer, however, lay in the more academic aspects of the game. I knew more about baseball, its technology and its ethos, than all the firemen and Store experts put together. Having read most of its literature, I could give a sizable lecture on the infield-fly rule alone, which only a thin minority of the townspeople knew existed. Gentleman Joe was held in some esteem for his strategical sense, yet he was the only man I ever knew who could call for a sacrifice bunt with two men out and not have a bad conscience about it. I remember one dismaying moment that came to me while I was watching a country semi-pro game. The home team had runners on first and third with one out, when the batter hit a ground ball to the first baseman, who stepped on first then threw to second. The shortstop, covering second, stepped on the base but made no attempt to tag the runner. The man on third had crossed the plate, of course, but the umpire, who was not very familiar with the subtleties of the rules, signaled a double play. Sitting in the grandstand, I knew that it was not a double play at all and that the run had scored, but when I went down, out of my Christian duty, to tell the manager of the local team that he had just been done out of a run, he told me I was crazy. This was the kind of brainpower I was up against.

That summer the local radio station, the one where we broadcast our Methodist programs, started a baseball quiz program. A razor blade company offered free blades and the station chipped in a dollar, all of which went to the first listener to telephone with the right answer to the day's baseball question. If there was no winner, the next day's pot would go up a dollar. At the end of the month they had to close down the program because I was winning all the money. It got so easy, in fact, that I stopped phoning in the answers some afternoons so that the pot could build up and make my winnings more spectacular. I netted about twenty-five dollars and a ten-year supply of double-edged, smooth-contact razor blades before they gave up. One day, when the jackpot was a mere two dollars, the announcer tried to confuse me. "Babe Ruth," he said, "hit sixty home runs in 1927 to set the major-league record. What man had the next-highest total?" I telephoned and said, "George Herman Ruth. He hit fifty-nine in another season." My adversary, who had developed an acute dislike of me, said that was not the correct answer. He said it should have been *Babe* Ruth. This incident angered me, and I won for the next four days, just for the hell of it.

On Sunday afternoons, we sometimes drove out of town and along hot, dusty roads to baseball fields that were little more than parched red clearings, the outfield sloping out of the woods and ending in some tortuous gully full of yellowed paper, old socks, and vintage cow shit. One of the backwoods teams had a fastball pitcher named Eckert, who didn't have any teeth, and a fifty-year-old left-handed catcher named Smith. Since there were no catcher's mitts made for left-handers, Smith had to wear a mitt on his throwing hand. In his simian posture he would catch the ball and toss it lightly into the air and then whip his mitt off and catch the ball in his bare left hand before throwing it back. It was a wonderfully lazy way to spend those Sunday afternoons—my father and my friends and I sitting in the grass behind the chicken-wire back-stop with eight or ten dozen farmers, watching the wrong-handed catcher go through his con-torted gyrations, and listening at the same time to our portable radio, which brought us the rising inflections of a baseball announcer called the Old Scotchman. The sounds of the two games, our own and the one being broadcast from Brooklyn or Chicago, merged and rolled across the bumpy outfield and the gully into the woods; it was a combination that seemed perfectly natural to everyone there.

I can see the town now on some hot, still weekday afternoon in mid-summer: ten thou-sand souls and nothing doing. Even the red water truck was a diversion, coming slowly up Grand

Avenue with its sprinklers on full force, the water making sizzling steam-clouds on the pavement while half-naked Negro children followed the truck up the street and played in the torrent until they got soaking wet. Over on Broadway, where the old men sat drowsily in straw chairs on the pavement near the Bon-Ton Café, whittling to make the time pass, you could laze around on the sidewalks—barefoot, if your feet were tough enough to stand the scalding concrete—watching the big cars with out-of-state plates whip by, the driver hardly knowing and certainly not caring what place this was. Way up that fantastic hill, Broadway seemed to end in a seething mist— little heat mirages that shimmered off the asphalt; on the main street itself there would be only a handful of cars parked here and there, and the merchants and the lawyers sat in the shade under their broad awnings, talking slowly, aimlessly, in the cryptic summer way. The one o'clock whistle at the sawmill would send out its loud bellow, reverberating up the streets to the bend in the Yazoo River, hardly making a ripple in the heavy somnolence.

But by two o'clock almost every radio in town was tuned in to the Old Scotchman. His rhetoric dominated the place. It hovered in the branches of the trees, bounced off the hills, and came out of the darkened stores; the merchants and the old men cocked their ears to him, and even from the big cars that sped by, their tires making lapping sounds in the softened highway, you could hear his voice, being carried past you out into the delta.

The Old Scotchman's real name was Gordon McLendon, and he described the big-league games for the Liberty Broadcasting System, which had outlets mainly in the South and the Southwest. He had a deep, rich voice, and I think he was the best rhetorician, outside of Bilbo and Nye Bevan, I have ever heard. Under his handling a baseball game took on a life of its own. As in the prose of the *Commercial Appeal*'s Walter Stewart, his games were rare and remarkable entities; casual pop flies had the flow of history behind them, double plays resembled the stark clashes of old armies, and home runs deserved acknowledgment on earthen urns. Later, when I came across Thomas Wolfe, I felt I had heard him before, from Shibe Park, Crosley Field, or the Yankee Stadium.

One afternoon I was sitting around my house listening to the Old Scotchman, admiring the vivacity of a man who said he was a contemporary of Connie Mack. (I learned later that he was twenty-nine.) That day he was doing the Dodgers and the Giants from the Polo Grounds. The game, as I recall, was in the fourth inning, and the Giants were ahead by about 4 to 1. It was a boring game, however, and I began experimenting with my father's shortwave radio, an impressive mechanism a couple of feet wide, which had an aerial that almost touched the ceiling and the name of every major city in the world on its dial. It was by far the best radio I had ever seen; there was not another one like it in town. I switched the dial to shortwave and began picking up African drum music, French jazz, Australian weather reports, and a lecture from the British Broadcasting Company on the people who wrote poems for Queen Elizabeth. Then a curious thing happened. I came across a baseball game—the Giants and the Dodgers, from the Polo Grounds. After a couple of minutes I discovered that the game was in the eighth inning. I turned back to the local station, but here the Giants and Dodgers were still in the fourth. I turned again to the shortwave broadcast and listened to the last inning, a humdrum affair that ended with Carl Furillo popping out to shortstop, Gil Hodges grounding out second to first, and Roy Campanella lining out to center. Then I went back to the Old Scotchman and listened to the rest of the game. In the top of the ninth, an hour or so later, a ghostly thing occurred; to my astonishment and titillation, the game ended with Furillo popping out to short, Hodges grounding out second to first, and Campanella lining out to center.

I kept this unusual discovery to myself, and the next day, an hour before the Old Scotchman began his play-by-play of the second game of the series, I dialed the shortwave frequency, and, sure enough, they were doing the Giants and the Dodgers again. I learned that I was listening to the Armed Forces Radio Service, which broadcast games played in New York. As the game progressed I began jotting down notes on the action. When the first four innings were over I turned to the local station just in time to get the Old Scotchman for the first batter. The Old Scotchman's account of the game matched the shortwave's almost perfectly. The Scotchman's, in fact, struck me as being considerably more poetic than the one I had heard first. But I did not doubt him, since I could hear the roar of the crowd, the crack of the bat, and the Scotchman's precise description of foul balls that fell into the crowd, the gestures of the base coaches, and the expression on the face of a small boy who was eating a lemon popsicle in a box seat behind first base. I decided that the broadcast was being delayed somewhere along the line, maybe because we were so far from New York.

That was my first thought, but after a close comparison of the two broadcasts for the rest of the game, I sensed that something more sinister was taking place. For one thing, the Old Scotchman's description of the count on a batter, though it jibed 90 percent of the time, did not always match. For another, the Scotchman's crowd, compared with the other, kept up an ungodly noise. When Robinson stole second on shortwave, he did it without drawing a throw and without sliding, while for Mississippians the feat was performed in a cloud of angry, petulant dust. A foul ball that went over the grandstand and out of the park for shortwave listeners in Alaska, France, and the Argentine produced for the firemen, bootleggers, farmers, and myself a primitive scramble that ended with a feeble old lady catching the ball on the first bounce to the roar of an assembly that would have outnumbered Grant's at Old Cold Harbor. But the most revealing development came after the Scotchman's game was over. After the usual summaries, he mentioned that the game had been "recreated." I had never taken notice of that particular word before, because I lost interest once a game was over. I went to the dictionary, and under "recreate" I found, "To invest with fresh vigor and strength; to refresh, invigorate (nature, strength, a person or thing)." The Old Scotchman most assuredly invested a game with fresh vigor and strength, but this told me nothing. My deepest suspicions were confirmed, however, when I found the second definition of the word—"To create anew."

So there it was. I was happy to have fathomed the mystery, as perhaps no one else in the whole town had done. The Old Scotchman, for all his wondrous expressions, was not only several innings behind every game he described but was no doubt sitting in some air-conditioned studio in the hinterland, where he got the happenings of the game by news ticker; sound effects accounted for the crack of the bat and the crowd noises. Instead of being disappointed in the Scotchman, I was all the more pleased by his genius, for he made pristine facts more actual than actuality, a valuable lesson when the day finally came that I started reading literature. I must add, however, that this appreciation did not obscure the realization that I had at my disposal a weapon of unimaginable dimensions.

Next day I was at the shortwave again, but I learned with much disappointment that the game being broadcast on shortwave was not the one the Scotchman had chosen to describe. I tried every afternoon after that and discovered that I would have to wait until the Old Scotchman decided to do a game out of New York before I could match his game with the one described live on shortwave. Sometimes, I learned later, these coincidences did not occur for days; during an important Dodger or Yankee series, however, his game and that of the Armed Forces Radio Service often coincided for two or three days running. I was happy, therefore, to find, on an afternoon a few days later, that both the shortwave and the Scotchman were carrying the Yankees and the Indians.

I settled myself at the shortwave with notebook and pencil and took down every pitch. This I did for four full innings, and then I turned back to the town station, where the Old Scotchman was just beginning the first inning. I checked the first batter to make sure the accounts jibed. Then, armed with my notebook, I ran down the street to the corner grocery, a minor outpost of baseball intellection, presided over by my young Negro friend Bozo, a knowledgeable student of the game, the same one who kept my dog in bologna. I found Bozo behind the meat counter, with the Scotchman's account going full blast. I arrived at the interim between the top and bottom of the first inning.

"Who's pitchin' for the Yankees, Bozo?" I asked.

"They're pitchin' Allie Reynolds," Bozo said. "Old Scotchman says Reynolds really got the stuff today. He just set 'em down one, two, three."

The Scotchman, meanwhile, was describing the way the pennants were flapping in the breeze. Phil Rizzuto, he reported, was stepping to the plate.

"Bo," I said, trying to sound cut and dried, "you know what I think? I think Rizzuto's gonna take a couple of fast called strikes, then foul one down the left-field line, and then line out straight to Boudreau at short."

"Yeah?" Bozo said. He scratched his head and leaned lazily across the counter.

I went up front to buy something and then came back. The count worked to nothing and two on Rizzuto—a couple of fast called strikes and a foul down the left side. "This one," I said to Bozo, "he lines straight to Boudreau at short."

The Old Scotchman, pausing dramatically between words as was his custom, said, "Here's the pitch on its way—There's a hard line drive! But Lou Boudreau's there at shortstop and he's got it. Phil hit that one on the nose, but Boudreau was right there."

Bozo looked over at me, his eyes bigger than they were. "How'd you know that?" he asked.

Ignoring this query, I made my second prediction. "Bozo," I said, "Tommy Henrich's gonna hit the first pitch up against the right-field wall and slide in with a double."

"How come you think so?"

"Because I can predict anything that's gonna happen in baseball in the next ten years," I said. "I can tell you anything."

The Old Scotchman was describing Henrich at the plate. "Here comes the first pitch. Henrich swings, there's a hard smash into right field! . . . This one may be out of here! It's going, going—No! It's off the wall in right center. Henrich's rounding first, on his way to second. Here's the relay from Doby . . . Henrich slides in safely with a double!" The Yankee crowd sent up an awesome roar in the background.

"Say, how'd you know that?" Bozo asked. "How'd you know he was gonna wind up at second?"

"I just can tell. I got extra-vision," I said. On the radio, far in the background, the public-address system announced Yogi Berra. "Like Berra right now. You know what? He's gonna hit a one-one pitch down the right-field line—"

"How come you know?" Bozo said. He was getting mad.

"Just a second," I said. "I'm gettin' static." I stood dead still, put my hands up against my temples and opened my eyes wide. "Now it's comin' through clear. Yeah, Yogi's gonna hit a one-one pitch down the right-field line, and it's gonna be fair by about three or four feet—I can't say exactly—and Henrich's gonna score from second, but the throw is gonna get Yogi at second by a mile."

This time Bozo was silent, listening to the Scotchman, who described the ball and the strike, then said: "Henrich takes the lead off second. Benton looks over, stretches, delivers. Yogi swings." (There was the bat crack.) "There's a line drive down the right side! It's barely inside the foul line. It may go for extra bases! Henrich's rounding third and coming in with a run. Berra's moving toward second. Here comes the throw! . . . And they *get* him! They get Yogi easily on the slide at second!"

Before Bozo could say anything else, I reached in my pocket for my notes. "I've just written down here what I think's gonna happen in the first four innings," I said. "Like DiMag. See, he's gonna pop up to Mickey Vernon at first on a one-nothing pitch in just a minute. But don't you worry. He's gonna hit a 380-foot homer in the fourth with nobody on base on a full count. You just follow these notes and you'll see I can predict anything that's gonna happen in the next ten years." I handed him the paper, turned around, and left the store just as DiMaggio, on a one-nothing pitch, popped up to Vernon at first.

The I went back home and took more notes from the shortwave. The Yanks clobbered the Indians in the late innings and won easily. On the local station, however, the Old Scotchman was in the top of the fifth inning. At this juncture I went to the telephone and called Firehouse No. 1.

"Hello," a voice answered. It was the fire chief.

"Hello, Chief, can you tell me the score?" I said. Calling the firehouse for baseball information was a common practice.

"The Yanks are ahead, 5-2."

"This is the Phantom you're talkin' with," I said.

"Who?"

"The Phantom. Listen carefully, Chief. Reynolds is gonna open this next inning with a pop-up to Doby. Then Rizutto will single to left on a one-one count. Henrich's gonna force him at second on a two-and-one pitch but make it to first. Berra's gonna double to right on a nothing-and-one pitch, and Henrich's goin' to third. DiMaggio's gonna foul a couple off and then double down the left-field line, and both Henrich and Yogi are gonna score. Brown's gonna pop out to third to end the inning."

"Aw, go to hell," the chief said, and hung up.

This was precisely what happened, of course. I phoned No. 1 again after the inning.

"Hello."

"Hi. This is the Phantom again."

"Say, how'd you know that?"

"Stick with me," I said ominously, "and I'll feed you predictions. I can predict anything that's gonna happen anywhere in the next ten years." After a pause I added, "Beware of fire real soon," for good measure, and hung up.

I left my house and hurried back to the corner grocery. When I got there, the entire meat counter was surrounded by friends of Bozo's, about a dozen of them. They were gathered around my notes, talking passionately and shouting. Bozo saw me standing by the bread counter. "There he is! That's the one!" he declared. His colleagues turned and stared at me in undisguised awe. They parted respectfully as I strolled over to the meat counter and ordered a dime's worth of bologna for my dog.

A couple of questions were directed at me from the group, but I replied, "I'm sorry for what happened in the fourth. I predicted DiMag was gonna hit a full-count pitch for that homer. It came out he hit it on two-and-two. There was too much static in the air between here and New York."

"Too much *static?*" one of them asked.

"Yeah. Sometimes the static confuses my extra-vision. But I'll be back tomorrow if everything's okay, and I'll try not to make any more big mistakes."

"Big mistakes!" one of them shouted, and the crowd laughed admiringly, parting once more as I turned and left the store. I wouldn't have been at all surprised if they had tried to touch the hem of my shirt.

That day was only the beginning of my brief season of triumph. A schoolmate of mine offered me five dollars, for instance, to tell him how I had known that Johnny Mize was going to hit a two-run homer to break up one particularly close game for the Giants. One afternoon, on the basis of a lopsided first four innings, I had an older friend sneak into The Store and place a bet, which netted me $14.50. I felt so bad about it I tithed $1.45 in church the following Sunday. At Bozo's grocery store I was a full-scale oracle. To the firemen I remained the Phantom, and firefighting reached a peak of efficiency that month, simply because the firemen knew what was going to happen in the late innings and did not need to tarry when an alarm came.

One afternoon my father was at home listening to the Old Scotchman with a couple of out-of-town salesmen from Greenwood. They were sitting in the front room, and I had already managed to get the first three or four innings of the Cardinals and the Giants on paper before they arrived. The Old Scotchman was in the top of the first when I walked in and said hello. The men were talking business and listening to the game at the same time.

"I'm gonna make a prediction," I said. They stopped talking and looked at me. "I predict Musial's gonna take a ball and a strike and then hit a double to right field, scoring Schoendienst from second, but Marty Marion's gonna get tagged out at the plate."

"You're mighty smart," one of the men said. He suddenly sat up straight when the Old Scotchman reported, "Here's the windup and the pitch coming in . . . Musial *swings!*" (Bat crack, crowd roar.) "He drives one into right field! This one's going up against the boards! . . . Schoendienst rounds third. He's coming on in to score! Marion dashes around third, legs churning. His cap falls off, but here he *comes!* Here's the toss to the plate. He's nabbed at home. He is *out* at the plate! Musial holds at second with a run-producing double."

Before I could parry the inevitable questions, my father caught me by the elbow and hustled me into a back room. "How'd you know that?" he asked.

"I was just guessin'," I said. "It was nothin' but luck."

He stopped for a moment, and then a new expression showed on his face. "Have *you* been callin' the firehouse?" he asked.

"Yeah, I guess a few times."

"Now, you tell me how you found out about all that. I mean it."

When I told him about the shortwave, I was afraid he might be mad, but on the contrary he laughed uproariously. "Do you remember these next few innings?" he asked.

"I got it all written down," I said, and reached in my pocket for the notes. He took the notes and told me to go away. From the yard, a few minutes later, I heard him predicting the next inning to the salesmen.

A couple of days later, I phoned No. 1 again. "This is the Phantom," I said. "With two out, Branca's gonna hit Stinky Stanky with a fastball, and then Alvin Dark's gonna send him home with a triple."

"Yeah, we know it," the fireman said in a bored voice. "We're listenin' to a shortwave too. You think you're somethin', don't you? You're Ray Morris's boy."

I knew everything was up. The next day, as a sort of final gesture, I took some more notes to the corner grocery in the third or fourth inning. Some of the old crowd was there, but the atmosphere was grim. They looked at me coldly. "Oh, man," Bozo said, "*we* know the Old Scotchman ain't at that game. He's four or five innings behind. He's makin' all that stuff up." The others grumbled and turned away. I slipped quietly out the door.

My period as a seer was over, but I went on listening to the shortwave broadcasts out of New York a few days more. Then, a little to my surprise, I went back to the Old Scotchman, and in time I found that the firemen, the bootleggers, and the few dirt farmers who had shortwave sets all did the same. From then on, accurate, up-to-the-minute baseball news was in disrepute there. I believe we all went back to the Scotchman not merely out of loyalty but because, in our great isolation, he touched our need for a great and unmitigated eloquence.

Joe's American Legion Junior team actually amounted to an all-star squad from all the country towns surrounding ours; it was easier to make the high school team first. On Tuesday and Friday afternoons we would ride in our red and black bus through the heavy green woods to the small crossroads towns to play the locals. The crowds would sometimes be in a foul frame of mind, especially if the farmers had got hold of the corn gourd early in the day. Since we were the "city boys," with our pictures in the *Yazoo Herald* every now and again, we were particularly ripe for all that boondocks venom. The farmers would stand around the field shouting obscenities at the "slickers," sometimes loosening up their lungs with a vicious organized whoop that sounded like a cross between a rebel yell and a redneck preacher exorcizing the Devil and all his family. More often than not, to compound the injury, we got beat. Yet far from being gracious in victory, those sons of dirt farmers rubbed our noses in our own catastrophes, taunting us with threats to whip us all over again in the outfield pasture, while their elders stood around in a group as our coach chased us into the bus and shouted, "You ain't such hot stuff, slickers!" or "Go on back to town now, boys, and get your *photos* took some more." One afternoon when I ruined the no-hitter the best pitcher in the county had going (he later made Double-A), with a broken-bat fluke into right field in the eighth inning, I thought those farmers might slice me in pieces and feed me to the boll weevils. "You proud of that little skinny hit?" one of them shouted at me, standing with his nose next to mine, and his companion picked up the broken bat that had done the evil deed and splintered it apart against a tree trunk. When we beat the same team two or three weeks later on our home field, I ran into their shortstop and catcher, two tough hardnoses, on Main Street the following Saturday. They sidled right up to me and waited there glowering, breathing in my face and not saying a word for a while. We stood nostril-to-nostril until one of them said, "You think you're somethin' don't you, bastid? Beat us at home with your crooked umpires. Next time you come see us we'll whup you 'til the shit turns green." And they did.

The next summer, when I made the Legion team, I finally came under the tutelage of Gentleman Joe, a hard taskmaster of the old school despite his unfamiliarity with "stragety," as he called it. Gentleman Joe would always have us pray before a game, and sometimes between innings when the going got rough. He was a big one for church, and began to remind me more and more of my old fourth-grade teacher. But his pep talks, back behind the shabby old grand-stand of our playing field, drew on such pent-up emotions, being so full of Scriptures and things of God's earth, that I suspected we were being enlisted, not to play baseball, but to fight in the Army of the Lord.

That was the team which won the Mississippi championship, beating almost everybody without much trouble. Before the final game for the championship in Greenwood, with four thousand people waiting in the stands, Gentleman Joe delivered the best speech of all. *"Gentle-men,"* he said, using that staple designation which earned him his nickname, "I'm just a simple farmer. Fifteen acres is all I got, and two mules, a cow, and a lot of mouths to feed." He paused between his words, and his eyes watered over. "I've neglected my little crop because of this team, and the weevils gave me trouble last year, and they're doin' it again now. I ain't had enough rain, and I don't plan to get much more. The corn looks so brown, if it got another shade browner it'd flake right off. But almost every afternoon you'd find me in my pickup on the way to town to teach you gentlemen the game of baseball. You're fine Christian gentlemen who don't come no finer. But I saw you gettin' a little lazy yestiddy, showin' off some to all them cute little delta girls in the bleachers. We didn't come way up here to show off, we come up here to *win!*" Then, his pale blue eyes flashing fire, half whispering and half shouting, he said: "Gentlemen, I want us to pray, and then . . . I want you to go out there on that field and win this Miss'ippi champi-onship! You'll be proud of it for the rest of your lives. You'll remember it when you're ole men. You'll think about it when you're dyin' and your teeth are all gone. You'll be able to tell your grandchildren about this day. Go out there, gentlemen, and *win this ball game for your coach!"* After we prayed, and headed for that field like a pack of wild animals, the third baseman and I shouted in unison, and we meant it: "Boys, let's get out and win for our *coach!"* That fall they gave us shiny blue jackets, with "Miss. State Champions" written on the back; I was so happy with that jacket I almost wore it out. And when my old dog Skip died of a heart attack trying to outflank a flea that had plagued him since the Roosevelt Administration, looking at me with his sad black eyes and expiring in a sigh as old as death, that is what I wrapped him in before I took him in my arms and put him in the ground.

Two or three years later, when we were past the age for Legion competition, I had my last confrontation with baseball. The owner of the tire store organized a semi-pro team, made up of college and high school players from around the state. There was a popular tire that year called the "Screaming Eagle," and thus we were the Yazoo "Screaming Eagles," the pride of the delta. Out of a roster of fourteen, one made it to the major leagues, one to a Triple-A league, and two to Double-A. That team won the Deep South championship, and at the national tournament in Wichita beat the U.S. Navy and ended up close to the top.

The state league we played in, making twenty-five or thirty dollars apiece a game, was composed of both delta and hill-country towns, and we played to big Saturday night crowds who had heard about the Screaming Eagles, under lights so faulty that it was difficult to see a ball coming at you in the outfield. Insects bigger than fifty-cent pieces caromed off the bulbs and zoomed around us in our isolated stations in the field, and the ground was full of holes, ruts, and countless other hazards. Playing center field one night in one of the hill towns, I went back to examine a sloping red mound of earth that served as the outfield fence; I discovered a strand of barbed wire eight or ten feet long, an old garbage can full of broken beer bottles, and a narrow hole, partially covered with Johnson grass, that looked as if it might be the home for the local rattlers. The most indigenous field of all was near a little delta town called Silver City. It was built right on a cotton field and was owned by the two young heirs to the plantation on which it sat, one of whom later made it all the way to the New York Yankees. The grandstand would seat close to two thousand people, but the lights were so bad you had to exert all your finer perceptions to discriminate between the bugs and the balls; this took genius, and tested one's natural instincts. It was here, in the state finals, that a sinking line drive came toward me in right field, with the bases loaded and two out in the first inning; I lost track of that ball the moment it came out of the infield. A second later I felt a sharp blow on my kneecap, and then I saw the ball bouncing thirty feet away over by the bleachers. "*Get* it boy! Stomp on it! Piss on it!" the enemy bleacher section shouted gleefully, and by the time I could retrieve it three runs had scored. Between innings our pitcher, who soon would be pitching in the major leagues for the Pittsburgh Pirates, looked at me wordlessly, but with a vicious and despairing contempt. Right then, with the world before me, I promised myself that if I ever made it to those mythical cities of the North, the ones I had dreamed about in my Brooklyn cap, it would have to be with a different set of credentials.

From **BASEBALL AND THE COLD WAR**
Howard Senzel

At Hebrew school, we used to play a game called Chinese baseball. This consisted of throwing a tennis ball against the back wall behind the Holy Ark. It would rebound into a cinder-topped parking lot of fielders. There were specific delineations for singles, doubles, and triples. Over the cliff was a home run, but there were those who were robbed by death-defying, climbing-down-the-cliff catches.

All baserunning and scoring took place only within the minds of the players, but the image was absolutely complete. The reality of the situation was no more than throwing a tennis ball, but this time in company, and that made the experience as total as any big-league game. Despite the limitations, we all had our baseball personalities. The bunter, just trying to get on base, would use position and angle rather than strength, and try to get the ball to fall just over a jutted shed roof. The power hitters would take a long run and shoot for the cliff. All the tactics, strategy, and drama of real baseball, we had off that back wall.

Even as a young child I knew, from my cousins, about Monopoly, Parcheesi, Clue, and The Great Game of Sorry, but my board game was All-Star Baseball. It was a simple affair. The board consisted of some glossy printing and two mounted spinners. The players consisted of round disks marked off in numbered sections. The numbers stood for various kinds of hits and outs. The game consisted of placing the disks over the spinners and awaiting fate's control of the spin.

It was a simple game, but still, the players were personalized. Each year, new disks were issued, based on last season's all-star team. Duke Snider had the largest angle of possibility for a home run, although my uncle's old set from the thirties was sometimes brought out by my cousin, and that had Babe Ruth, with a home-run angle even larger than Snider's. It was my understanding that the game was scientifically designed so that if you played an entire season of games, each cardboard disk would reproduce the exact performance of that player in that season. Even though I knew baseball wasn't like that, I trusted the statistics to intensify the metaphor. And besides, if you could have Duke Snider, Willie Mays, and Hank Aaron on the same team, you didn't like to ask too many questions.

I played with my cousins and always kept score. Since the action existed only as an abstraction, keeping score was all that the game actually was. I kept the score sheets in the bottom of my night table, until the drawer was so full it cracked. Then I threw them all out and began again. The summer we moved to the suburbs, where I didn't know anyone, I played a ninety-nine-game season of all-star games between the National and American League teams of the previous year. At the end of the season, I computed every imaginable statistic for every player. It was not quite science. Four hundred hitters were quite common, and the average number of runs per game was nearly twenty, more than double the number of runs produced in real baseball. As I look back and see the amount of energy and concentration that went into the cardboard disks and spinners, I am amazed by the way this game was able to pull me into total transcendence. At school, I was never very good at arithmetic. But I did all of the computation for all the various averages, and I was accurate. Arithmetic was a discipline, and something I was not good at, but baseball statistics were simply the logical extension of the need to know. They had to be done correctly, and besides, they were never a chore if you knew that at the end of the arithmetic you would have an up-to-the-minute batting average.

When I was about twelve, David Friedman, my old KPAA captain and my friend, sent away for a very expensive, fancy, mail-order game called APBA. What the initials stood for is something I never inquired about and never found out. I spent many days of my life playing that game, but really it came too late. I had moved to the suburbs and begun to dream of driving automobiles and chasing after fast women before APBA ever had a chance to get its hooks into my imagination. Had the game come into my life when my dynasty of internal baseball was ascending, rather than collapsing, who knows how different my life might have been.

The game was very complicated, with many throws of different-size dice. There were different categories of pitchers, and the meaning of the roll of the dice varied accordingly. The batters were thrown with double-digit dice, allowing for the possibility of nearly every number between 11 and 66. A card for each batter translated the roll of the dice into that batter's performance, scientifically calculated on the basis of last year's actual performance. It was all very scientific and as manager you could duplicate the strategy decisions of real baseball. Yet the transformation from board game to mental baseball was never made for me by APBA as it was by All-Star Baseball. The trouble with the game was that it made you feel that you were always on the verge of mastering it, when it was clear that the game required at least a lifetime of devotion just to be comfortable with its mechanics. I kept waiting for the time when I would be able to jump up after throwing the dice and yell, "Eleven, home run, we win, yippie!" But that was a point I never reached. I seemed forever stuck at a primitive stage. The roll of the dice was always followed by "Eleven . . . Let's see, right-handed pitcher, Class C . . . No plus or minus, right? . . . Okay . . . Let's see, Roy Campanella . . . eleven . . . I think it was a home run, just let me check and make sure I looked in the right column."

What strikes me all these years later is not that APBA failed to consume me, but the extent to which it was given its chance. During that winter, my friend and I did manage to get through the entire National League season. That represents about six hundred games. And with the countless readings of all the cumbersome charts and tables, our commitment represents, by the standards of ordinary behavior, an overwhelming devotion to APBA baseball. Partly, this had to do with the scale of the game's price tag and our respectful desire to get our money's worth. But much more than this was the fact that we were not baseball novices. We knew the world of internal baseball, and we knew all kinds of other forms of transportation to get there. APBA was complicated, but nothing was more complex than real baseball, and so, with our difficulty, we came to believe that we were approaching a more complex, more exciting, and, therefore, a higher form of internal baseball.

———————

As I watched the vehemence with which Mrs. Tiant's noisemaker whirled, I realized that this was no minor religious feast, but the noisemaking of the romantic rallies of the earliest days of trade-union organizing. Luis Tiant's wife united an East European Jewish rite to the romantic union marches of the Industrial Revolution, and to the World Series. Here was this great Cuban lady, storming the knitting mills of Lancashire, denouncing the Jew's villain, and rooting for her husband. And so beautifully was he pitching that the comparison seemed justified. Nearly.

———————

And now I could remember Teddy Gold. In 1970, a young radical named Theodore Gold, who had been a leader of SDS at Columbia University, joined the Weathermen and went underground. A short time later, he was killed in the townhouse explosion in New York's Greenwich Village. He died attempting to execute the highly dangerous and extremely risky political act of calling for a civil war in order to see if the citizens will take you as seriously as the authorities. He died trying to make the bombs that would announce the revolution to a population that had to finish making their car payments before they could contemplate anything so drastic. But Ted Gold died for an ideal. And however remote his dream might seem to other people in other times, his seriousness cannot be doubted. He risked, and sacrificed, his life for what he believed.

And what he believed in was the truth of his own alienation. That this society and its institutions and human relationships were so bankrupt, corrupt, disordered, and awful that it would be worth risking his life in order to set in motion the forces that would change them. The first step was to destroy the illusions and the myths that hold up the institutions, and then perhaps even the odd bit of federal real estate or corporate headquarters.

And because he was known to be thoughtful, and intelligent, and serious, and because he gave his life, we also know that Ted Gold thought about these things. And thought about these things to a point where he was driven to become a bomber.

And in the end, Ted Gold was the Weatherman, the bomber, part of the fringe dismissed as lunatic by regular America. A very marginal member of society, indeed. Of all the kinds of people that this society produces, none had less stake in things as they are than Ted Gold. None was less committed to the preservation of traditions and institutions. None more desperate for change, and none more eager for total change. Ted Gold was not just willing to participate; he was willing to give his life.

And at the same time, Ted Gold was a fanatic follower of the New York and, later, the San Francisco Giants. He read the box scores every morning. And he was quoted as saying that he would have to wait until Willie Mays retired before he could become a true communist.

Now, the radical understanding of the function of professional baseball is: circus. Its effect was to divert the people from their natural inclination to think about their lot, and to keep them from getting restless. It was an opiate. It gave people room in which to tolerate intolerable circumstances. For a good radical, it was a joy of childhood, but definitely not worthy of serious consideration for anyone seriously political.

And baseball was also hero worship, and the star system, and the worst kind of indulgence in the American cult of the rugged, unique, superior individualist. A good communist was not interested in baseball. And so Ted Gold, who was committed enough to sacrifice his life for the cause, could not think of himself as a good communist. He was not prepared to give up baseball.

And now, in the middle of the World Series, near the very last moments of the baseball season, I finally understand Ted Gold's position.

Alienation is emotional, but radicalization is an intellectual process. Proposition, conclusion, and then anger. The process of becoming a radical is not only creating but channeling anger. And as the propositions and anger increase, they begin to form a pattern. It changes the way that the world is perceived. It changes the way that you live and the things that you want from life. The illusion is that the process is one of genuine rebirth, causing a new and different human being to emerge from the same consciousness. But the evidence is to the contrary.

The evidence is that there are depths beyond which an intellectual process cannot go. The evidence is that there are aspects of your own identity so strongly established that they cannot be penetrated by conviction, not to mention thought. There are things about our own identity that we cannot alter by decision. And baseball is one of those things.

The baseball fan does not decide, and in fact cannot decide, about baseball if it has seeped into the deepest sense of self. Because if baseball is there, that is who you are.

It is not that I realized I was declaring myself for baseball, but just that I got so totally and un-self-consciously into the baseball that I forgot all about the work. And it is not that I abandoned my job, but that the excitement of the baseball caused such disarray in my mind and my notes that categories dissolved. And I could feel every bone in my body vibrating to the beat of the detente. And then, "From across the water came Cuban Pete, He was doin' the boogie to the rhumba beat," came from my record player, and Hank Snow's voice synchronized all the other patterns. It's the rhumba boogie done the Rhumba-Cubanal style. It's Luis Tiant pitching. It's Fidel Castro being respected instead of patronized, imperialism revenged. It's a reminder of the passions that baseball produces, and a mutual forgiveness between my childhood and myself. And, of course, it is regulation baseball.

The baseball was superb, which should have been enough. And it was more than enough, but the evidence for my personally observed system had begun to go awry. The Tiant family had started to go to Hollywood. In the last game of the Series, they entered into a comfort with their celebrity. They were now mugging for the camera in ways that suggested they might have had a few lessons during the rain.

And their son, Luis, now aiming for immortality and even higher tax brackets, began to mix the metaphors in my mind. Luis Tiant, as he pitched, began the recounting of the storming of the Moncada Barracks, the young revolution's bleakest hour and most severe defeat. The stage had been set for the triumphal march into Havana. Instead, Tiant fell apart and was chased out in the seventh inning.

The ceremonial first pitch of the seventh game was thrown out by Joey Tramontana, a crippled boy representing the Jimmy Fund. The announcer told us that the Jimmy Fund was an old Boston Braves charity for crippled children that was taken over by the Red Sox when the Braves left for Milwaukee. A communal health problem in a culture which has destroyed community, I thought. But what did that make of the politics of the ceremonial first pitch, and wasn't it ever so slightly perverse to be looking there?

The national anthem was sung by the Winged Victory Chorus of the U.S. Third Army Airborne Division. They wore green sequined tuxedos and destroyed Boston's image as a city of conservatories. They were also a mistaken context for organized baseball. Baseball has prospered and streamlined its image for the corporate era. What were they doing, singing in sequined tuxedos?

But the World Series ended, and with it the impossible threads that I had felt obliged to pursue. And besides, I had relearned the joys of baseball and the subtleties of Cuban detente it might contain. There have been some hard knocks. Luis Tiant will be remembered as a King, but the very nature of the Series did not allow for the kind of solo heroism that political consideration desired. National television exposure, as well as diplomatic recognition, would have to wait. Detente, in a pretty successful trial balloon, was nevertheless set back a few cosmic places in the grand order of things. But Luis Tiant planted a metaphor in the consciousness of the American television public that was certain to bear fruit, one day. Just not today.

The media, as fickle as any superficial fan who pays attention to the World Series and nothing else, shifted their focus to the winning Cuban. A newspaper report of the last game highlights Tony Perez. The story wanders off the game and tells how, fifteen years ago, a teen-age ballplayer named Perez got discouraged and decided to return home to Cuba.

"Cuba had just fallen into the hands of Fidel Castro, and he had suddenly banned Cubans who played in America from going back, once they came home."

One sentence later, Perez was saying nice things about baseball, and in return, he was certified a World Series hero. Anyone who has studied the case will remember the president of the United States imposing an embargo, but no matter. My professional expert opinion on the matter is that the baseball expert at the State Department's Cuba Desk had staked not only some political judgment, but probably a lot of money, on Luis Tiant and the Boston Red Sox. And though Tiant came through beautifully, all the money behind Boston was lost. Hostility followed regret, and revenge was taken in the only area available. Tony Perez's heroism would be used to throw one last baseball insult at Fidel Castro. It was a small-minded exercise in bitter face-saving. Too insignificant a matter to alter the movement of baseball detente. Too futile a gesture, even, to mollify a bureaucrat's gambling losses.

The World Series was finally won by Cincinnati, the tie-breaking run being scored on a bloop single by Joe Morgan, with two out in the ninth inning of the seventh game. Which was typical. This was the most even match there ever was, and it produced the most exciting baseball anyone has ever seen. As World Series go, this was a jewel, and a classic, and, some said, the greatest ever.

For me, this World Series was baseball's final seduction. I found out many things in the course of the baseball season. But the World Series' final note rang in the deepest part of myself that I found, and that was baseball.

As I look back to the images of amazing baseball, there are too many instances too memorable to be contained in any one event. I think of Luis Tiant, bending and twisting and studying center field in the middle of his windup; baserunning with his face as much as his legs; playing both cat and mouse to Joe Morgan's famous lead off first base. And by contrast, in between Tiant's appearances, Reggie Cleveland throwing sixteen straight pitches to first base to hold Morgan, all of them, eventually, in vain.

And that glorious sixth game. Tiant's shellacking, Dwight Evans's catch, Bernie Carbo's second pinch-hit home run, and Carlton Fisk's game-winning hit, a home run worthy of announcing a candidacy upon. And too many more feats simply to catalogue. They were all part of the dramatic pattern, and therefore more spectacular than their story will ever sound. I have never seen a more interesting sequence of heroic activities organize themselves into a baseball game. Not to mention my new respect for the subtleties of Cuban detente.

And so, amidst tears and laughter, and songs of praise of motor oil, antifreeze, and beer, the cameras cut directly from the world champions' locker room to the Johnny Carson show, and the summer ended. Pete Rose, still covered in World Series sweat, had just finished saying, "I wish opening day was tomorrow." I did too.

And though this is certainly not the time or place to ask, there is a part of me that has been in turmoil all this time, and which still asks me, Why this baseball? Why not Greek tragedies and symphonies? Why not economics, history, and philosophy? And if it must be so esoteric, why not something closer to a master plot? Why get stuck in a metaphor that does not even hope to ring universal?

And now, finally, I can answer that question, because this baseball is now a part of me that I can see. And I can see that it runs deeper than other culture. Not traditional philosophy, and not traditional history, because in my identity, baseball runs deeper. Baseball is so deeply rooted that it is not subject to will. Baseball is the strongest, least vulnerable, and most confident piece of myself that I am in touch with. And so I am able to see all I see, and do all I do, through the metaphor of baseball. And no other framework could do this for me, because no other framework could ever allow me the same kind of access to myself.

And so it is by baseball that I am able to examine and express myself. And now this no longer seems odd or embarrassing to me. This is who I am.

CURVEBALL

Charles Barasch

That curveball,
that terrible hummingbird,
dropped over the plate
so soft, *so real*,
like a pear or breast,
striking me out.

I love the pitcher.
I sit on the bench cursing him.

That curveball was the wheel,
was wine, was cooked food,
was Stonehenge.

SECOND BASE & OTHER SITUATIONS

Geoffrey Young

Baseball is a team game of individual achievement. For example, there are no other feet but yours in the batter's box, you've got the bat in hand. You're waving it, your feet are set. But the pitcher, he's got the ball, he starts it up, he can throw it where he wills. You must react, you must wait and see where it's going, can you hit it. From the bench you hear, "Good eye," and "Green light."

You're playing second, you make a diving catch of a one-hop grounder almost behind the bag, but you can't get your body and glove and arm back in position (sitting) quickly enough to make the short toss for the force out on the runner sliding into second. Sensation of the dream's slow-motion time, great stop goes for naught.

Men on first and second no outs, hard hit ball to shortstop, you notice the runner at second has had to wait until the ball passes him before advancing to third, you come across second for the flip from short for one out, then fire to *third base* yelling "Tag him!" your throw just misses runner's back, is caught, runner runs into the glove double play.

Line drive hit right at you, not a knuckler, it's got just a hint of top spin on it, you put glove up near chin, but top spin carries the ball down a hair, the drive bounces off the heel of your glove for an error. Next guy up drives in two runs.

A ball in the gap, fast runner on first, you go out to get the relay arms raised yelling "Hit me in the head" it's a one-hop peg from right center, shortstop's yelling "Home!" you turn no time to aim and fire in one motion to the plate, throw's a strike in the air catcher's so stunned he's not sure what's happened in the collision the runner's out, has held on.

Single to left past the shortstop in the hole on a damp night, the ball will be wet you round first notice left fielder down on one knee just coming up with the ball, you turn it on for second, slide head first as ball comes in high and slightly to the left of the bag.

Last inning of first game of the year, you're up a run, men on first and second, one out, a hard hit ball to you at second, perfect game-ending double play ball hits pocket of glove and in that haste to turn it over get possession of the ball which bounces off fingers reaching for it, you scurry to get the force at second god-damn nerves!, you look at the pitcher, say nothing, next guy up doubles, both runners score, you lose.

A. You're going badly, nothing's dropping in, let's face it, you're swinging like a preschooler with a drumstick, so even when your team is winning, you have a hard time feeling it.

B. "My stats! My stats!" Secret pleasure in idle moments wondering what your average might be, because you went five for five hitting perfect shots to places where they *wasn't*. Team's under .500, but the wife looks great, kids're angels asleep.

You play in a local slow-pitch tournament, costs each player $5 to enter, double elimination, couple of guys don't show up, have to use a guy behind the plate who's never played, or rarely, lose two straight, not a single ground ball hit to you in 14 innings.

You don't slide because you're eager to get dirty, to skin your knee or decorate your butt, but because you've got to get to that base as fast as you can, and without running past it. You have no choice, whistle of ball in air at your ear.

Fielding grounders: as ball jumps off bat, *instant reading* by quick eye which sets body moving toward the ball in a rhythm that allows fielder maximum ease in stopping the ball and with feet gliding underneath body comes up from its crouch in one motion the ball in hand arm throwing hard to first.

A first baseman who scoops out your worst throws. Baseball is a team game of individual achievement. Single after single after single.

You boot an easy grounder (drop easy fly ball), look up at nearest teammate, say something horrendously accurate about the nature of the universe, and god, propagation, motherhood, try and laugh it off, comes out putrid bile, you turn quickly inward, get head back in game, how many outs? spit in pocket, crouch for next pitch, poised, eager, unforgiven by contemptuous self but forgotten in surge of action, moving toward ball, or bag.

Popping up with men on base. Or a chance to win it, two outs, man on second, tie game, last of ninth, hit an unmitigated bullet right back at pitcher who sticks up his glove in self-defense, ball sticks in pocket, you never get a foot out of the box. Extra innings. Shortstop flips you your glove.

Say it's raining slightly, your team is being crushed. Your outfield has misplayed or dropped outright FIVE balls, and like drunks your team has been struggling for purchase in the muddy batter's box. You might come away feeling terrible, be inclined to drink postgame draft beer to excess, out of anger, but you don't. A blow-out is a blow, but it's not even that. Nor is it the rain, which *is* dangerous. No. You're almost elated because of two great double plays, the second of which was pure accomplishment under the guise of routine execution. Three-hop grounder to third playing fairly deep, fields it clean, throws a ball chest high to you coming across second for one, you get rid of the ball in a blink to first *with* something on it, beat runner by half step, side retired, you're running in (light-headed) to take your turn at the plate. Wet softball, two good throws.

Pitcher backing up third prevents overthrow and a free base. Calls time.

Baseball puts you on the defensive. In the field, you don't know where the ball will be hit, or when. As a batter, you don't know exactly where the pitcher will throw it, or how fast, with what arc, two strikes on you. You may anticipate, you may guess, you may cheat a half step, you might squeeze 'em, but you *must* react, you *must* adjust to the ifs of velocity and direction. Readiness is half. Not knowing is what makes the game compelling. Those first few steps. Having thought it, before it happens. The edge, a foot either way. You're all attention, what to do, when to do it, this vividness alone, *per se*, for itself.

SPRING TRAINING

Lynn Rigney Schott

The last of the birds has returned—
the bluebird, shy and flashy.
The bees carry fat baskets of pollen
from the alders around the pond.
The wasps in the attic venture downstairs,
where they congregate on warm windowpanes.
Every few days it rains.

This is my thirty-fifth spring;
still I am a novice at my work,
confused and frightened and angry.
Unlike me, the buds do not hesitate,
the hills are confident they will be
perfectly reflected
in the glass of the river.

I oiled my glove yesterday.
Half the season is over.
When will I be ready?

On my desk sits a black-and-white postcard picture
of my father—skinny, determined,
in a New York Giants uniform—
ears protruding, eyes riveted.
Handsome, single-minded, *he* looks ready.

Thirty-five years of warmups.
Like glancing down at the scorecard
in your lap for half a second
and when you look up it's done—
a long fly ball, moonlike,
into the night
over the fence,
way out of reach.

THE ANXIOUS FIELDS OF PLAY

Richard Hugo

By the mid-thirties, when I was ten or eleven, baseball had become such an obsession that I imagined ballparks everywhere. In the country, I visualized games in progress on the real grass cattle were eating. In the city as I rode down Fourth Avenue on the bus, the walls of warehouses became outfield fences with dramatic doubles and triples booming off them. Hitting was important in my fantasies. Pitching meant little except as a service necessary for some long drive far beyond the outfielders. I kept the parks small in my mind so home runs wouldn't be too difficult to hit.

The lot across the street from my grandparents' house was vacant and whenever I could get enough neighborhood friends to join me we'd have a game there. In center field a high board fence bounded the west side of the Noraines' backyard. It was about a hundred feet from the worn spot we called home plate. The right-field fence, a good forty feet away at the imagined foul line, ran east and bordered the north side of the Brockermans' yard. "Over the fence," I yelled, "is a home run." "Over the fence," said Mr. Brockerman from his yard, hoping to keep his windows intact, "is out." "It's our game and we can make the rules, and besides you can't even get a job," I yelled back. It was a cruel remark. The Depression was on and my grandfather was the only man in the neighborhood who had steady work. A few years later when I was old enough to realize the hopeless state of things for men during the Depression, I wanted to apologize to Mr. Brockerman, but he had long since moved away. No left-field fence. Just some trees and the ground of the Burns's yard, looking more trampled than the ferns and grass of the vacant lot.

One evening the men in the neighborhood joined us for a game. I was so excited, I bubbled. Growing up with my grandparents, I missed the vitality of a young father. I ran about the field loudly picking all the men for my team. My hopes for a dynasty were shattered when a grown-up explained that we might have a better game if we chose even sides. Days after, I trudged about the neighborhood asking the fathers if they would play ball again, but no luck.

When my grandparents had the basement put in, a concrete full-sized basement replacing the small dirt cave where Grandmother had kept her preserves, a pile of gravel was left on the north side of the house. Our house was the only house on that side of the block and in my mind the woods to the north became a baseball field. The rocks—smooth, round, averaging about the size of a quarter—were perfect for my purpose.

I fashioned a bat by carving a handle on a one-by-four and I played out entire nine-inning games, throwing the rocks up and swatting them into and over the trees. Third base was a willow tree. Second base was (I knew exactly in my mind) just beyond the honeysuckle and the giant hollow stump that usually held a pool of rainwater inside its slick mossed walls. Many times that pool reflected the world and my face back at me in solitary moments. First base, not really important because I seldom hit rocks that way, was vaguely a clump of alders.

I knew exactly how far a rock had to sail to be a home run. It had to clear the fence I dreamed beyond the woods. My games were always dramatic and ended with a home run, bases loaded, three runs down, two out, the count three and two, bottom of the ninth. How did I manage that? It was easy. I could control my hits well enough to hit three singles to load the bases because my notion of what constituted a single was flexible. Then I'd select a rock whose size and shape indicated it might sail well, and clobber it. If, for some reason, it didn't sail far enough to be a home run, I simply tried again.

Inning after inning, I swatted rock outs, rock singles, rock doubles, rock triples, and rock home runs. I was the Yankees and also my opponents, the Giants. The only major-league ball I heard was the World Series. It was carried on the radio and the Yankees were usually playing. The Yankees also had the most glamorous stars. Sometimes I played out the entire series, all seven, letting the Giants win three. The score mounted. The lead changed hands. Then the last of the ninth, when Babe Ruth, Lou Gehrig, or Joe DiMaggio broke it up. I don't remember now if Ruth still played with New York when DiMaggio joined the team but on my Yankees they were teammates.

One game, the dramatic situation in the ninth, a strong wind was blowing, as usual from the south. I tossed a flat round stone, perfect for sailing, and caught it just right. I still can see it climb and feel my disbelief. It soared out over the trees, turned over once, and started to climb like a determined bird. I couldn't have imagined I'd ever hit one that far. It was lovely. It rose and rose. I thought it might never stop riding that high wind north. It crossed the imaginary left-field fence before its flight became an aesthetic matter, and it disappeared, a dot, still climbing, somewhere over Rossner's store on the corner of 16th and Barton. I believe that rock traveled about two blocks. Why not? Joe DiMaggio had hit it.

I couldn't see the neighborhood beyond the trees. I simply drove the rocks out over the woods and imagined the rest, though sometimes I heard doubles rattle off the sides and roof of the community hall in center field just beyond the woods. A few years later I realized how dangerous my Yankees had been, spraying stones about the neighborhood. During my absence in World War II, the woods were wiped out by new housing.

One Sunday I left the house to play off somewhere and so was gone when my Uncle Lester from Tacoma showed up without warning to see if I wanted to go with him to watch the Seattle Indians play in the Pacific Coast League. When I got home and found I'd missed the chance, I wept bitterly and whined against the fates. I was still whining and sobbing when my uncle returned on his way back home. He must have been touched by my disappointment because he returned the following Sunday and this time I was ready. It was kind of him. He saw that I was a bored, lonely boy. Grandfather had few passions outside of the house and the yard, and no interest in baseball.

When I was old enough and had some money, I went to the Sunday doubleheaders alone, catching a bus downtown and transferring to a trolley—an hour-long trip from White Center. I was there by ten o'clock when the park opened and waited for the players to arrive. I collected autographs of course and saw several stars on their way to the big leagues, including Ted Williams, who was hitting around .260 with San Diego. I took it all in, hitting practice, infield practice, then the two games. I went filled with anticipation, heart pounding, but I sat, untypically for someone my age, quietly in the stands watching the game. Recently my Aunt Dol, Lester's widow, told me that in church I would sit so quietly for a small boy that people remarked on it. I can remember that despite my nervousness and anxiety, I also had moments when I was unusually patient and quiet. I could wait for hours with nothing to do. Given the drabness of life with my grandparents, I had developed ways of entertaining myself in my mind.

In 1936, I was a seventh grader and a substitute on the Highland Park Softball Team. That was something. Seldom did anyone but an eighth grader make the team, even as a sub. "You can beat eggs. You can beat cream. But you can't beat Highland Park's softball team." That was our yell, and the vowel repeat of "beat cream" intrigued me even then. The last game of that season, Mr. Fields, the coach, sent me in to pinch hit. I was twelve and had never been in a league game before. I was excited and frightened and people seemed to swirl, the other players, Mr. Fields, and Miss Shaefer, our other coach. My hero, Buss Mandin, our star pitcher, was watching. The world was watching. The pitcher was no longer another boy, he was a stranger from another universe. The ball came, surely too fast for any mortal to hit, yet as slow as if dreamed. I don't remember swinging. The bat seemed to swing itself and I saw the ball lining over the shortstop hole into left field, a clean single. Mandin, Fields, and Shaefer smiled approval from the sidelines as I held first. I had found a way of gaining the attention and approval of others and I was not to let it go for nearly thirty years.

In the eighth grade next year, I was the softball team catcher. Ralph Lewin, a short thick powerful boy, was the pitcher. He was good. I was good too and not afraid of the bat—a consideration at that age. I crouched quite close to the hitter and didn't flinch when he swung. Actually, the closer you squat to the batter the easier catching is.

One night Ralph and I were at Betty Moore's house. She was the cutest girl in school and somehow I was supposed to be "with her." We were on a sun porch, the three of us, all thirteen years old. Betty's older brother and another boy his age had girls in the darkened front room and were necking. Ralph urged me to kiss Betty but I was far too scared. He said to me, with disdain, "This is what you do," and he kissed her. I tried to keep my composure and I said, "Oh, is that it?" or something like that and humiliation flooded my stomach. They went on necking. I had never seen a man kiss a woman before except in the movies, and I'm not putting anyone on when I say that I really thought people kissed only in films. I can never remember being kissed as a child nor did I ever see any show of affection between my grandparents. I walked out, my face flushed with shame, through the dark living room where one of the older boys yelled some insult at me, and finally, after years of groping, into the fresh air outside, free and alone. I walked the mile home, degraded and in anguish, and as I cried my tears created a secondary glow around the streetlights. I wanted to be like Ralph Lewin, like Betty Moore's brother, like anybody else. At home, my grandparents were already asleep, and I sat alone, as I did so many times in that still house, and stared into the solitary void I was certain would be my life.

But on the ballfield Ralph and I were social equals. One day we played the alumni, now freshmen and sophomores in high school, and I struck out, fooled badly on a change of pace. The fans laughed. Maybe I couldn't do anything about the humiliation I'd suffered in Betty Moore's house, but I could do something about it on the ballfield. I promised myself no one would ever fool me again on a change of pace, and I kept my promise. I developed a technique of hitting late, of starting my swing at the last possible moment to avoid being tricked. Nearly all my hits for the next thirty years were to my off field, right field. Over the years, whenever players asked me why I hit to right and never pulled the ball, I told them a half-truth. I said I hit better to right field. That was true. When I hit to left, I tended to grind the ball into the dirt. But I never told them the real reason.

That final year in grammar school we won the championship of our league in an extra-inning game against E. C. Hughes. They had beaten us out of the soccer championship in an overtime game just a few months before and the softball win felt good. I looked to the city play-offs with confidence. In my small world, how could any team be better than ours? Our first playoff game we were defeated by a team of seven Orientals, two blacks, and a tall Jewish short fielder by the score of 14 to 0. Despite my working-class background I was lucky to grow up knowing prejudice was wrong, but I remember thinking then that minority people possessed some sort of magic.

My hitting was my ticket to acceptance. That first summer out of grammar school I spent with my mother in Bremerton, and I joined a softball team. The opening game was played in a pasture, very like the pastures I'd imagined into ballfields years before, and I hit a single, a double, a triple, and two home runs. My standing with the other boys, strangers just a few days before, was insured. The summer was mine.

After that I turned to hardball for several years. In the Park League I began as a pitcher but one day a shower of triples and home runs convinced me that either second base or the outfield was where I really belonged. The summer I was fourteen I played second base on the Boulevard Park Merchants. All the other players were adults except for my buddy, George Zimmerman, who lived in Boulevard Park and had me try out for the team. I also made the American Legion Team in West Seattle and hit around .350 for the season.

Often a ballgame gave me confidence I could find nowhere else. Once, playing center field in a Park League game when I was around fifteen, I memorized the lineup of the opposing team, and in the last inning, score two to one in our favor and the other team threatening with men on base and two out, I detected a player batting out of turn. The umpire checked and called the batter out.

In high school, though I made the squad all four years, I spent three of them on the bench. I knew the coach, Lloyd Doty, was reluctant not only to cut pitchers but even to try to distinguish between pitchers and players who called themselves pitchers. So I hung in there calling myself a pitcher and became a batting practice ace. Park League experience had taught me three things about my pitching. One, I had exceptional control for a boy; two, I was easy to hit; three, when

I was hit, the ball went a hell of a long way. I was indispensable to the morale of the starting hitters. "Just throw your fastball, Richard," Coach Doty said.

In my senior year, a starting outfielder was caught burglarizing a clothing store and was sent up for a year. I declared myself an outfielder and played every game in right field. I had a miserable season, made errors, failed to hit consistently. My desire for acceptance was so overwhelming in high school that out in the field or at bat I was dizzy with tension and fear of failing in front of the students. I remember I played better when we were away at other schools.

I played semi-pro ball in the city leagues after that and did well. Just after I turned nineteen, I was called into the service. In the army, the chances to play were few, and I seized them when they came. I remember playing second with some sharp players, one of them a professional, at Logan, Utah, where we held infield drills on the Utah State campus quadrangle. I put everything into it, whipping the final throw of each infield round from second to home in a taut rope that sang through the thin mountain air as the spectators gasped. I remember playing third base in a monastery courtyard at the Army Air Corps rest camp on Capri, while the monks and a Red Cross girl with gorgeous legs looked on. I did not relax on a ballfield. I always played my best no matter how makeshift the game.

I was discharged in June of '45, and I immediately joined a semi-pro team in the city league. It was clear to me by then that I was fouled up sexually and I was drinking more and more. I even played a game drunk and hit a triple far over the right fielder's head. I ended up at third base gagging. The run had made me sick and the manager took me out.

I turned out for the University of Washington team in the spring of '46, and made the squad for a few weeks until I was caught playing intramural softball and cut. That summer I played on another semi-pro team but was told to get out by the grim manager after the fourth game when I made the mistake of trying to joke with him after we'd lost a close one. That hurt, the sudden hostile and permanent rejection when I was only trying to be friendly. I remember saying good-bye to one of the players, and though I barely knew him, I was close to tears. I felt I was losing something I loved, and with my life so void of satisfaction, the loss seemed monumental. The good-bye I was saying to whoever that player was seemed a big good-bye to many things.

I went to school, off and on, majoring in creative writing but tiring badly after three or four quarters. Then I'd go out and find a menial job somewhere. I worked in warehouses and at a steel mill, then in California at an ammunition magazine. In the summer of '47 I went back to softball, to a team in West Seattle. Several members were old friends from high school, and they were good players. I came to the team after the season started and it took awhile before I got into the lineup, but by the end of the season I was the catcher. It felt good crouching close to the batter as Jimmy Gifford's pitches broke past the batter into my glove for the third strike and I wheeled the ball down to Ed Schmidt at first base to start the infield throw around.

For the next thirteen years, I played softball in the West Seattle Class A League. The first year we lost the championship to a veteran team, the West Seattle Auto Dealers, in a playoff game. But we had the nucleus of a good team, as well as the camaraderie of young men who had known each other for several years, and in 1948 we became the power of the league. By then I had studied two quarters with Theodore Roethke and was working on poems at home in the evening, when I wasn't out drinking. I was still living with my grandparents who were nearing the end. With no sex life, there seemed little reason for me to move out. I was frozen, a perpetual fifteen, but after a bad two or three years, I was playing ball again and loving it. My appetite for acceptance, for the approval of others, was satisfied on the ballfields, if nowhere else.

Ken Gifford, Jim's brother and one of my high school chums, played third base. John Popich, four or five years younger than Gifford and I, played shortstop, and his cousin, Walt, about my age, played second. Ed Schmidt, also a high school friend, played first. That was the nucleus of the team. When Jim Gifford went to Seattle University to play basketball and pitch softball, Mimo Campagnaro, a strange hypochondriac who threw best on those days he complained of a wrenched back or a devastating headache, became our pitcher. Stinkey Johnson, another high school friend, was the backup pitcher to Mimo. For years, it was like we were still kids, or so it seemed to one of us.

The last scheduled game of the season in 1948, we found ourselves again playing the West Seattle Auto Dealers. We were tied in the standings for first place, so again the championship was on the line. With two out and the tying run on second in the last of the seventh, I drilled a single up the middle to send the game into extra innings. (Oh, Joe DiMaggio.) Ed Schmidt was managing and, though not a demonstrative man, he couldn't hide his delight in the first-base coaching box. We won in the bottom of the eighth.

I remained after the others went home. Dark clouds were moving in from the southwest. The field seemed lonely and forlorn, abandoned to the dusk. I luxuriated in the memory of the game just completed, and in some odd way I felt at one with the field deserted to the wind. Several times I visited ballfields in the fall and winter and sat alone in the car remembering some game I'd played there, as the rain fell or leaves blew across the empty grounds.

I cultivated a casual, joking attitude on the field to hide the seriousness with which I took each game. But I betrayed that seriousness by showing up earlier than the others and sitting around the park alone waiting for the equipment to arrive. Whenever players were late, I kept an anxious lookout. (Two more and we'll have nine and won't have to forfeit.) I took that anxiety into the batter's box. I doubt that in those nearly thirty years of ball, I ever batted relaxed. Because hitting was so important, I developed ways of countering my anxiety. I managed to remove any idea of competition from my mind by ignoring the pitcher as a human being until he vanished and only the ball remained. If I was aware of the pitcher as a man, I was finished.

John Popich was just the opposite. He had to hate the opposition. "Let's beat these bastards," he would say without one touch of humor. He grew up in Riverside, where West Marginal Way parallels the Duwamish River, the son of Yugoslavian immigrants, and life for him was an endless fight. Like most of those who grew up in Riverside, he had moved to middle-class West Seattle. I think he suffered conflicts that many children of immigrants do: the society pulling him one way, his loyalty to his heritage pulling him the other. He often spoke with fondness of Yugoslavian dishes his mother prepared. And he insisted, perhaps too much, on poking fun at the Italians on the team—Mimo and his brother Freddie; Robert Rimpini, an outfielder; and Morrie Capalato, another outfielder, Italian-Jewish by background, who owned a small grocery in Alki. Popich's remarks usually implied the superiority of Yugoslavs. His cousin Walt, from the same area and circumstances, but emotionally far less complicated, suffered little conflict. When he spoke of Riverside, which he had left behind for good, it was usually as "those people."

Physically, John was easily the most gifted player on the team—fast, unusually strong, well coodinated. From his shortstop position, he fired accurate cannon shots at Schmidt who took them easily in his cool, unhurried way as if they were easy tosses. Popich had one failing that prevented him from realizing his potential. He couldn't adjust his aggressive instincts to conditions. One game, he flew out every time up trying to power the ball against a hopelessly stiff wind. With Schmidt's cool, he could have played professional baseball.

One game, at Alki Field, I was run over in a play at home. That was the one play I hated. It is always open season on the catcher, and later, during my last four or five years, I gave up blocking the plate and started tagging runners like a third baseman, flashing in once with my hands and getting out of there. This time, I made the mistake of taking Popich's streaking relay squatting on my haunches. The ball and runner arrived at the same time and the runner, seeing how vulnerable I was, ran me down. His knee crashed into my head and I rolled back, green stars exploding. I remember lying there on the plate, holding the ball for a moment before my right hand involuntarily relaxed and the ball dribbled out. I was taken out, of course. I had double vision and my right arm ached from a stretched nerve trunk, a neuritis that stayed with me for three months. The run tied the game.

In the last of the seventh, Popich hit the longest home run I've seen in softball. The bases were loaded at the time, and the ball went far over the head of Jack Marshall, a fast young left fielder. It must have landed 150 feet beyond him as he ran back and he had already been playing deep. I believe it would have cleared many left-field fences in baseball parks. With my double vision, I saw two unbelievable drives sailing over two Jack Marshalls, and eight runners scoring.

Popich's home runs were raw power, shots that seemed to take less than a second in flight. Schmidt's were just the opposite. In one game, he unloaded two home runs and with his classic swing the balls didn't seem hard hit at all. They soared slowly like lazy birds, beautiful to watch, like the rock I'd hit that day. Popich batted third, Schmidt fourth, and I followed, swinging the bat like I was swatting off demons, driving the ball late into right field. Despite our hitting, we were primarily a defensive team. In a typical game, we would grab an early lead, then play flawless defensive ball. Once we got the lead we seldom added to it. We concentrated on defense as if we considered the game already won. Usually, it was.

Most of the others were married and getting on with their lives. I took the scorebook home and computed averages. When I listened to professional games on the radio, I often lined out a score sheet on a piece of paper, using the blunt back edge of Grandmother's bread knife for a rule, and scored the entire game sitting alone at the table in the kitchen. I watched my dissolute life passing. Sometimes with anger and resentment that exploded into verbal abuse of friends when I was drunk and filled me with shame the next day when, terrified I'd end up friendless and alone, I made embarrassed apologies. Sometimes with frustration when I refused to admit my defeat and sought out women only to find myself unable to conquer my timidity. But mostly with sadness and the intense love of simple compensations like softball and fishing.

One day, before a game at Lincoln Park, I'd come early as usual, and was sitting in the grass near some boys in their middle teens. They were talking about girls and chewing the tender root ends of grass blades. "Sharon's easy," one of them said, "Jesus, she's easy." He was smiling. Ten years younger than I was, and already they knew more about life than I believed I ever would. I looked away through the trees at the sea. Somewhere out there beyond me was a life of normalcy and I was certain I would never be a part of it. It was farther than the islands I could see. It was beyond reach. It was a sad moment and I wanted the players to come and the game to begin.

Within a few years we had become a smooth, balanced team. Jim Gifford came back. He was now one of the best throwers in Seattle and could have pitched AA ball. Gordon Urquhart replaced Walt Popich at second base and we formed the best team I've ever played on. Urquhart and I managed the team, or rather I should say Urquhart managed the team on the field and I planned strategy with him over a beer at our sponsor's place, the Blew Eagle Cafe. The strange spelling occurred during the Depression. Gino, the original owner, first named it the Blue Eagle Cafe, but when the Roosevelt administration launched the National Recovery Act in the early thirties, it adopted as its symbol a blue eagle. Every time a radio announcer said, "Look for a blue eagle," Gino got free advertising. The government insisted he comply with some law by changing the name, but Gino complied only by changing the spelling. The possibilities for obscenity were too good to pass up.

We went through the league undefeated, the first team to do it since the twenties, and that season I played in the most perfectly played game I can remember. Neither side made a mistake. Jim Gifford threw a no-hitter. The opposing pitcher threw a two-hitter. We won late in the game on a triple by our center fielder, Jim Burroughs, and an infield out. I remember it well because it again reflected the way I felt about things in general and my poems in particular. If something was good in itself, well done, it made no difference whether it was important or not, nor whether it had an audience. Here was a game in a Class A softball league at Alki Playfield in a city in the Far West, one of thousands of such games going on all over the country with practically no one watching, and yet the game itself had been played with a perfection that to me made it important. I was constantly looking for perfection in my poems. It was a handicap really, because in my drive for perfection I rewrote poems completely out of existence. I was blind to all the mistakes I can see there now, but had I seen them then, I would have rewritten again and again until the mistake was gone. And while I didn't realize it then, the reason I had to rewrite so much was that making real changes was so difficult. Each rewrite was almost the same thing over, done with the hope something would change and that, in turn, would trigger other changes that would finally result in a perfect unit of sound. My perfectionism was really a symptom of stagnation. No matter how I tried, my poems, like my life, were going nowhere. Later I tried to handle this theme in a long poem called "Duwamish Head." That's where the Duwamish is backed up by the sea and no longer seems to flow.

Gordon Urquhart was the most interesting person I played ball with. By lucky accident we found ourselves working together at Boeing and I got to know him well. He surmounted setbacks and adversity with a resiliency I found monumental and he had a great sense of humor. He had been a marine NCO in Korea in an outfit overrun by the Chinese. He found himself one night standing in the dark, firing wildly as Chinese soldiers in bewildering numbers rushed by all around him. He was hit in the leg and, typical of him, took charge of the survivors he could find the next morning and led them back to safety, hobbling on his wounded leg.

He loved his wife and she died, strangled in an asthmatic seizure while he held her, help on the way too late. I remember the voice over the intercom at work telling him to call home and his hurried departure. I offered my awkward condolences a few days later when he returned. "Yes," he said, "it was a shock." He was most composed and his grief never surfaced, despite his emotional honesty. Later, he remarried and went on his indestructible way. An alder. A catfish. Those were my two private nicknames for masters of survival.

Gordon loathed the idea of privileged people, people on top. He used to say sarcastically, "What's happening to your precious Yankees?" when they were losing. He also hated Sugar Ray Robinson, and was outraged when Robinson got a championship fight against Bobo Olson, while Tiger Jones, who had beaten Robinson, was ignored. Of course, I loved Robinson and the Yankees because they had class, which, to paraphrase Henry Reed, in my case I had not got. Like my grandfather, who identified with Henry Ford, I appreciated the most successful, especially those who had what I thought of as style—those who won and looked good doing it. Urquhart was a winner who identified with the underprivileged, but only those who tried. (In my poems, I was on the side of the losers who lived their defeat.)

Urquhart's hatred of privilege was so intense, I think his own drive for success must have involved some conflict. I even imagine he may have disliked himself for it. The first time I met his father, he told me with undisguised bitterness that Roosevelt had broken him. I didn't get the story clear, but it seemed to involve large holdings of beef Mr. Urquhart had had in Montana in the thirties, a situation sure to profit him considerably until the federal government had made beef available at low prices or for free to the poor. Something like that, as I remember. This seemed to have ruined him for good, because he still dwelled on it with considerable anger despite the years that had gone by. I remember I was bewildered by it because my world was so small and immediate that to hate Roosevelt years after his death seemed a little like being pissed off at Xerxes.

Whatever Urquhart's relation was with his father, it must have involved intense attitudes about success and failure. When Robinson knocked out Gene Fullmer, I was delighted. Urquhart, of course, was furious and suggested at lunch the next day that New York money had bought Fullmer to take a dive. Fullmer was Urquhart: without style or grace, tough and aggressive, and, probably most important, from a remote area where he could not benefit from the New York publicity centers. Urquhart had moved to Seattle from eastern Montana. Like Fullmer, he was a fighter from the moon. Urquhart was assailing Robinson, when I said, unexpectedly (even I didn't expect it and had I thought about it probably wouldn't have said it), "Isn't what you really don't like about him is that he is a success?"

I might have accused him of murder. He was stunned and flashed into anger. I could have crawled away and died. I apologized later for the obvious hurt he had felt but he was still angry and accepted my apology with something less than graciousness. Some people may think it odd that I would apologize when his anger demonstrated I was probably right. Let them. One of my favorite quotes is Valéry's: "I can't think of anything worse than being right."

Urquhart had little natural ability. He looked terrible in practice. He booted grounder after grounder. Made bad throws. He could never have made any team as good as ours had we not known how good he was once the game started. I never remember Gordon making an error in a game, and although not a consistent hitter, he seldom failed when it counted. Unlike most softball players he took his competitive instincts to his job and I've heard he has risen quite high in the Boeing company. I daresay he did it on plenty of hard work and guts, clawing away, refusing to be beaten. He lacked the physical gifts of Popich, the fast reflexes of Ken Gifford, or the cool smoothness of Schmidt. Yet, more than anyone on the team, he was responsible for the best season we had. I find it hard to think of him in a high executive position. He was never good at hiding his feelings, an honesty not usually found in corporate executives. I can't imagine him as cold or manipulative, or anything really but a nice, tough, and resilient man. I remember him vividly because we played ball together. That was our link. We both loved playing, he with his honest intensity, and I with my intensity hidden behind my jokes because I knew if it surfaced it would ruin my ability to play.

Years after I was finally able to have sexual relations with women, I continued to play ball, both in the West Seattle League and in the Boeing League (employees only). Our West Seattle team got old, like that team we had first beaten out for the championship, and we found ourselves coming in second more often than first in the league. I published some painting poems in *Contact*, one of the best of the early West Coast magazines, and for the picture on the cover sent in a photo of myself in a Boeing All-Star softball shirt. I took a kind of perverse delight (still do) in not looking like a poet, and I enjoyed appearing on the cover looking like a jock alongside the pictures of the other contributors, some of them terribly affected shots (face half-hidden by smoke in the coffeehouse gloom), when inside the magazine my poems, with reproductions of the paintings that had triggered them, were by far the artiest items there.

Bob Peterson, the San Francisco poet and now a good friend, was poetry editor. He is also a baseball nut and, I think, entertains fantasies of himself as a star pitcher. When, for the contributors' notes, I sent in my Boeing League–leading batting average of .541, he reduced it to .400. "No one," he said, "would believe .541." "They would if they had seen the pitching," I wrote back. There were younger and much better players on our Boeing team, several of them top players in the city leagues, but they didn't take our games seriously and tried only to see how far they could hit the ball. I was still hitting as intensely as always to right field no matter how absurd the score or weak the opposition.

A friend named Bill Daly pitched for that Boeing team. Bill made a remark one day to Dick Martin, the third baseman, that had a lot of wisdom: "Dick, I was thinking the other day how much time we've put into this game all these years. What if we'd put that time into work, making a living. We'd probably be rich." Bill also pitched against us in the West Seattle League, and though I knew his stuff well, he struck me out one game. He did it with a drop, not too much on it, that came in high and outside and dipped into the strike zone. I'd seen it all the way, saw it drop into my favorite spot, and I never pulled the trigger. (Good-bye, Joe.) I walked away, the message clear, remembering many times I'd slammed that pitch deep into the right center field gap, had seen the outfielders turned and running as I rounded first on my way to a triple or home run. My reflexes were going and I knew it as I sat down and waited for the inning to end. I didn't feel sad. I didn't feel any sense of loss. I didn't feel humiliated at striking out as I once would have, though I was still intensely trying to avoid it. More than just the reflexes had gone.

The only good sports poem I can remember reading was one called "Cobb Would Have Caught It" by Robert Fitzgerald. Whenever I tried to write about baseball or softball, I found myself thinking about the game itself and the poem kept turning into a melodramatic sports story with the winning hit coming at the crucial moment. (Oh, Joe DiMaggio. Oh, beautiful rock sailing downwind high over 16th and Barton.) I was interested in the score, not the words.

In the summer of '72, two of my students were playing softball in Missoula and I started going to the games. I foolishly put my name on the roster one night at the last minute to avoid a forfeit and before the season was over I played four games, a fat middle-aged man standing in the outfield, being eaten by mosquitoes and wishing he could lose twenty years for an hour and a half. My first time at bat in a serious game (serious because the pitcher was throwing hard) I lined a double over the right fielder's head. Anyone else would have had a home run. I hobbled into second just as surprised as the spectators. The last game I played I pulled off a running one-handed catch before a large crowd that went wild. I couldn't believe it when the ball, blurred by sweat and fear, hit my glove and stuck there as I ran full tilt toward the foul line. But now only luck was on my side and luck has a way of running out. I loved those late triumphs but I could also laugh at them.

I took interest in the whole scene, not just the game. Except for those times I was obliged to play to prevent forfeits, I sat in the stands and took note of the spectators as well as the game, of the players' wives and children, of the players from teams not on the field. One night I watched a player's wife play with a small child. It was beautiful. *She* was beautiful, a full, warm woman who radiated affection. I imagined myself coming home to her from work tired and putting my head in her lap. Another wife kept score with intense dedication, marking each play in the book, always with the score, inning, and number of outs ready for anyone who would ask. Though she was in her thirties and the mother of three children, her flesh looked soft and virginal like that of a high school girl.

The player-spectators who interested me were working people of the old cut, posturing, clowning, awkward, self-conscious, never quite accepting themselves, kidding the players in the field with loud, sometimes crude, always good-natured insults. They drank lots of beer. They also turned me through parts of my life I'd neglected for a long time and I suppose I loved them for that.

I thought again about those tiny worlds I'd lived in with far more desperation than I hoped any of them would ever know. I thought of Ingmar Bergman's film *The Naked Night* (sometimes called *Sawdust and Tinsel*), where the degraded protagonist and his wife have finally only each other with whom to face an arrogant humiliating world. How the crutch we once needed to hobble through life remains in our closet long after our leg has healed. How Gordon Urquhart could fight through his setbacks and his complicated attitudes about life to a kind of success while my best hope of avoiding defeat was to turn values around with words, to change loss into victory. How John Popich came to the field with his physical gifts, hoping in seven innings to win the battle he would probably never win. How failures are in many ways successes and how successful people, those who early in life accepted adult values and abandoned the harmless fields of play, are really failures because they never come to know the vital worth of human relationships, even if it takes the lines of a softball field to give them a frame. How, without play, many people sense too often and too immediately their impending doom. After nearly thirty years of writing, I was ready to try a softball poem.

MISSOULA SOFTBALL TOURNAMENT

This summer, most friends out of town
and no wind playing flash and dazzle
in the cottonwoods, music of the Clark Fork stale,
I've gone back to the old ways of defeat,
the softball field, familiar dust and thud,
pitcher winging drops and rises, and wives,
the beautiful wives in the stands, basic, used,
screeching runners home, infants unattended
in the dirt. A long triple sails into right center.
Two men on. Shouts from dugout: go, Ron, go.
Life is better run from. Distance to the fence,
both foul lines and dead center, is displayed.

I try to steal the tricky manager's signs.
Is hit-and-run the pulling of the ear?
The ump gives pitchers too much low inside.
Injustice? Fraud? Ancient problems focus
in the heat. Bad hop on routine grounder.
Close play missed by the team you want to win.
Players from the first game, high on beer,
ride players in the field. Their laughter
falls short of the wall. Under lights, the moths
are momentary stars, and wives, the beautiful wives
in the stands now take the interest they once feigned,
oh, long ago, their marriage just begun, years
of helping husbands feel important just begun,
the scrimping, the anger brought home evenings
from degrading jobs. This poem goes out to them.
Is steal-of-home the touching of the heart?

Last pitch. A soft fly. A can of corn
the players say. Routine, like mornings,
like the week. They shake hands on the mound.
Nice grab on that shot to left. Good game. Good game.
Dust rotates in their headlight beams.
The wives, the beautiful wives are with their men.

It struck me as a crude poem and for a while I didn't like it. It seems to be discussing its own meaning. But one day, I came to believe that the crudeness was right, at least for that poem.

The summer of '73 I returned again to watch a few games. It was pleasant saying hello to a lot of nice people, most of whom ask little from life or from others. A few inquired if I was going to play again and I told them not a chance, but I felt a little proud that they had asked. One night a big husky girl, who played on one of the women's teams in town, brought a group of handicapped young people to watch one of the men's games. Some of them seemed retarded, others afflicted with physical and neurological problems. From all I've written here, I should not have to explain the following villanelle I finished a few months ago.

THE FREAKS AT SPURGIN ROAD FIELD

The dim boy claps because the others clap.
The polite word, handicapped, is muttered in the stands.
Isn't it wrong, the way the mind moves back.

One whole day I sit, contrite, dirt, L.A.
Union Station, '46, sweating through last night.
The dim boy claps because the others clap.

Score, 5 to 3. Pitcher fading badly in the heat.
Isn't it wrong to be or not be spastic?
Isn't it wrong, the way the mind moves back.

I'm laughing at a neighbor girl beaten to scream
by a savage father and I'm ashamed to look.
The dim boy claps because the others clap.

The score is always close, the rally always short.
I've left more wreckage than a quake.
Isn't it wrong, the way the mind moves back.

The afflicted never cheer in unison.
Isn't it wrong, the way the mind moves back
to stammering pastures where the picnic should have worked.
The dim boy claps because the others clap.

I think when I played softball I was telling the world and myself that futile as my life seemed I still wanted to live.

FROM ALTITUDE, THE DIAMONDS
Richard Hugo

You can always spot them, even from high up,
the brown bulged out trying to make a circle
of a square, the green square inside the brown,
inside the green the brown circle you know is mound
and the big outside green rounded off by a round line
you know is fence. And no one playing.

You've played on every one. Second base somewhere
on the Dallas Tucson run, New Mexico you think,
where green was brown. Right field outside Chicago
where the fans went silent when you tripled home
the run that beat their best, their all-season
undefeated home town Sox. What a game you pitched
that hot day in the Bronx. You lost to that left hander,
Ford, who made it big, one-nothing on a fluke.
Who's to believe it now? Fat. Bald. Smoking your fear
of the turbulent air you are flying, remembering
the war, a worse fear, the jolting flak, the prayer.

When air settles, the white beneath you opens
and far below in some unpopulated region
of whatever state you are over (it can't be Idaho,
that was years ago) you spot a tiny diamond,
and because you've grown far sighted with age
you see players moving, the center fielder
running the ball down deep, two runners
rounding third, the third base coach waving hard
and the hitter on his own not slowing down
at second, his lungs filled with the cheers of those
he has loved forever, on his magnificent tiny way
to an easy stand-up three.

ORDERING INFORMATION FOR
THE ORIGINAL ANTHOLOGIES
AND SUBMISSIONS TO FUTURE ANTHOLOGIES

The older anthologies are no longer available in bookstores but may still be purchased directly from North Atlantic Books—(*Baseball I Gave You* . . . at $20.95, in whatever edition is available; *The Temple of Baseball* at $14.95 in paperback or $29.50 in hardcover; and *The Dreamlife of Johnny Baseball* at $10.95 in paperback and $22.00 in hardcover). The prices all include shipping but do not include sales tax for Californians. We will also provide sets of all of these anthologies at $35.00 (paperbacks only) or $45.00 (hardcovers where available). For an additional $5.00 on the sets we will add a copy of the one companion basketball anthology, *Take it to the Hoop*, edited by Daniel Rudman. *Io* #10 is completely out of print, though for an incidental reason: it happened to include the first publication of a student at the University of Maine named Stephen King (a poem you can find in the present anthology), and his collectors have bought all the copies. Orders, as well as submissions of work for future baseball anthologies (with a self-addressed, stamped envelope if return of the material is desired), may be sent to: North Atlantic Books, 2800 Woolsey Street, Berkeley, California 94705.

Richard Grossinger